STORIES OF OUR LIVING EPHEMERA

STORIES OF OUR LIVING EPHEMERA

Storytelling Methodologies in the Archives of the Cherokee National Seminaries, 1846–1907

EMILY LEGG

UTAH STATE UNIVERSITY PRESS
Logan

© 2023 by University Press of Colorado

Published by Utah State University Press
An imprint of University Press of Colorado
1580 North Logan Street, Suite 660
PMB 39883
Denver, Colorado 80203-1942

All rights reserved

 The University Press of Colorado is a proud member of the Association of University Presses.

The University Press of Colorado is a cooperative publishing enterprise supported, in part, by Adams State University, Colorado State University, Fort Lewis College, Metropolitan State University of Denver, University of Alaska Fairbanks, University of Colorado, University of Denver, University of Northern Colorado, University of Wyoming, Utah State University, and Western Colorado University.

ISBN: 978-1-64642-520-4 (hardcover)
ISBN: 978-1-64642-521-1 (paperback)
ISBN: 978-1-64642-522-8 (ebook)
https://doi.org/10.7330/9781646425228

Library of Congress Cataloging-in-Publication Data

Names: Legg, Emily, author.
Title: Stories of our living ephemera : storytelling methodologies in the archives of the Cherokee National Seminaries, 1846–1907 / Emily Legg.
Description: Denver, CO : Utah State University Press, [2023] | Includes bibliographical references and index.
Identifiers: LCCN 2023021433 (print) | LCCN 2023021434 (ebook) | ISBN 9781646425204 (hardcover) | ISBN 9781646425211 (paperback) | ISBN 9781646425228 (ebook)
Subjects: LCSH: Cherokee National Female Seminary—Archives. | Cherokee National Male Seminary—Archives. | Cherokee Indians—Education. | Cherokee Indians—Folklore.
Classification: LCC E97.6.C35 L44 2023 (print) | LCC E97.6.C35 (ebook) | DDC 398.2089/97557—dc23/eng/20230727
LC record available at https://lccn.loc.gov/2023021433
LC ebook record available at https://lccn.loc.gov/2023021434

This book will be made open access within three years of publication thanks to Path to Open, a program developed in partnership between JSTOR, the American Council of Learned Societies (ACLS), University of Michigan Press, and The University of North Carolina Press to bring about equitable access and impact for the entire scholarly community, including authors, researchers, libraries, and university presses around the world. Learn more at https://about.jstor.org/path-to-open/.

Cover illustration © Camilla McGinty for Uweyv Art & Design

For my children, Oliver and Iris,
And the light you've brought to this world.

For my husband, Adam,
And the strength you've lent me along the way.

And for those who came before, those who are here, and those who will follow,

These stories are for you.

CONTENTS

PART 1: ᏅᎲᏂᏫᎩ ᎢᏗᏍᏛᏫᎵ: ANITSALAGI IDIGALVLADI, CHEROKEE STORIES

Preface   5

PART 2: ᎧᏢᎬ: DZPᏍᎬ SᎾᏏᏓᏋ, KALVGV: ANOTLVSV DUNADADUDALV, EAST: MAKING RELATIONS

1. Origin Stories: Our Stories, Our Ways, Our Knowledges   29
2. Wolf Wears (Eurocentric) Shoes: Indigenizing the Archives   57

PART 3: ᎤᏬᏢ: ᎤᎠᏎᎢ ᎢᏍᏬᏎᎢ, UYVTLV: UGOHVI VGATAHVI, NORTH: SEEKING KNOWLEDGE THROUGH

3. Archives Out of Story: Severed Relations and Indigenous Worldviews   81
4. Storying Duyuk'ta Together: Indigenous Storytelling as Rhetorical Methodology   108

PART 4: ᎤᏚᎵᎬ: ᎤᏍᎢᎲᎠᏍ ᎠᏕᎳᏍᏗ, WUDELIGV: USQUANIGODV AGADOHVSDI, WEST: KEEPING THE WISDOM

5. Stories Emerging from Dusty Boxes: Finding Duyuk'ta at the Cherokee National Seminaries   133
6. "Where Bright Thoughts Like Rivers Flow": Composing With and for the Cherokee Nation   169
7. "To Keep Alive Tradition": Survivance and Writing at the Cherokee National Seminaries   196

PART 5: ᎤᏓᎾᏬ: TSᎵᏐᏯTEᏂᎵ SᎾᏏᏓᏋ, UGANAWU IGATIHAIGVNEDI DUNADADUDALV, SOUTH: MAINTAINING RELATIONS

Gadugi: Working Together (An Epilogue of Sorts)   223

References   243
Index   251

STORIES OF OUR LIVING EPHEMERA

PART 1

DhCWY TJSꝹWJ: anitsalagi idigalvladi
Cherokee Stories

*Then take our wreath, and let it stand
An emblem of our happy band;
The Seminary, our garden fair,
And we, the flowers planted there.*

*Like roses bright we hope to grow,
And o'er our home such beauty throw
In future years—that all may see
Loveliest of lands,—the Cherokee.*

From "Our Wreath of Rose Buds" by Corrine, a
Cherokee Female Seminary student (1854)

PREFACE

It was Easter Sunday afternoon in 1887 at the Cherokee Female Seminary, a quiet day except for the high wind. The girls who had remained at the school over the holiday were spending the afternoon quietly resting in the lounging garments. In Ida Collins closet, her prettiest dresses and blouses were scented like spring flowers. The recital of last evening had been a great success; and she, like the other girls who were becoming so well accomplished, had performed in a most creditable way. Below the window, the girls could hear the words of an itinerant preacher, one who smoked all the time and not one usually taking a part in the programs. Then they started smelling smoke. They ran to the window. "Fire!" they heard a girl cry. The preacher had knocked the ashes from his pipe—fire, ashes and all—into the unfinished column, with its collection of small dried shavings and bits of other debris. There was a glow, a flame, and the draft from the wind caused the fire to break into an uproar of conflagration. Below, they could hear the younger girls dragging their trunks across the floor. Like a sleepwalker, Ida began to snatch her wispy new spring dresses and blouses from their closet racks and to go running down the hall with them. Taking them to the window, she opened the window and threw her clothing out to whatever fate it might encounter, in the high wind. (Fry 1988, 101)

Ida Collins Goodale's narrative of the Easter Sunday fire at the Cherokee Female Seminary brings voice to the well-known event in Cherokee history. After starts and stops due to funding and the US Civil War that brought havoc and instability to Cherokee society, the Cherokee Female Seminary had reached an almost twenty-year uninterrupted stride out of the prairies of Park Hill, Indian Territory. Yet the carelessness of an outsider mixed with the high winds of land that wasn't always the Cherokees' took that away in one day. As the grounds of the seminary lay blanketed by the dressings and belongings of students, Ann Florence Wilson, the principal of the Cherokee Female Seminary, ran back into the burning seminary building to save one important piece of school property—the gradebook. Soon, the students from the neighboring

Cherokee Male Seminary, who had abruptly left Easter Sunday services as soon as someone burst in shouting the female seminary was on fire with no regard for the bewildered preacher, arrived and began collecting the garments that decorated the shrubs and trees of the prairie, remarking on who they remembered wearing what as they returned each one to the women, while the students of the female seminary had made sure everyone was out safely, ensuring that no lives were lost. The women who had been attending the seminary were now scattered, much like their garments, in various directions after the fire, with some continuing their education at the Cherokee Male Seminary, some returning home, some headed off to other schools, and some married (Fry 1988, 102). While the Cherokee Female Seminary would be rebuilt in Tahlequah two years later, the fire took everything with it that day—everything, that is, except for that one gradebook, three sturdy brick pillars, and the perseverance of the Cherokee people to rebuild and restore an education system. Even so, twenty-three years later, a similarly devastating fire occurred on Palm Sunday in 1910 at the Cherokee Male Seminary (which at that time was run as a coeducational facility) and destroyed the entire building that coincided with the newly formed state of Oklahoma's takeover of all of the Cherokee's educational systems, including the still-standing Cherokee Female Seminary.

As a Cherokee Nation citizen and a descendant of some of the many Cherokee women who attended the female seminary, I grew up in those tallgrass plains of Oklahoma hearing this survival story of Cherokee education from my elders, who would often begin by explaining how the Cherokee had always seen themselves as a people who first learned to write from Sequoyah's syllabary and continue writing when learning at the Cherokee Male and Female Seminaries. These stories of Sequoyah and the seminaries live and breathe alongside many other traditional stories about Rabbit, Wolf, Selu and Kana'ti, and stories of our ancestral lands "back home"; however, for how important these cultural institutions are in Cherokee identity, all that physically remains from the seminaries is extremely limited in scope and scattered across archives in libraries, boxes, and files all over the United States. Because of fires that devastated both seminaries and the forced takeover by the Oklahoma State government in the early 1900s, these scant archives of both seminaries unfortunately leave behind material traces of living stories that have as many gaps as there are teeth.

What I did find during my archival research on the seminaries mirrored the removal policies of the federal government during the nineteenth century. What few material artifacts remained of this important time in Cherokee history were curated through approaches to archival science that championed classifying systems based on Eurocentric epistemologies (Duchein 1992). Because of the removal of the stories and Cherokee culture from these artifacts, the resulting written histories that exist of the Cherokee Female Seminary as well as its counterpart, the Cherokee Male Seminary, are overshadowed by narratives of removal, assimilation, and erasure—far from the stories of a celebration of Cherokee identity, survival, and perseverance I grew up with. These narratives informed by Eurocentric research methods still colonize and silence Cherokee ancestors' voices to this day, creating discord between the living stories of the Cherokees and the written histories about them. To speak to, with, and through that discord, I return to the scattered archives of the Cherokee National Seminaries to recover the histories of the Cherokee National Seminaries from colonized practices of research by critically weaving together student writing, recovered pedagogical practices, and the remaining archival artifacts from the tumultuous nineteenth century with multiple strands of Cherokee traditional stories that serve as an Indigenous theoretical and knowledge-making lens.

Building on archival research and the work of decolonial and Indigenous scholars, this book recovers the complicated histories of Cherokee education and the Cherokee women who received that education from dominant histories that simplify their existence as an extension of assimilation and deny the Cherokee people a heritage of survival and resistance during the nineteenth century. Throughout the book, I assert that Indigenous storytelling encourages scholars and researchers to retool dominant methods used in existing colonial structures to do the day-to-day work of knowledge-making that makes decolonized recovery work possible. When we re-tool our methods, we can do more than recover underrepresented histories; we reframe our historical narratives in ways that can teach us about our own contemporary experiences as scholars and teachers, especially in the ways that we are culturally positioned within academics.

DhGWY iSWᏸT DZPᏰE (ANITSALAGI VGATAH-VI ANOTLVSGV): CHEROKEE KNOWLEDGE-MAKING

At a very early point in my research, I was intimately aware of three points of data I had collected—the Cherokee stories of storytellers, my grandmothers' stories, and the colonized stories of archival boxes across the United States. This was the moment I realized that my research needed to be guided by more than already accepted archival research practices. My research needed to be complicated and practiced through a methodological approach that could navigate these complex, interwoven stories. What's more is that I also felt the cultural imperative to actively practice my embodiment as a Cherokee scholar through the ways I needed to think about writing about my research in addition to doing decolonial research through Indigenous methodologies, and without doing so my work may only replicate the colonial systems already in place. As Linda Tuhiwai Smith explains:

> The problem is that constant efforts by governments, states, societies and institutions to deny the historical formations of such conditions have simultaneously denied our claims to humanity, to having a history, and to all sense of hope. To acquiesce is to lose ourselves entirely and implicitly agree with all that has been said about us. To resist is to retrench in the margins, retrieve 'what we were and remake ourselves'. The past, our stories local and global, the present, our communities, cultures, languages and social practices—all may be spaces of marginalization, but that have also become spaces of resistance and hope. (Smith 2012, 4)

To me, embodying resistance and hope in research necessitates synthesizing Cherokee traditional beliefs and practices with contemporary Indigenous research methodologies and writing this book in a way that follows a distinctly Cherokee path of understanding and ceremony grounded in the practices of balance and community, known as SGAᏛ (*duyuk'ta*). As a way to embody the practice of SGAᏛ (*duyuk'ta*), my role of a researcher is better understood as taking on the role of a listener and a storyteller. At each point in my research, I position myself in traditional Cherokee stories before listening to the stories out of the archives, whether they are told by material artifacts, written narratives, or ephemera of nineteenth-century students. In that reciprocal exchange between listener and storyteller, I also share my own story so that I can acknowledge my own relations in a good way and follow my own path, especially as it becomes woven within other Cherokee stories.

As a new parent who hopes to raise children who develop a deep appreciation for their Cherokee roots, I've sought out Cherokee stories in various bookstores so that we can begin to read and learn together. Typically, the stories that get printed for children are Cherokee animal stories—stories about Rabbit and Bear, why Possum's tail is bare, why Mole lives underground, and other similar anthropomorphic tales. It's easy to see why these stories get published in children's literature in our Disney-fied children's culture in America. However, as I have discussed, it's not the content of these stories that have power, and these aren't just children's stories of simplistic adventures of forest animals. The Turtle Island Liars' Club tells these same stories, often called the "how" and "why" stories. Chris Teuton explains, "These stories tell about how our world was made and how animals came to be the way they are today. On the surface, they seem to be about the physical world. But kids aren't fooled. If you listen closely, you'll see that these 'how and why' stories are about how our thoughts and actions transform ourselves and the world" (Teuton 2012, 194). We shouldn't be fooled either by a Eurocentric coding of stories, for they hold much more power than a nugget of content, much more than entertainment and escape, and much more than a close analytical reading of a canonized text.

As you read the chapters in this text, I ask you to work to embody the ceremony of SGAO° (*duyuk'ta*) as well by opening yourself up to your own stories, listening carefully to the stories of Cherokee education, paying attention to teachers such as Rabbit and Wolf, and putting yourself in relation with these cultural locations as part of your own knowledge-making process. Keep in mind that sometimes stories are slow to unfold, taking along a meandering path as we wander in our knowledge-making. The pathways, especially as they wrap around the (re)positionings of worldviews, ontologies, and epistemologies, may seem like the long way around through a book about the Cherokee National Seminaries; however, the long way around helps shift our ways of thinking from the hidden systems of Eurocentric means of gaining knowledge to Indigenous practices of participatory knowledge-making. The long way around gives us the time and space to listen and listen carefully to the stories that are being shared. Together, as a community of listeners and storytellers, we are making knowledge with the Cherokee ancestors and archival materials they left in a ceremony of learning.

OF JOURNEYS AND ACKNOWLEDGMENTS: A STORY OF RECIPROCITY

As you might have realized by this time in the preface, this book is certainly an educational and pedagogical history of nineteenth-century Cherokee, and yet, it is also a book about the ways we make and understand those histories through storytelling research methods. Rather than approaching this book by asking *what it is*, think of this book of a journey, with each storying leading you along to experience knowledge rather than just being told the who, what, where, when, and why. Because, as you read, I hope you'll realize that this book didn't come into being by asking those five familiar W-questions. My own experiences and stories shaped my interactions with the material artifacts, people, and stories I also learned along this writing journey. While storytelling is almost always associated with spoken word, writing as a means of storytelling is the material practice of unveiling a path through the kind of knowledge work that storytelling accomplishes. As the stories are told, my hands weave together the words as they appear on the digital white space before the blinking cursor. And yet, this process of sharing stories about my research, stories about the ways my ancestors taught me to do archival research in a good way, and stories about the ways to hear that they were still telling us took much longer than the "academic" archival research process took.

Thinking about the journey this book has taken and the ways others have shared their stories with me causes me to pause briefly and contemplate those who helped create the invisible threads that are tied together from the beginning to the end—my grandmothers. Without this pause to acknowledge them, the work they contributed so deeply to this book remains invisible since the knowledge they leant falls outside of the academic citation protocols. My Nana, Mary Lee (Haury) Moon, taught me early on that the everyday was worth documenting and that good stories came from these very real and lived experiences. In her house, where I spent a good portion of my childhood, were tiny, lined notebooks filled with her perfect cursive, scattered on various surfaces and stored in a handful of "junk" drawers. These were the kinds of notebooks that were usually used for grocery lists, calorie counting, Christmas gift ideas, random phone numbers, reminders, and the like. While these things certainly could be found in her notebooks, she also quietly wrote down stories of what she had experienced that day or what she noticed. I don't know if she ever expected us to read those little notebooks, but stories of the everyday in them are priceless memories stored on faded paper. She also quickly adopted to new technologies, like picking up the earliest Gameboy to play Tetris "to keep her mind sharp" as well as buying the newest camcorders on the market. While we could always count on her asking my Papa to make sure to record every candle blown out at birthdays, every loud laugh while reading birthday cards, every "Ooo, ahhh, hey . . . that's great!" uttered after a Christmas present was opened, she also would set up the camcorder and just record. Much to the chagrin of the extended family, this often included setting up the camera during the huge Thanksgiving dinners that spilled from the kitchen, through the eating area, and intro the den. While there is nothing quite as unsettling as being surreptitiously filmed while eating the largest meal of the year, once the camcorder sank into the background these videos captured not just the stories we told and created but the ways those stories came into being. She was the documenter of the family, and I learned just how this subtle yet important work happens.

My other grandmother, Mary Leota (Holmes) Legg, also documented life, not always in the everyday, but in the far reaches of history. She had a knack for family history and dedicated years of her life to working at the Family History Center, pulling together the genealogies of my grandfather's side and her side as well, all with the intention of writing these histories down into books to share with her kin and descendants. She would bring history books and notes home with traces of family history and create binder after binder of carefully indexed, cross-referenced sources. When looking through these binders, we joked about how it would be nice to see some of her handwriting, but she was so meticulous, she had typed out every note, label, and source. Everything was kept and everything was documented. Without her tireless work, our family wouldn't have been enrolled with the Cherokee Nation, as my great-grandmother, who was on the Dawes Rolls, had passed away when my grandfather was just eighteen months old. While her own family was of European descent, she took care to reconnect our family to our Cherokee past and, in turn, keeping our Cherokee heritage possible for our descendants. While she had written documentation of our families, she also took to heart every story and had the amazing ability to recall relative after relative, explain how we were connected, and share stories of them. When she knew her life was getting close to ending, she didn't pull any punches. Instead, she pulled me over, knowing that I was writing a book with some family history, and asked me to help her and my grandfather record some of their history. With my computer recording them, my grandpa started with the facts: where he was born and when, who his family was, who he lived with when his mother passed away, where he went to school, and so on. He ended with a quick story about how he proposed to my grandma in a letter (that he kept on the fireplace mantel along with their first picture together), and said, "Well, I think that's about it." Speaking up in her thick, Oklahoma accent, Grandma let out a huff and interrupted, "Well, Carl, that's not what she wants to hear. She wants to hear the stories, not just the facts." After a brief kerfuffle of documenting ideologies passed between the two of them, she made him start over. But this time, she made sure to interrupt with the stories.

Sadly, both of my grandmothers passed away before this book went to print. My Nana, Mary Lee, always wanted to hear updates of what I was writing, how it intersected with my research, and where in the publication process it was. She died just before I received my peer reviews, but not before she had a chance to read the earliest complete draft of my manuscript. I received the call that my Grandma, Mary Legg, had passed away not even ten minutes before I found out that my manuscript had been fully supported by the peer reviews and the contract became official. In a way, their invisible guidance is woven deeply through these pages. Nana, teaching me the values of everyday stories, and Grandma, teaching me the importance of keeping the stories in with the documentations. Their influences are on every page turn, and without either of them, my journey would not have started. There is no book in your hands without them.

While my grandmothers' quiet influences shaped this book, those familiar with the academic publishing machine and the path to tenure might recognize that my writing this book humbly began in a graduate seminar the same semester I was asked to submit my dissertation prospectus. Under the thoughtful guidance of my dissertation chair, Pat Sullivan and committee, Jenny Bay, Samantha Blackmon, and Thomas Rickert, those research notes turned into a successfully defended dissertation. Three days later in that summer or 2016, my son was born, full of light and life and very little need for sleep. I went from the confident, newly christened PhD to the insecure new mother and new faculty member in a matter of weeks. Along that path, my relationship to my research and writing struggled, while the Eurocentric structure of the dissertation caused me to stumble as I tried to rework the text into something much more akin to the Indigenous knowledge-making my research was supposed to champion. Yet through that time, my husband, Adam Strantz, kept me going, offering me his strength when I was at my weakest. He would sit and listen as I paced the room, talking through my book. He came along with every research trip, often taking our son around museums while I hung out in the archives, digging for clues. To this day, his knowledge of Oklahoma history rivals anyone's thanks to those long museum days with a sleeping toddler in a stroller.

As I began the trial by fire with my husband that is parenthood, I realized that I needed the guidance of my mothers, grandmothers, and ancestors before me to raise my children in ways that were responsible to their Cherokee culture, to their relationships, and to the world (and everything) within them. And yet, I had this book manuscript reminding me that my work and writing was slow with every annual activities report due to my chair. Stories are like that, though. They take their own time to unfold and in the middle of them, we don't see our linear sense of beginning or ending. During this time of what felt like stagnation in my research and writing, I decided to turn to gardening and finding a more (literal) grounding of who I was becoming. Besides, if I could get plants to grow in ground that had been left untended for years, perhaps I could get those words to grow on a page that definitely felt like had been untended for years. Like many stories, the details get a little fuzzy between failing to grow a decent crop of corn in Ohio (of all places), having so many tomatoes that I didn't mind sharing with the squirrels in that midwestern August heat, and preparing for coursework for the upcoming semester that I began to see the relationships that were forming between the different ways I was gaining knowledge. I realized that, like a budding garden plot, a dissertation needed to be reworked and resown in ground that had been tilled, fertilized, and respected with each rock I (and the hand tiller) took out of the ground that has then ended up in my son's rock collection. In Ohio, I found many colleagues and friends, both local and across state lines, who offered to read and give feedback along with words of encouragement. Even more, their friendships steered me back to an understanding of what self-care truly looked like. It was during this time and with their gracious help that I also went back to cultivating my love of reading, which had slipped away somewhere in the sleepless nights of parenthood followed up with the pressure pot of the tenure track during the day.

Somewhere along this path, I picked up Robin Wall Kimmerer's book, *Braiding Sweetgrass: Indigenous Wisdom, Scientific Knowledge, and the Teaching of Plants*. While part of me was hoping it would help me grow corn in Ohio, the lessons went much deeper and were much more entangled with what I was struggling against in my own writing. Through her, I learned that relationships grow with reciprocity, responsibility, and restoration (Kimmerer 2013). In her teachings about the relationship between goldenrods and asters, mothers and children, humans and Earth (and all of the other-than-human relations within), she explains:

> Responsibility to the tree makes everyone pause before beginning. Sometimes I have that sense when I face a blank sheet of paper. For me, writing is an act of reciprocity with the world; it is what I can give back in return for everything that has been given to me. And now there's another layer of responsibility, writing on a thin sheet of tree and hoping the words are worth it. Such a thought could make a person set down her pen. (152)

Writing is reciprocity—a line I have circled, underlined, and drew hearts around in my now worn copy of her work. *My* writing is reciprocity toward my ancestors, who share their knowledge through stories and through this writing; I am responsible to the knowledge they have generously shared. *My* writing is also reciprocity to all of those names and stories I mentioned here, whose experiences have quietly shaped each word on the page. *My* writing is reciprocity to those who will come after me, reading through these stories in their own lifetimes. Through the sharing of reciprocity and responsibility in my writing, I finally caught the deep knowledge that my ancestors and those at the Cherokee National Seminaries had been sharing all along: Writing is *restorative*. For the Cherokee, the syllabary helped restore a nation; the seminaries, through their teaching, helped restore a community; and the shared stories about them continue to restore the Cherokee people. All it took for me to finally hear those teachings was loving grandmothers, gracious family and friends, a failed corn plot, and a new book (and a lot of patience and listening).

ᎣᎯᏍᎦᎤᎰ (WINIDUYUK'TA, DIRECTIONS)

Just as Kimmerer discusses the restoration of the land and the healing of the Earth (2013, 326), the lessons the Cherokee students at the seminaries had poured over have turned into the act of healing for myself. What I learned is that writing *with* my ancestors provides the same restorative act of healing a broken Earth through the pathways of a childhood dream, the pursuit of knowledge, the want of teaching others, and in turn, being taught more about myself and the traumas of a mixed-blood existence. Similarly caught in the tensions of white-presenting and culturally (and politically) Cherokee, the students at the Cherokee seminaries helped me understand that restoring the archives with Cherokee knowledge and culture would lead to stories that love us back, restore us, and heal us. Such is the way of stories when grown through the Indigenous wisdoms of understanding our relationships in the world. As I began to see the ways that these students navigated the tensions of white-presenting assimilation with their words, language, and stories, I understood that Cherokee knowledge-making is much deeper than the words presented on the page. Thinking through the practices of the Cherokee, I turned to the Cherokee medicine wheel and cardinal directions to guide my process back to writing after my pen had been silent. The Cherokee medicine wheel, when embodied and materially practiced, steers us through the directions of the world around us. Each path is taken in ceremony and reflection of the ways we work together in ᏍᎦᎤᎰ (*duyuk'ta*), balance. It is here, in ceremony, that my dissertation, pruned through Eurocentric academic processes, finally began to thrive in the teachings of Cherokee culture. As I carefully took apart each chapter, followed through on stories that had yet to be heard during the research process, and found their places in

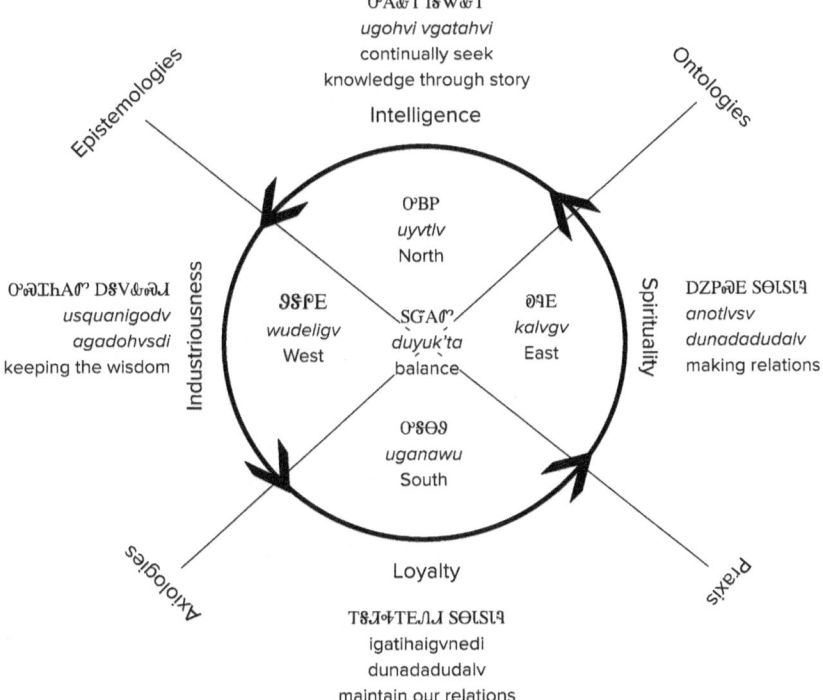

Figure 0.1. Map of the Cherokee medicine wheel as a research methodology.

ceremony along the medicine wheel, this book began to take the shape that you find it in today. Along the way, I also gave up my need to try to make the corn grow and instead let the goldenrods and asters return to my garden beds to bring the bees back to my tomatoes, okra, and beans.

While this written medium can cause the knowledge to stagnate, as it is always presented in the same way, I have consciously organized each chapter through Cherokee ceremony, the living practice of embodied cultural knowledge. To do so, the structure of this book follows a traditional Cherokee path through the cardinal directions in a counterclockwise method: east, north, west, and south.

The four directions, expressed as spirituality, intelligence, industriousness, and loyalty, organize the book into four sections. When mapped onto the contents of this book, the following structure unfolds: part one (east) complicates Eurocentric means of archival work and historiography by acknowledging and making relations with the histories of the Cherokee National Seminaries with Cherokee ontologies and traditional stories; part two (north) develops archival research praxis grounded in

Cherokee epistemologies to build relationships between the archival artifacts from the seminaries and Cherokee traditional storytelling practices; part three (west) recovers disciplinary histories at the Cherokee National Seminaries by applying and maintaining Indigenous storytelling methodology; and part four (south) makes connections between learning from our ancestors and a progressive rhetorical history at the Cherokee Female Seminary, storytelling, contemporary Indigenous experiences, and pathways for Indigenous and settler scholars to enter into an accomplice-based relationship with Indigenous methodologies. By entering into research and writing through ceremony, this path establishes Cherokee ontologies and epistemologies (spirituality and intelligence) as a process of building relationships within research with the accountability and maintenance of those relationships through applied methodologies (industriousness and loyalty) in contemporary Indigenous experiences in higher education and Eurocentric political systems. I have also structured my book into seven chapters throughout these four sections as a means to maintain the metaphysical importance of the number 7 that is represented through Cherokee Clan structures and council houses. Just as the medicine wheel follows the embodied practices of Cherokee basket weaving, these sections and chapters are woven together following the cultural and materialist practice of weaving Cherokee double-walled baskets (Awiakta 1994; Driskill 2016), which follow the counterclockwise directional paths as the reeds are woven around the ribs of a traditional Cherokee basket.

One of the key takeaways from the Cherokee medicine wheel model and organization is that knowledge-making *with* Cherokee ancestors and storytelling in this way takes time. So, while this book is indeed a rhetorical and pedagogical history of the Cherokee National Seminaries, the ceremonial pathways to understand and listen to those stories is slow and methodical. In this sense, this book provides an Indigenous storytelling way of presenting the deep layers that Cherokee ontologies, epistemologies, language, culture, and history are carefully woven together. What began as a typical dissertation had to be prepared, the reeds of knowledge stripped of their Eurocentric bark, soaked in water to create a pliable organization out of once rigid and friable runners, and re-woven following centuries-old ways of basket weaving and knowledge-making. These were the lessons my grandmothers were trying to teach me, and it wasn't until I slowed down and took time to deeply listen that I began to understand that this kind of knowledge-making was happening on *their* time. And it was *good* time. As I finally put the finishing touches of story into this manuscript, I looked out of the windows in the sunroom where I spent a good deal of a pandemic writing and would lose my train of thought in the goldenrods I didn't pull from the flowerbed lining the road in front of our house. I remembered the words of Robin Wall Kimmerer:

> *Wewene*, I say to myself: in good time, in a good way. There are no shortcuts. It must unfold in the right way, when all the elements are present, mind and body harnessed in unison. When all the tools have been properly made and all the parts united in purpose, it is so easy. But if they're not, it will be futile. Until there is balance and perfect reciprocity between the forces, you can try and fail and try and fail again. I know. And yet, despite the need, you must swallow your sense of urgency, calm your breathing so that the energy goes not to frustration, but to fire. (2013, 352)

When asked about the theoretical uptakes of this book for particular audiences, my first response is to channel the wisdom of Kimmerer and remind everyone: *in good time and in a good way* toward balance and ceremony. Like stories, the path to knowledge and theoretical uptakes (in an academic sense) meander through important shifts in the ways we do things and a (re)positioning in our relationships to story and knowledge-making to strip away the deeply embedded tendencies of Eurocentric meaning-making. My hope is that in presenting the stories of the Cherokee National Seminaries to you in this way you also may be a part of the ceremonial restorative act that is grounded in ontological and epistemological reflection; reciprocity both to and from the ancestors who maintain these stories, histories, and Cherokee culture; and the focus on SGAO (*duyuk'ta*, balance) that brings a healing fire to the archives as well as to ourselves as researchers and writers as the stories of the seminaries return that healing back in cyclical reciprocity.

ENTERING INTO CHEROKEE CEREMONY

To begin by weaving, my research enters into ceremony by beginning in the east, ᎧᎸᎬ (*kalvgv*). By telling Cherokee stories alongside the histories of the Cherokee seminaries, an example of tribally run education during the nineteenth century, I complicate our pedagogical histories and previous histories of the Cherokee seminaries by interrogating our origin stories in chapter 1. By questioning our origin stories, I turn my focus to the ways that these stories have severed the Cherokee seminaries archives from the stories they are telling when we approach our research through Eurocentric means of recovery work and historiography. As such, I draw specific attention to archival research as a space of conflicting stories and tensions between dominant and nondominant research practices in chapter 2. On one hand, the archivist maintains distance and seeks out provenance and origins of the artifacts to develop a classificatory system for the archive collection. However, the other story, as I have explained, is that by definition this mode of classification is inherently colonial in practice and serves to sever the relationships of those artifacts. That dark, dusty, often neglected space of the library where the things to research are tucked away in standardized gray archival boxes that keep their contents hidden from the scholar's eye is a place of colonization and oppression if the researcher is not attuned to those histories and stories. To talk about the archive as a place, Derrida begins with the concept of the *arkhe* as the base of archive. He writes, "Arkhe . . . names at once the commencement and the commandment. This name coordinates two principles in one: The principle according to nature or history, there where things commence—physical, historical, or ontological principle—but also the principle according to the law, there where men and gods command, there, where authority, social order is exercised, in this place from where order is given—nomological principle" (Derrida and Prenowitz 1995, 9). In other words, the archive, coded with the concept of *arkhe*, is the place where things begin and power originates—both starting points. It is a place, and a present gathering of whatever power is being exercised at any time and at any place. When the power of that place is contextualized through colonial and Eurocentric views of research, the power of place and the stories contained as part of that network are something that researchers need to acknowledge. Even today, archives are places of Eurocentric power as artifacts held by federal institutions are threatened by the removal of artifacts from their Indigenous homelands when these federal institutions are placed up for sale or change hands (Johnson 2021). Yet, despite the forced erasure of these Indigenous histories and removals, the material evidence that remains is stories and documents that still speak to us. To strip the archival documents from these histories told and presented by the Cherokee Nation denies the researcher the stories that the archives themselves are asking us to listen to. This history and the archives of the seminaries are then caught between the oral stories of Cherokee teachings and the assimilation narratives and policies of the nineteenth century that are often told and retold throughout history books. The first part of this book seeks to place the institutional histories of the Cherokee National Seminaries, the remaining ephemera of the seminaries and legal documents from the creation of the seminaries, and Cherokee stories back into relation with one another, DZPoᎤE SᏕLSᏞᎱ (*anotlvsv dunadadudalv*, making relations).

After entering through and with stories, the book makes its way through the north, ᏅᎯ (*uyvtlv*) and builds on the theories and epistemologies developed in the first two chapters in order to develop archival research reflective practices (praxis). In doing so, we can uncover and navigate the tensions between colonization, assimilation, and gender in the Cherokee Female Seminary and its artifacts (Legg 2014, 73–74). Because of the complicated and colonized state of the history of the Cherokee Female Seminary, the archival research and historiography of this time in Cherokee history calls for an indigenized methodological approach to archival research. As researchers, we ramble through the archives, searching for that historical data that seems to emerge out of the various boxes we sift through to increase our general knowledge and help us dream of new knowledges (Connors 2016). But our rambling and inventive knowledge-making is tied to place—a place of power and a place of politics (Bieseker 2006). My work then turns to Cherokee ancestors to seek the knowledge of understanding the ways that Eurocentric methods of research and Enlightenment-era archival processes have erased the cultural bearings of the seminaries. By seeking knowledge with our ancestors, I ground my recovery work with and in Indigenous theories and epistemologies in order to develop archival research reflective practices (praxis).

Specifically, in chapter 3, I draw upon the living oral archive of Cherokee stories, and I expose Eurocentric worldviews in materialist stories that create part-to-part relationships, such as Latour's actor-network theory (ANT) and Ingold's environmental meshworks. To weave, I turn to Cherokee stories, such as "Grandmother Spider," that bring together the researcher, the artifacts, and their cultural ecologies within an Indigenous worldview that relates the part to the whole in relationships. By grounding materialist theories within an Indigenous worldview, this chapter extends *all our relations* as Indigenous materialist ontologies that constitute a reflective and process-driven praxis (practice as theory-work). It is through these Cherokee stories that Indigenous teachings situate archival research as a sustaining process of relationship-building and knowledge-making between researcher, artifacts as participants, environments, technologies, and cultural practices together. As I rambled through the archival places at Northeastern State University, I approached my research with the same desire to find a new knowledge through points of historical data that I hoped may decenter the histories of rhetoric and composition. I brought with me experiences and stories from my own family and my own research background in Indigenous histories, Cherokee practices, and Indigenous philosophies. As I also sifted through yellowing folders and gray boxes, I tried to listen to the stories these documents were telling. I reflect back to that moment, and the archives were also listening back to me. Acting as agents in this participatory knowledge-making praxis, the archives listened and acted against their predetermined cataloging and classifying. They existed in that moment as material remnants of these teachings and once again were a part of that Indigenous relationship shared through storytelling. Those colonial structures no longer shaped the archive, and the archives listened by dispossessing bias and assumptions made through those structures.

I assert that for these reasons, we need Indigenous methodologies, specifically storytelling, to do recovery work and to understand how these stories can retain power in already powerful places. As a means of decolonizing research, chapter 4 calls for an Indigenous approach to archival research that is grounded in Indigenous theory-making, that is, storytelling. Making the move to Indigenous storytelling in archival work begins the decolonial work of dismantling colonial power structures in research and moves to navigate these colonial systems in a way that is rhetorically and culturally networked and situated. In order to resituate myself, my story, and the artifacts in the archives that I encountered, I needed to reframe my own knowledge-making through constellating and relationship-building in basket weaving. When we frame basket weaving as more than just an activity and as a cultural and embodied practice (Driskill 2016), we begin to situate ourselves within Indigenous ways of being in relation. By situating my research within Indigenous ontologies of all our relations (Powell et al. 2014; Weaver 1997; Wildcat 2001b), I reflect on the rhetorical and methodological practices of all our relations as taught through traditional Cherokee stories in order to uncover the materialist impulses (Bennett 2010; Ingold 2008; Barad 2007) in research. Indigenous storytelling methodology impacts archival practices and the disciplinary histories of rhetoric and composition and encourages participatory knowledge-making practices that ask researchers to engage in human- and object-centered ecologies. I argue that these methodologies are absolutely necessary in order to de-center the histories of rhetoric and composition and to push the boundaries to relandscape our disciplines so that other stories and voices are heard and recognized. Once we make these moves, we can start the process of bridging together our stories, seeking out "all our relations" in rhetoric and composition histories. When analyzing institutional archival artifacts such as blueprints and legal proceedings, stories, such as "Wolf Wears Shoes," situate researchers as colonial settlers and uncover a theoretical and cultural positioning in the archives. Using the rhetorics of Cherokee storytelling as an Indigenous intervention with other theories of networked ways of knowing and ecologies (Barad 2007; de Certeau 2013), this chapter develops a networked knowledge-making praxis so that we may re-tool dominant methods of research that exist within colonial structures and top-down knowledge-making practices.

By indigenizing our archival research methods, we enter a balanced relationship within our research that does the work of sustaining materialist and networked ᏍᎩᏚᎩ (sgadug, Cherokee for "community"). Uncovering this research path opens up the archives so that we can listen to the Indigenous histories of the Cherokee National Seminaries. Sustaining ᏍᎩᏚᎩ (sgadug) calls for researchers to understand the actions of ᏚᏳᎩᏛ (duyuk'ta, Cherokee for "honest") as a right, and balanced spiritual path that is created through storied practices. All of these storied practices encourage participatory knowledge-making that ask researchers to engage in human- and object-centered ecologies within the ᏍᎩᏚᎩ (sgadug). Our path through the north reminds us as scholars to continually seek knowledge through story, ᎤᎪᏫ ᎢᏡᎦᏛᎢ (ugohvi vgatahvi) in all our relations, even if those relations are buried deep in the ephemera of dusty archival boxes and prepares us as we enter into story and to seek knowledge with Cherokee ancestors in the ᏭᏕᎵᎬ (wudeligv, west). The heart of this book finds its place in the west, ᏭᏕᎵᎬ (wudeligv), the direction that turns us to ways of keeping the wisdom, ᎤᏍᏆᏂᎪᏛ ᎠᏓᏛᏍᏗ (usquanigodv agadohvsdi). While Western philosophies draw distinct lines between the ontological and epistemic, Indigenous ontologies and epistemologies of storytelling come together in order to recover, reacquaint, and relate our beings and ways of knowing. After developing an Indigenous methodology for archival work, I turn to ways of keeping that wisdom as an active practice that employs storytelling. Storytelling acts as a methodological framework in the Cherokee National Seminary archives that reimagines the role of Cherokee culture through the impact that Cherokee education had on the Cherokee people during this tumultuous time in history. From these recovered histories that emerge through the application of Cherokee traditional stories with archival artifacts, we gain a nuanced understanding of the ways that Cherokee used education as a pathway that navigates survival and resistance.

The insights we can gain from this wisdom of nineteenth-century Cherokees serve as a case study for histories that challenge Eurocentric models of education and assimilation narratives. In chapter 5, I frame institutional documents such as blueprints, tribal law documents, and course catalogs through the Cherokee stories of Selu and Kana'ti that teach Cherokees ways to understand balance and gendered relationships. By applying the teachings of Selu and Kana'ti to the recovered artifacts and stories of the seminaries that are placed within the intersections of gender, race, and colonization, my archival research complicates assimilation narratives of Indigenous education, and instead offers a culturally motivated means of institutional practices and pedagogies. Answering Royster's call to relandscape rhetoric and composition, the histories of the seminaries that have been buried in archival practices provide a culturally Indigenous landscape that complicates our understanding of the origins of composition and rhetorical pedagogies.

Chapter 6 turns to the writing practices of nineteenth-century Cherokee and constellates the turn to literacy alongside the pedagogical means of teaching writing at the seminaries. In this chapter, I trace the relationships the Cherokee have with writing from the ancient stories of the Ani-kutani, a priestly clan of the Cherokee who used writing as a means of restricting knowledge and creating a hierarchical power structure within Cherokee society to the development of Sequoyah's syllabary as a means to retain sovereignty when faced with aggressive policies of erasure that Andrew Jackson ushered in. Through these stories, we learn that, for the Cherokee, writing was a material orality, and teaching writing in a way that acknowledged the material orality of the Cherokee meant developing and adapting writing pedagogies grounded in materialist methods. Courses at the seminary, such as Object Lessons, taught Cherokee students that writing was best learned through experience and that experience was gained through material exposure and relationship-making.

To further contextualize the progressive role of tribal education and literacy practices within the Cherokee Nation (Nelson 2014; Brown 2018; Justice 2006), I offer an analysis in chapter 7 of Cherokee student writing from student newspaper publications that range from 1850 to 1880 that I recovered in my archival research. By building on Ellen Cushman's work on the Cherokee language as perseverance (Cushman 2011) and situating the use of the Cherokee language as ontological, chapter 7 analyzes student writing that is published in the Cherokee language and pushes back against other publications that frame these newspapers as evidence of assimilation. These student writings and the publication practices of including both English and Cherokee stories follow a model created by the Cherokee Nation in their tribal newspapers and also uncover the roles of Cherokee women that follow traditional matrilineal structures. As part of an exchange program with other seminaries and colleges during the nineteenth century, these newspapers and student writings perform the dual role of navigating an expectation to perform "white" while Cherokee while maintaining sovereignty by centering the Cherokee language, which would be seen but not accessible to a white audience, through student writings that are for a specifically Cherokee audience. We know from oral stories as well as documentation that the Cherokee were an agrarian society with a robust political structure based on a clan system that set up the governmental structure for each of the Cherokee towns. The pastoral images that the Cherokee students describe, however, are not entirely accurate representations of Cherokee life and, in fact, seem to mirror the colonial settlers' images of the "noble savage." Were the Cherokee so far removed from their culture that they believed the settlers' stories of who they were in the past? The details about the specifics of Cherokee culture, including references to the stomp grounds, stickball, Green Corn Ceremony, and subtle repetitions of the role of the hunter, Kana'ti, and the Corn Mother, Selu, make it almost impossible to think that the Cherokee had forgotten who they were. Instead, what the students have done is create a mirrored existence through their writing of what the dominant society believes of the Cherokee. In all of these stories in the newspapers, the Cherokee students remark on how they are no longer this "noble savage" of white narrative dominance. By doing so, they shift their past and their culture onto a metaphorical past and culture that can be "erased" by claims of civilization. By recovering nineteenth-century Cherokee women's writing, my archival research situates writing practices at the Cherokee Female Seminary as embodying indigeneity in Eurocentric educational systems and exemplifying what Joshua Nelson calls "progressive traditions" that seek a third path of identity through rhetorical acts of survivance and cultural balance (Lyons 2000; Stromberg 2006) as a response to the realities of assimilation at a time of Native removal legislation and marked erasure.

Turning to the south, ᎣᎦᏃᎥ (uganawu), in the Afterword, I share the ways we can strive to maintain our relations, ᎢᎦᏗᎭᎢᎬᏁᏗ ᏚᎾᏓᏚᏜ (igatihaigvnedi dunadadudalv), by constellating Indigenous histories and the lessons we have learned from our ancestors with contemporary experiences of Indigenous peoples. Eurocentric histories have taught us to think that the past and our ancestors belong in museum displays and protected in archives, but our stories teach and steer us otherwise. Our pasts and our presents are cyclical and relational, and our ancestors are still with us, teaching us, through story. Colonization displaces our ancestors and their stories in the past as if our survival after the Trail of

Tears was not grounded in our traditions and practices that resisted and survived. For Cherokees now, we can turn to and listen to our ancestors who have so much to teach us about walking the path between survival and resistance. In order to maintain these relationships, I ask us to begin questioning the borders and boundaries we place between our research practices and our ways of being and knowing in the world. If Enlightenment thinking can construct a viable research method still in practice today, so too can Indigenous practices reframe our research methodologies in lasting ways. Storytelling, when it is recognized as such, transcends our borders between scholarly research and ways of being in the world. Even more than a methodological framework, the participatory nature of storytelling is a lived and embodied act that sustains a community of knowledge-makers across time.

It is here in the south that I synthesize connections between storytelling and the histories of the Cherokee National Seminaries so that we can see our current academic practices in ways that are reflective, performative, and transformative. Rather than a linear history that tells us to learn from a fixed past, I argue for a cyclical, relational, and material knowledge-making from communities that transcend temporal boundaries. In doing so, my book constellates the progressive rhetorical pedagogies at the Cherokee Female Seminary, storytelling, contemporary Indigenous experiences, and current methodological and pedagogical applications so that we may also walk the path between surviving and resisting colonial strongholds within academic institutions. By synthesizing these connections between nineteenth-century and contemporary academic experiences, I articulate the ways a colonial institution can be indigenized from within through storytelling and sharing contemporary experiences of Native American sovereignty within the walls of ivory towers. By reflecting on my archival work, I draw upon the experiences and writing practices of nineteenth-century Cherokee women who had to navigate the insider/outsider positionings of being Indigenous within the academy. By putting Indigenous practices in relation with academic experiences, I offer ways that those who are positioned as settlers in Indigenous knowledge-making practices can act as accomplices so as to join in *with* a community of knowledge-makers. These communities are woven together through story, ancestors, and all our relations through the ways that network individual knowledges within lived experiences that are culturally and rhetorically situated. Through these practices woven in both the content and structure in this book, we (Indigenous and settler scholars alike) can reflect on our own pathways in ceremony and work to Indigenize our teaching, our writing methods, and our storied ways.

Ultimately, the stories I tell in this book fall into such categories as Indigenous methodology, revisionist history, disciplinary landscaping, and archival research. Given that this story is also steeped in Indigenous teachings, locations, and culture, my aim is to tell a story through interdisciplinary constellations realized through Indigenous storytelling methodologies so that the stories here can speak of the Cherokees' own histories of composition teaching in the Cherokee seminaries. Always mindful of the Indigenous ways of being that I invoke in this book, I weave together Cherokee stories, Cherokee language, and Indigenous epistemologies in conversation with contemporary theories of materialism and object-oriented ontologies. By weaving together these approaches, my work reaches beyond illustrating interdisciplinary scholarship to performing, modeling, and actively participating in interdisciplinary scholarship through decolonial and Indigenous lenses. Through an interdisciplinary and Indigenous weaving of archival research, Cherokee stories, theoretical work, and historiography, this book steers us back to several present realities—the reality that the archives of the Cherokee National Seminaries have always already been Indigenous even in a colonized state; the reality that our methodological need to navigate and resist colonial structures still is present; and the reality that we, as scholars, must seek reflective practices that are constantly aware of our own cultural ecologies.

And so, let us breathe in together slowly, ready for the stories to unfold, so that we may work together to keep the fire of ᏚᏳᎪᏛ (*duyuk'ta*, balance) burning . . .

PART 2

ᎤᏄᎬ: ᏓᏣᏅᏒᎬ ᏕᎤᏓᏚᏓᎸ

kalvgv: anotlvsv dunadadudalv
East: Making Relations

Having grown up in a Christian household, we often began the holiday season with the story of John the Baptist, who appeared to prepare the people for the coming of Christ. "Prepare the way! Prepare the way!" he heralded, reminding us that every important moment and story that comes with it should help prepare the way for the advent of what is to come. While this story may ring more familiar to a wider audience than the Cherokee stories of councils of animals who prepared the Earth for the coming of our people, these stories serve as their own preparation and reminder that preparing and entering into ceremony requires us to actively come together to listen and participate. As so, ᎤᏄᎬ *(kalvgv, the east) serves as our herald to prepare us to make relations through and with the stories that bring us together so we may listen for the knowledge that is yet to come.*

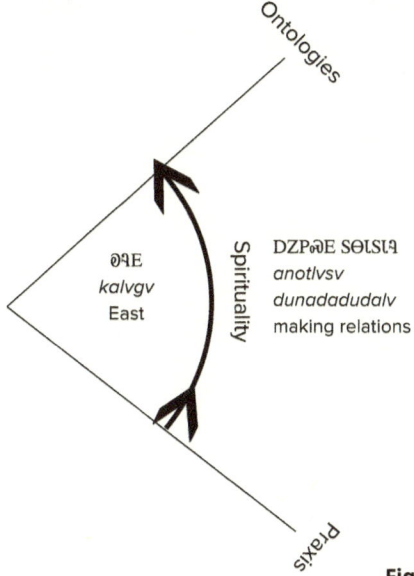

Figure 1.0. East: Making Relations.

1
ORIGIN STORIES
Our Stories, Our Ways, Our Knowledges

LISTENING FOR OUR GRANDMOTHERS' STORIES: A CAUTIONARY TALE OF ARCHIVAL RESEARCH

In those long and hazy summers of childhood, I would go looking for my Cherokee grandmothers in museums, unaware I was caught within the colonial teachings that the best place to find "my people" were in the quiet corners of displays about America's "exotic" past. As misguided and perhaps naive as these early museum wanderings were, I felt the pull to find some sort of balance between the material existences of my grandmothers that seemed lost and the stories of them that felt so alive every time I went to visit my grandparents. Each summer in Bartlesville, Oklahoma, I'd become reacquainted with my grandmothers. I'd always hear of them through stories that were often told after Sunday dinners of fried catfish and crappie, cucumbers, and tomatoes fresh from the garden and over the drone of golf or basketball on the television. These stories had convinced me that some material remnant of them may be living on, hidden somewhere in those curated museum displays of imperfect artifacts that showed off their authenticity with evidence of daily use from so long ago. Early on, I had made the connection between family and history by listening intently about how my family didn't always live in Northeast Oklahoma, of how a Trail of Tears brought them there, and of how my Cherokee great-grandmother had once walked through the halls of the magnificent Cherokee Female Seminary building in Tahlequah when she attended school to become a teacher in rural Cherokee lands. Those stories made it feel as though they could bring forth some spiritual connection with those artifacts kept at length behind the glass barriers in museums as I would carefully scan each display for something that was made recognizable from all of those Sunday dinners.

As those childhood summers came and went, I eventually convinced myself that I would settle even for just a name on an unassuming placard somewhere in the museum at Woolaroc Wildlife Preserve, a wildlife

https://doi.org/10.7330/9781646425228.c001

refuge with a museum that, after spending a few hours roaming outside in the bright heat of Oklahoma Augusts, always seemed so invitingly cold and dark to me as the A/C hummed overhead. When Woolaroc disappointed, I would squint my eyes to read the names of the donors in the Cherokee section of the Five Civilized Tribes Museum in Muskogee to see if, by some mistake, my grandmothers gave up their Cherokee artifacts before asking if my family might want to hold on to them. Even trips to the Cherokee Nation Heritage Center in Park Hill didn't seem to bring me any closer to finding my grandmothers beyond an invite from the docents to do some genealogy by reading the Dawes Rolls. As they were being helpful and patient, I didn't want to tell them that I had, of course, *seen* my grandmothers there, but those documents never opened up to let me *hear* them. Still, I had a look and tried to listen. As I sat down with the genealogist, I admitted that I knew they were on the rolls as I was an enrolled Cherokee citizen. At that point, she got excited and asked for my Cherokee family's name so she could pull out other documents and histories that were piled high on the cold, metal shelves of an almost forgotten room. But as quickly as she got excited, her demeanor (and mine) changed as I mentioned the name Nix. She had never heard of the Nix family and didn't know anyone by that name. I figured as much, as that was not a new story I had heard that day. As much as I tried to find them in those museums of curated histories, the names Nix, Armor, and Lowery never appeared alongside the more celebrated names Ross, Ridge, and Starr even though my childhood innocence convinced me that they all must have been friends and neighbors like some Cherokee version of six degrees of Kevin Bacon, or to us Cherokees, six degrees of Will Rogers.

Looking back, this quiet search for my grandmothers was my own way of navigating through the distance I felt from my own Cherokee heritage. In many discouraging ways, my silenced grandmothers seemed like a success story for colonialism and assimilation handed down through familial events that followed the death of my great-grandmother, Lucille Irene Nix, when my grandfather was only eighteen months old. Her land allotment she received through the Dawes Act had passed to her husband, Eldon Legg, who was not Cherokee. When he remarried, Lucille's land went to my grandfather's step-brothers, a part of my family history that is rarely discussed or acknowledged. The Indian Removal strategy enacted its generational trauma and tried to remove the "Indian" from my family and myself to save my assimilated contemporary existence. And yet, I know now that there was also generational strength at work as well. In a gentle wash of their wisdom to imbue a love of learning in me and perhaps even a little of their own desires to escape that Oklahoma summertime heat, my parents and grandparents forged a path for me to resist those systemic colonial strategies by helping to build and maintain a relationship with my culture in one of the few ways accessible to Cherokee living away from traditional communities. While her land eventually did return to my family, in this regard, my story wasn't unique among Oklahoma Cherokees, and it also wasn't completely over. My grandmothers may not have been in those corners—perhaps by their own design—but their stories filled my head and heart. And I wasn't done looking for ways to listen.

Driving down a rural, dusty road on my way to Tahlequah during the waning daylight of oranges, pinks, and purples was a familiar drive that retraced the many trips I had taken in those early, formative summers of childhood. I was looking for my grandmothers again, but this time I was motivated by that familiar research itch a young graduate student gets in the early days of dissertation writing. Although I had grown up in central Oklahoma, the northeast part of the state always felt more like home to me. Maybe it was the unassuming highway signs declaring "Entering the Cherokee Nation" or the ways that wheat fields melted into rolling grasslands and hills dotted with stunted blackjack oak trees, but I felt at ease there. Like so many other Cherokee, my family had been removed from their homes in Tennessee during the late eighteenth century, as white settlers encroached on the lands that were home to the Overhill Cherokees and which eventually would be flooded to become the Tennessee River Valley reservoir. With hopes to establish themselves as cattle ranchers, my family relocated west to Indian Territory, and eventually settled in the Cooweescoowee District of the Cherokee Nation near Vinita as they were able to receive a handful of land allotments near the now ghost town of Centralia. I knew the area well—as a kid, summer days meant traveling back to these places, with their familiar pile of gray rocks that served as corner fence posts peeking out from scraggy groves of blackjack trees near old houses built from the same red, orange, and gray stones. While visiting my grandparents, we'd spend time fishing for crappie, driving down country roads, picking wild blackberries with a snake-poking stick in hand, and wandering around the remnants of Centralia, which nature was taking back, where they grew up. I always tried to make time to listen to stories of aunts, uncles, cousins, and all my ancestors who I'd come to know more intimately as my grandmother took on the role of family genealogist. During these times, I learned about my relatives, my heritage, and Cherokee history. It was also my grandmother who would tell me about our connection to the seminaries and how my great-grandmother, Lucille, who I learned had died of tuberculosis she had contracted before my grandfather was born, was once a student there when it was a teaching college. Surely, I had convinced myself, Lucille had stories for me to listen to hiding somewhere in the archives.

Content by being at home in the Cherokee Nation and motivated to take on the role of Researcher, I started my official research trip with a nostalgic visit back to the Cherokee Nation Heritage Center, convinced that Great-Grandma Lucille would somehow be there ready to tell me stories in 2013. Once again, I looked up at the great and mighty pillars of the old Cherokee Female Seminary and listened intently for them to tell me about what education meant for the Cherokee and for me, a modern Cherokee woman trying to succeed along my own path in higher ed. In one of those chicken-and-egg dilemmas, I've tried to consider if it was the fact that I had been steeped in the collegiate stories of my grandparents, great-grandparents, and beyond or the fact that I always saw college as a liberating and self-defining moment in my life that drew me to the stories of my relatives as they attended schools in rural Oklahoma and Kansas. Opting to celebrate the both/and of my experience, I have been drawn to the histories of higher education and what it means for someone like me, a Cherokee from Oklahoma, to attend and find ways to give back to my own community from a space that felt far from the tallgrass prairies. What I did see, however, was the simple idea that a formal higher education did not have to exist away from those back country dirt roads. Because the Cherokee National Seminaries were among the first higher educational institutions established "out west," education had always been associated with the same prairies and hills I was so familiar with.

BEGINNING IN THE EAST: THE ORIGINS AND (DIS)LOCATIONS OF STORIES IN RESEARCH

I've told and retold this story more times than I can remember in various contexts—academic ones like conferences, published works, job talks, and everyday contexts to whomever would listen or shared my interests in anything Cherokee or education related. But perhaps the reason I've told this story so many times is that the stories of the Cherokee National Seminaries have never left me and are now a part of the ways I navigate my own existence. The seminaries are stories of my people, of my ancestors, and of my educational fabric, putting my research interests square in the "chicken or egg first" conundrum. But that's what stories do. Stories make us. They make our understandings and they share our knowledges. Stories lead us to new knowledges as well in those emergent encounters. There's always a moment right before a story begins, where a decision is made and the discourse shifts frames. The storytelling shifts can surprise us in the subtlety through a change in body language as we settle in for the tale, or stories can break in with their directness through the phrase "One time, back when," as we lean on the colloquial rendering of the fantastical "Once upon a time." Then, there are those times that something subconsciously creeps up and by just a laugh and a quick "remember when?" we find ourselves with a story. In those moments, shared across cultures and times, we enter into a shared framework of active telling, listening, and drawing together as we perhaps have something to learn from each other. It's always good to start with stories, as stories are at the core of what we know about our existence, whether your existence is found in Genesis, the Brahma, Skywoman, a big bang, or countless other ways of being and knowing. Stories are a good place to start because they bring us from nothingness to somethingness, not just in the beginning but again and again with each utterance and remembrance.

When we come together in story, we enter into ceremony through ᎣᎯᎬ (*kalvgv*, the east) as the stories we shape, share, and listen to bring us together for that suspended moment in time as we enter into a storytelling framework. Our stories are the opening of our ceremony, just as Indigenous groups use sage, sweetgrass, drums, and other means to quiet all our relations for ceremony and prepare them to listen, not just with one sense, but with their whole bodies, mind, and spirit (Archibald 2008, 76). This is why we begin in the east on the Cherokee medicine wheel. Just as the sun rises in the east to prepare us for the day, the Cherokee enter into council through the east, walking counterclockwise, to listen to stories that help make relations between the clans. This act is always deliberate and an embodied act steeped in practice to prepare our minds and bodies for what we will hear, discuss, and reflect on as a community. So, as with the sun, our stories bring us together and prepare us to make relations so that we may be respectful and reflective listeners, prepared for stories whose meanings may not always be what they seem on the surface (Archibald 2008, 76). Yet, by entering into ceremony, we become ready—heart, mind, and body—to begin the act of making relations not just with those around us but with the stories primed to guide us.

Once you hear a story and really take time to listen, that story takes root, holding strong together the stories it gathered along the way with yours. You are a part of it, and it is a part of you. And that's all there is.

This is the power of stories, as Thomas King reminds us, and so, I begin here with a story.

A long time ago, before we had books and before we had schools, we needed stories to teach people. These stories would teach us of the animals, how things came to be, and how to live in the world, treating each other with respect and care. Yet there was a time when we didn't have our stories, so this is the tale about how we got our stories. Once, a long, long time ago, there was a group of people who lived by themselves and could talk to the animals. Everyone, including the animals, spoke the same language, and everyone got along. However, one day, the people started to fight as people generally do. Argument after argument led to people not talking to one another. The arguments led to people pushing each other. The pushing led to fighting, the fighting led to stealing, and eventually people were so angry with one another, they began to hit so hard that they could kill one another. The Creator didn't like what had happened to the people, so he divided them up into groups of four. Each group was sent out in four different directions: North, South, East, and West. Once each group got to their destination, they were confused, as they had never lived in this place. They didn't know where the water was, what the plants were, how to get ready for winter—everything was unfamiliar to them. The Creator felt sorry for them and wanted to help them while they still were learning their lesson. So, he sent them dreams. These dreams taught them about the animals, plants, fish, medicines, what to eat, and what to do. With these dreams, the people began to learn and grow. Soon, they once again got along with each other in their new homes. The Creator sent another gift so that the people would remember and never forget these things. The Creator sent them Stories—stories about the animals, the plants, and how to do things. Each time the people would tell these stories, they would remember the Animals, the Plants, and how to take care of them and take care of each other.[1]

Stories, once they are told, take root and grow. The more they are told, the deeper the roots go, and the more that we can learn from them. This is why Cherokee start with stories in the east and why we enter into ceremony with our research in the east with stories as well. All of our knowledges have been given to us through story—our origins, our medicines, our relations, and how we are

---

1. Adapted from Kathi Smith Littlejohn in *Living Stories of the Cherokee*.

to exist as a part of this world. Stories prime us to enter into a discourse of learning through listening, and these stories take their place and grow through the connections we begin to make and realize through additional stories. Just like a birch tree grove and the mycelium networks that grow all around us, yet imperceptible on the surface, our stories provide a fertile and every-connected way of linking knowledge to experience to practice. We begin with these stories so that the cycle can keep on, never searching for a linear end. They are the networks that tie our epistemologies to our ontologies; and so, we begin in story.

Just as the Cherokee tell stories to remind them how to exist in the world, stories are used to shape worldviews, highlight what is culturally important, and provide connections to the past. The Cherokee story of the origins of storytelling make these connections meaningful, explaining that each time a story is retold, the people have more to learn and grow from it. In this sense, stories for the Cherokee are never fixed on a singular origin, but stories are living means that constantly (re)originates to make knowledge. Yet, in a Eurocentric sense, we often think of origins as tangibly connected to a moment fixed in time, signifying the beginnings of lasting trends, ideas, institutions, and even the eventual persons we become. We perpetuate this notion of fixed moments as stories and legitimize them through written histories that reside on library shelves. As these histories take up residence on shelves, our scholarly citation practices reinforce their legitimacy, morphing them into the capital H "Histories" that lay claim to the origins of scholarly thought. Cheryl Glenn and Jessica Enoch recognize the rhetorical work and power that the origin stories of rhetoric and composition have had on the shape of the field's understanding of its own histories and what historiographers have done to counter the ubiquity of these origins by explaining the ways that more traditional methods of research "strived for objectivity and truth, while contemporary historiographers make claims for unqualified objectivity in their reach for the 'truth'" (Glenn and Enoch 2010, 11). Rhetoric and composition historiographers, when encountering the rigidity of history and origin stories in the field, have gone to work "revisiting the archives, scouting out new ones, rewriting, and often overturning history" (Glenn and Enoch 2010, 11). This turn to recovery work in historiography has been fueled by feminist methodologies that opened up the landscapes of rhetoric and composition to include the overlooked stories of African Americans, Native Americans, Chicanx students, women teachers, non-English-speaking students, and more (Glenn and Enoch 2010, 14–16). Where the singular history of rhetoric and composition once resided, the stories of underrepresented yet influential peoples live. Where the origin story of rhetoric and composition once legitimized the discipline, the stories of rhetoric and composition shape our futures. These stories matter.

Yet, when we do archival work, the available archives are often sites where Indigenous peoples, histories, and cultures are actively "unseen," especially as the federal and state governments worked to dissolve tribal sovereignty and obtain artifacts and materials for their own Eurocentric archives and museums as a tactic to keep Indigenous peoples as relics of the past[2] (King 2017). Malea Powell explains this cultural practice of unseeing Indigenous peoples, such as the Cherokee, in the origins of the Euromerican-focused and colonizing American dream narratives. Centering around stories of settlers as brave men who tamed the wilderness, these narratives unsee Indigenous peoples who had already established vast nations and developed sustaining cultural practices. Powell explains, "For the colonizers, it is a necessary un-seeing; material Indian 'bodies' are simply not seen so that the mutilations, rapes, and murders that characterized this first-wave genocide also simply are not seen." Such "Un-seeing Indians," continues Powell in detailing the materiality of this first-wave genocide, "gave (and still give) Euro-Americans a critical distance from materiality and responsibility, a displacement that is culturally valued and marked as 'objectivity'" (Powell 1999). This objectivity is especially present in archival practices that are tethered to Enlightenment thinking, and it clouds our ability to see Indigenous histories in archival boxes. Ultimately, one of the underlying conditions of the disciplinary histories of rhetoric and composition is that they rely on what was deemed worthy enough to be archived, given space, maintained, and held by institutions. This unfortunate aspect of historiography is that it ultimately invites an origin story that is male-centric and exclusionary of BIPOC (Black, Indigenous, people of color) and women. What this means is that recovery work and historiography, especially for Indigenous peoples and their stories, remains a colonized space where even the act of researching history is granted only to those in power. Indigenous peoples have been removed from historical work in part

---

2. Lisa King has written extensively on Indigenous rights to self-representation in museums in her book *Legible Sovereignties: Rhetoric, Representations, and Native American Museums.* Her work argues that to be seen, Indigenous self-representation and sovereignty is balanced between what their sovereign rhetorical goals and the needs of a wider audience.

because of the simplification of oral cultures and the notion that a culture is unable to produce history without writing.

According to Hayden White, narrative (a mode of oral cultures) is simply not seen as an accepted form of theoretical application in research methods; rather it is still a discourse that serves as a representation of events (White 1984, 2–4). As if to mirror White, Walter J. Ong reiterates this point by focusing on the oral-literate binary, explaining that these narrative events spoken as utterances are "impossible to 'examine,'" because they remain in the realm of the oral and lack the materiality of writing (Ong 2009, 98). The idea that oral cultures lack a thingness to examine, to look back on, means that there is slippage in meaning and veracity in stories (or at least the possibility of such loss), making the historical indistinguishable from fiction and other forms of narrative. Like Ong's argument that utterances are unable to be examined, White argues that this lack of material reflection emphasizes the simulacrum and mimesis of the event, rather than the lived, historical event (White 1984, 3). Even if the so-called discursive narrative is an accurate representation of historical events, these oral stories are regarded as hearsay and lose all legitimacy without the value-added literate medium of writing. Their arguments feed into the common place notion that all history is fiction, which is often repeated inside and outside of academic parlance. Because of the claims that writing adds legitimacy and story as historical representation is unexaminable, Indigenous people are denied the rhetorical space and academic legitimacy to tell their histories through traditional methods, especially through oral narrative. "Just when minorities are insisting on telling their own histories," Craig Womack explains, "they find out that history is fiction—and perhaps, not fiction having the virtues that novelists and storytellers celebrate" (Womack 2008, 353). If stories are fiction, only a reflection of reality, where does that leave the Indigenous historian? Where does she turn to dismantle the colonizer's claim if her words are mere vestiges of reality, unacceptable to those in power?

As the saying so often goes, "History is written by the victors," and it's not a far stretch to add, "Research methods are established for the victors." Even in archival research, there is a clear need for methodologies that respond to colonial power structures that are felt deep within academic spaces—methodologies that are attuned to the voices of oppressed peoples and seek to work with these communities rather than talk about these communities as othered subjects. Aimé Césaire, in his influential 1955 *Discourse on Colonialism*, spoke clearly to the ravages of colonization and othering of subjugated peoples in Africa, Latin America, and the Caribbean. His work illustrates the power dynamics between the colonizer and the colonized and especially rings true when research is involved in these unbalanced power structures (Césaire and Kelley 2000, 42). Little is left for researching Indigenous histories as more than "an instrument of production" (Césaire and Kelley 2000, 42) to fill the coffers of academic research and publications. For Césaire, "colonization = 'thingification'" (Césaire and Kelley 2000, 42), which underlines the pressing need for research methodologies that expose the thingification of colonization. Beyond exposing colonization, methodologies must also seek to dismantle these power structures in which the colonizer has emphasized that Indigenous peoples, their cultures, and their knowledges are somehow uncivilized, placing them "lower on the evolutionary chain," and must be eradicated through exposure, conquest, and assimilation (Mallon 2012, 1–2). Insomuch that I value the work that archival research can do and the promise of scholarship that could potentially speak back to the rhetoric and composition origin stories, I knew that traditional methodologies to archival research, or even accepting archival research as a guiding methodology, would not suffice. To conduct my research in a good way, in a way that the Cherokee Origin of Stories has led me, I begin by centering my work through indigenist methodologies that champion the inventiveness of the archives through both written and memorialized artifacts as they are understood through Cherokee stories and relies on different research methods that serve to revisit our colonized histories and methods that grow out of Indigenous practices of storytelling.

As I began my archival research to recover Indigenous pedagogies and Cherokee writing at the Cherokee National Seminaries during the nineteenth century, I knew I was caught in these intersections of coloniality, gender, indigeneity, and assimilation rigidly laid out in a linear path in the archives. My turn to decoloniality is shared within the community of scholars invested in cultural methodologies, especially relying on Indigenous rhetorical scholars, like Andrea Riley Mukavetz, who explains that "Native rhetorics positions its scholarship and teaching within decolonial theories and social movements because of its commitment to privileging indigenous ways of knowing, acknowledging one's complicity in colonial rhetorics, and developing options for creating and sharing knowledge that does not use colonial rhetorical practices" (Riley Mukavetz 2014, 109). In order to decolonize and resituate myself and the artifacts in the archives that I was encountering, I needed to return to Indigenous worldviews of the Cherokee culture I position myself in and reframe my own ingrained knowledge-making through constellating and relationship-building. "A constellation . . . allows for all the meaning-making practices and their relationships to matter," the Cultural Rhetorics Theory Lab explains, "It allows for multiply-situated subjects to connect to multiple discourses at the same time, as well as for those relationships (among subjects, among discourses, among kinds of connections) to shift and change without holding a subject captive" (Powell et al. 2014) turning to constellating practices in archival research, scholars can decolonize archival practices that keep us in the rigid linearity of archival methods and make knowledge in relation with the artifacts and ephemera by listening to their cultural networks, peoples, and stories.

STORIES OF THE ORIGINS OF THE CHEROKEE NATIONAL SEMINARIES

What follows, then, is a story of the ways that the Cherokee developed and maintained an educational balance between progressive educational philosophies and traditional Cherokee culture and stories at the Cherokee National Seminaries. This story follows other academic predecessors who have encountered colonial shadows in their research. Julie Reed, a historian at Penn State University, writes about the ways that Cherokee maintained a balance between their traditional culture and societal structures to care for Cherokee orphans through an early educational system that promoted a sovereign collective welfare (Reed 2016). Because the nineteenth century was an incredibly unstable time in Indigenous history in the United States, the Cherokee continued to approach the cultural instability through a dedication to balancing acts that maintained a Cherokee identity, as Joshua Nelson's book *Progressive Traditions: Identity in Cherokee Literature and Culture* demonstrates. In addition to focuses on the nineteenth century, Cherokee scholars, such as Kirby Brown and Daniel Heath Justice, continue documenting the ways that the Cherokee maintained tribal sovereignty through their writing and continued to spread a national identity through their writing (Brown 2018; Justice 2006). Ultimately, all of these stories follow the practice of "restorying," as Quo-Li Driskill names the practice of storytelling that both restores and continues Cherokee traditions (Driskill 2016, 1), especially highlighting the ways Cherokee culture, colonized through archival practices, still continues and is present in the archives. As Cherokee people say, "We are still here,"[3] and as our archives say, "We are still telling stories."

---

3. "We are still here" is a phrase used by the Cherokee in public spaces, such as the Smithsonian's National Museum of the American Indian, to remind a white/ Eurocentric audience that Cherokee culture is not a relic of a past time that still

ONE ORIGIN STORY OF THE CHEROKEE NATIONAL SEMINARIES

The origin of the Cherokee National Seminaries, some of the first tribally run institutes of higher education, have roots in the early 1800s during the time that President Andrew Jackson made it his mission to remove and erase Indigenous nations from the southeastern United States. Even though the Cherokee Nation was formally established as a sovereign and autonomous government in 1794, the newly established United States immediately sought to undermine the sovereignty of the Cherokee Nation, located primarily in the present-day southeastern United States. One of the landmark Supreme Court cases, *Cherokee Nation v. Georgia*, directly stripped the tribal government of autonomy and sovereignty. This case, brought forth by the Cherokee Nation in 1831, sought a federal injunction against the State of Georgia, which passed laws denying the Cherokee rights within their boundaries. Rather than hearing the case, the US Supreme Court ruled that it had no federal jurisdiction in the matter because the Cherokee Nation was a dependent nation and wards of the state. Although the Supreme Court a year later instead ruled the Cherokee Nation as sovereign in *Worcester v. Georgia*, President Andrew Jackson did not uphold the court's ruling and instead instituted removal policies. After the actualization of the Indian Removal Act of 1830, the Cherokee, Chickasaw, Choctaw, Seminole, and Creek were rounded up from their homes, imprisoned in the middle of their towns behind fences, forcibly marched across the country, and relocated to what is now Oklahoma. The relocated Cherokee Nation began the process of reestablishing their government in Indian Territory (Oklahoma).

The newly established government valued education for the Cherokee greatly and enshrined their values in the Cherokee Constitution of 1839, writing, "Religion, morality, and knowledge, being necessary to good government, the preservation of liberty and the happiness of mankind, schools and the means of education, shall forever be encouraged in this Nation" (qtd in Starr 1921, 225). The council further emphasized the role of the Cherokee tribal government in the implementation of a tribally run school system, writing, "That all facilities and means of the promotion of education, by the establishment of schools, and the diffusion of general intelligence among the people shall be afforded by legislation, commensurate with the importance of such objects, and the extent and condition of the public finances; and all school which may be, and are now in operation in this National, shall be subject to such

---

pervades some of the knowledge people might have of American Indians, and that Cherokee culture and people are still living, practicing, and being Cherokee in our modern society.

1830
- Indian Removal Act

1831
- Beginning of Trail of Tears (forced march from Cherokee homelands to Indian Territory)

1839
- End of the Trail of Tears

1846
- Cherokee Council passes act establishing both seminaries near Park Hill, Indian Territory

1851
- Students begin arriving at seminaries & classes begin

1856
- Financial issues force the seminaries to pause accepting students

1861
- Continued financial problems and tribal upheaval caused by the start of the Civil War force the seminaries to close

1870
- After re-furnishing the seminaries after the upheaval of the Civil War, the Cherokee Nation reopens both seminaries are begins admitting students

1887
- Female Seminary burns down; complete loss

1887
- Dawes Act (Allotment Act) passed by federal government, requiring tribal nations to distribute reservations lands to individual tribal members

1889
- Female Seminary, now rebuilt in Tahlequah, starts admitting students; Curtis Act completely dissolves tribal governments, including the Cherokee Nation

1909
- Newly formed state of Oklahoma takes control of the seminaries from the Cherokee Nation; Cherokee Women join the Male Seminary, now run as a co-educational facility for Cherokee citizens

1910
- Male seminary building burns down completely, ending the co-educational institution

Figure 1.1. Timeline of the Cherokee National Seminaries.

supervision and control of the National Council as may be provided" (qtd. in Starr 1921, 225). By November of 1846, during the annual session of the National Council, the Cherokee Nation passed an act that furthered the tribal nation's dedication to supporting their nationhood and sovereignty through a national system for higher education for the Cherokee. This act jointly established the two nonsectarian national seminaries, one for men and one for women, "in which all those branches of learning shall be taught, which may be required to carry the mental culture of the youth of our country to the highest practicable point" (Cherokee Advocate 1847). Being established in less than ten years after the Trail of Tears, the Cherokee National Seminaries stood as an act of defiance and resistance against President Andrew Jackson's removal policies that sought to diminish tribal sovereignty not even ten years prior.

Seen as a shining beacon for Cherokee education and a source of national pride for the Cherokee people, the seminaries quickly became well established in the new Cherokee Nation. However, the early successes of the Cherokee National Seminaries were short-lived due to outside pressures from the national political scene during the 1850s and 1860s, and the seminaries both faced extreme hardships throughout their early tenure. During the Civil War, the Cherokee Nation had to close both seminaries due to lack of operating funds as well as the civil unrest that the Cherokee faced during this time.[4] The political pressures from the Civil War forced the Cherokee Nation to close both seminaries in the 1860s as the Cherokee Nation was torn between the Union and the Confederacy. While the seminaries were closed, the buildings were looted and stripped of materials, caught between the pro-Union faction of the Cherokee Nation and the pro-Confederacy faction. Both seminaries reopened during the 1870s after years-long efforts to reclaim the buildings, furniture, books, and other necessary supplies that were plundered during the war years. While the seminaries were once again opened to Cherokee Nation citizens, the stability was unfortunately not long-lived. On Easter Sunday in 1887, the Cherokee Female Seminary suffered a devastating fire. While no students were harmed, all that remained from the fire were a few books, including the gradebook, and the tall, brick pillars of the seminary building. Yet, even with this devastating fire, the dedication to higher education did not end. By 1887, the Cherokee Nation built a new female seminary in the nation's capital, Tahlequah, which still stands and is one of the major buildings of present-day Northeastern State University.

As the seminaries entered a new century, the nation was once again subjected to changing federal policies that impacted every part of Indigenous nationhood during this time. With the passage of the Curtis Act of 1889, the federal government all but dissolved tribal governments, and the Cherokee Nation was formally dissolved in 1906, prior to the admittance of Oklahoma into the Union. Ultimately, a newly established Oklahoma fought and won control of the female seminary

---

4. While the Cherokee Nation was not recognized as a state during the Civil War and the years leading up to it, the Cherokee were involved in numerous ways during this time, to the point that the Cherokee Nation was as factionalized as the United States. When the US government abandoned Fort Gibson, the Cherokee took over as all federal presence was removed. The citizens of the nation were divided among the Cherokee that were slaveholders and the Cherokee, who formed the Keetowah Society, who were pro-Union. As the United States warred, the Cherokee established both pro-Union and pro-Confederate regiments and joined their respective causes against each other.

in Tahlequah, purchasing it for $40,000 in 1909 (Agnew n.d.). At this point, the Cherokee continued the education of its women at the male seminary, which was now treated as a coeducational seminary. While educational operations were relinquished to the newly established Oklahoma State government, the US government continued to force policies focused on assimilation and allotment onto the tribal nations, which resulted in the Dawes Commission and the opening of Indian Territory to white settlers. The coeducational seminary continued until March 24, 1910, when yet another devastating fire completely destroyed the male seminary building (Starr 1921, 243). The story of the Cherokee National Seminaries is always lingering and ready to surface in the Cherokee Nation in northeastern Oklahoma. Whether it's passing by the imposing yet graceful Seminary Hall while walking down the streets of Tahlequah, visiting museums that showcase images of nineteenth-century women at the seminary playfully smiling in candid pictures of their walks through town, or remembered through family tales of their own relatives who went to the seminaries for some time, the Cherokee people of Oklahoma find the moments to recall the histories of the seminaries.

While mundane features might be left out, these histories are often buttressed with many of the more personal elements, such as the time Ann Florence Wilson, longtime and beloved principal of the Cherokee Female Seminary, bravely faced the fire that destroyed the seminary to rescue the gradebook. While the seminaries ceased to exist shortly after statehood, they live on and remain as vibrant in the minds of the Cherokee people as ever. However, outside of the Cherokee Nation, the history and ties to early nineteenth-century education of the seminaries are barely seen or heard. Even though the Cherokee National Seminaries exist and share a parallel history with the explosion of higher education in the United States during the nineteenth century, the importance of this cultural landscape is simply overlooked. To the outside, the seminaries are cast as another cog in the painful process of assimilation and erasure as they are often mistakenly seen as another example of federal- and missionary-run tribal education in the United States that is emblematic of the horrendous conditions and assimilation through federally run boarding schools such as infamous Carlisle Indian Industrial School. What is also erased when the history of the seminaries is collapsed to a mention is the importance of education to the survival of Cherokee culture, the building of nationhood, the careful use of writing and rhetoric by the students, and the impact that this cultural location cultivates within the histories of nineteenth-century higher education. My hope in telling this history alongside the history of nineteenth-century education is that the stories weave together to provide historians and scholars in rhetoric and composition with a fully realized cultural tapestry of our diverse and intercultural origins in order to disrupt the single narrative origin story.

RED BRICKED LANDSCAPES OF THE NINETEENTH CENTURY AND THE SHADOWS OF CURRENT-TRADITIONALISM

The nineteenth century is often recognized as a key moment for our higher-education system and an origin of our modern educational practices. It's easy to see why: the nineteenth century marked a " 'red-brick' explosion" in both England and the United States, borrowing its name from the construction of red brick buildings on newly platted universities (Parker 1967, 344). While formal education began as early as 1591, the number of universities in England remained steady at seven until 1828. However, the young United States established more than seventy universities after 1828, many of which are still operating today. It is during this era of rapid education progression that many scholars in rhetoric and composition have turned to as a focus for historical recovery work, producing in-depth histories about the early days of modern rhetorical study and the origins of composition studies during the "red brick explosion" of the nineteenth century. These histories and origins are found in the pages of works such as Albert Kitzhaber's influential 1953 dissertation, *Rhetoric in American Colleges, 1850–1900*, John C. Brereton's *The Origins of Composition Studies in the American Colleges, 1875–1925*, James Berlin's *Writing Instruction in Nineteenth Century American Colleges*, as well as many others. One of the distinguishing features in all of these texts is the method of recovery work that focused on the tangible evidence of education that steered scholars away from narratives that had been passed down through institutional threads. Many of these recovered histories rely on institutional archives as sources of retained pedagogical practices, especially since the nature of pedagogical practices often is documented through various pieces of ephemera, if those pieces even remain. While recovering nineteenth-century pedagogies can be a daunting task even for the most diligent scholar, the lasting impacts of scholars like Kitzhaber, Berlin, and Brereton are the models they provide to begin this work. Kitzhaber's *Rhetoric in American Colleges, 1850–1900*, turns to the material locations of our pedagogical histories—the libraries and archival boxes filled with remnants of the everyday lives of students in old textbooks, pictures, newspaper clippings, and scrapbooks.

His analysis of nineteenth-century textbooks begins the work of finding our entrenched composition practices as well as provides a method for historians and scholars to follow. In addition, *Archives of Instruction: Nineteenth Century Rhetorics, Readers, and Composition Books in the United States* (Carr, Carr, and Schultz 2005) is another clear example of how scholars have creatively relied on archival material to recover pedagogies during the nineteenth century. As a means to combat the "forgetfulness" of pedagogy and overlooked literacy artifacts, the authors explain that their work functions as both a recovered history as well as a means to continue to do recovery work through the analysis of the cultural impulses and pedagogical practices illustrated in textbooks from that time (Carr, Carr, and Schultz 2005, xiii). By contextualizing ephemeral pieces through cultural practices, these scholars have laid a foundation of disciplinary history and an origin story that connects the oldest roots of the discipline to contemporary teaching practices. Indeed, archival work has certainly been productive and necessary for recovering histories, the archive can still produce an authoritative origin story, even though the archive is the seat of rhetorical and historical invention. Yet, Malea Powell speaks out strongly against the tendency to emphasize this origin story through our historical research, explaining, "Our discipline's inclination to fetishize the text above the body, combined with the narrowness of vision that insists on connecting every rhetorical practice on the planet to Big Daddy A and the one true Greco-Roman way does not exactly build a sustainable platform for the continued vibrancy of our disciplinary community" (Agnew et al. 2011, 121). She calls for a turn away from colonial discourse and asks rhetoric and composition scholars to "rely on rhetorical understandings different from that singular, inevitable origin story" (Agnew et al. 2011, 122). This is certainly true for rhetoric and composition research that is conducted in the archives, and while these connected narratives of nineteenth-century composition pedagogies are indeed useful to the field and necessary work, I argue that our limited focus stems in part from the accessibility of archives situated within northeastern universities that were attended by men during the nineteenth century.

The beginnings we settle on create locations for our discipline's histories, and these locations often are seen as the spaces of our pedagogical practices. For example, Brereton's work of gathering materials and summarizing the emerging narratives gives us an example of extensive and careful archival work that serves as a model for tracing histories through the textbooks and student work hidden in archives that were long overlooked (Brereton 1995). While Brereton's text remains influential because of the depth of archival research, he is also clearly aware of the limitations set up by his methods to produce a seemingly decontextualized and male-dominated history of composition, explaining that up until the 1900s and in spite of the red brick explosion of universities, only 15 percent of all college students were women (Brereton 1995, 19). He situates this lack of diversity with his methods of assembling his text. While there are many examples of student writing in other research libraries, Brereton explains, he had access to Harvard's library and to those texts that were preserved from that time and housed in the library (Brereton 1995, xv–xvi). Even as our discipline asks us to push the boundaries of our origins, as historians and scholars, we are often constrained by the accessibility of archival materials, as Brereton reminds us. Harvard's composition practices locate an origin for our discipline because of the archives available and the accessibility to materials in those archives. Because of the value given to Harvard by the dominant society, the materials that form our histories are also value laden because they were considered worth archiving. However, when working with institutions that lacked access to this cultural valuing, we are restricted in the materials that make our histories. Our materials cast shadows, hide our landscapes, and argue for a singular origin and singular story.

While there is a finality in artifacts, the stories we tell continue beyond the archives. These stories shape the ways we understand the world around us, and like the Creator, are given to us to help us understand ways to exist. But what happens when these stories are shaped on a colonized materiality of the past? What shadows do they cast? As Jacqueline Jones Royster argues, "what we choose to showcase depends materially on where on the landscape we stand and what we have in mind. The imperative is to recognize that the process of showcasing space is an interpretive one, one that acknowledges a view and often rescopes that view in light of aesthetic sensibilities—values, preferences, beliefs" (Royster 1996, 148). I open with this conversation motivated by Royster to emphasize a point: The disciplinary history of rhetoric and composition is indeed landscaped—through histories, archives, and institutions. The available and accessible archival evidence has shaped the history of rhetoric and composition through Harvard's composition program and textbooks in part because Harvard's curriculum was highly documented, leaving behind material traces for historiographers. This robust documentation should not be any surprise, even to the most casual historian—Harvard is still considered the shining light of American education and, even more, Harvard's English program during the nineteenth century was on the forefront of education reform and established a pattern that other colleges began to follow. In fact, by the 1900s, Harvard's English program was the most prominent and influential English program in the United States (Kitzhaber 1990, 33). Because of Harvard's influence, claim to preeminence, and robust archives, it's easy to see why historiographers are drawn to Harvard as an origin of modern education and fertile grounds for an origin story that can legitimize and uplift a disciplinary history, especially rhetoric and composition, which had be relegated to the drudgery of academic service.

And so the story goes that Harvard's rise to prominence began under Charles Eliot, during the second half of the nineteenth century, who promoted the practical application of rhetoric to speaking and writing, rather than a discipline to study for the sake of study and knowledge alone (Kitzhaber 1990, 32). With a disciplinary shift to practical application, Eliot's educational reforms resulted in what is known as the Harvard Plan, which became a model of entrance examination for colleges during this time. Because Harvard's entrance requirements included an examination in English studies, preparatory schools began to focus more of their curriculum on composition and literature; yet even with these cross-institutional curriculum changes, Harvard's admitted students still struggled when writing about subjects other than what they had studied for the entrance exam. While the Harvard Plan pushed the lower schools to adjust their curriculum, these schools did little else to prepare students for more advanced writing. Because the Harvard Plan was so influential, all of the colleges that adopted the entrance examination model were challenged by students who were woefully underprepared (Kitzhaber 1990, 43). The ultimate result of this pattern of students passing their entrance exams in English and struggling beyond is that colleges needed to adapt their own curriculum to compensate. This curriculum, now known as current-traditionalism, focused on the transferable mechanics of writing and decontextualization of rhetorical moves; that is, formal rules of grammar that did not always allow for flexibility in writing. In combination with Parker's explanation that these now "service" courses were often taught by itinerant faculty, innovation and deviation from current-traditionalism seemingly halted for decades to the point that even today we still are discussing the value or constraints of the five-paragraph essay in freshman composition courses. current-traditionalism has become the long shadow cast on the early histories of educational reform and progressive approaches to rhetoric and composition that also occurred alongside Harvard during the nineteenth century to the point that our disciplinary history seems rigidly single-stemmed.

Pruning our disciplinary history through Harvard and current-traditionalism, no matter how influential these approaches were, ultimately emphasizes the connected origin narratives of the discipline's histories that are located in male-dominated, northeastern colleges of the nineteenth century. However, just as the field develops a history that stems from one branch of nineteenth-century education, scholars are actively answering the call and revising these histories to be more inclusive. To help us maintain a diverse history of composition teachings and rhetorical theory, we can look outside of Harvard and other male-centered teaching instructions as not just a response to these uncontested histories but as a way to "re-landscape" our discipline, as Royster calls us to do (Royster 1996). As ubiquitous as the Harvard plan and current-traditionalism has become in the histories of not just rhetoric and composition but also English departments, there is the need to constantly remind ourselves that these histories are also contextualized and not universals. Why did current-traditionalism take hold when it did? Kitzhaber points to a confluence of events: the rise of land grant universities through the Morrill Act, the Harvard reports placing the blame of the lack of preparedness in writing on lower schools, the superficial means of addressing those problems through a one-size-fits-all approach to composition studies, and the impact of the German model of education that introduced electives and specialization to the college curriculum (Berlin 1984, 17, 47). All of these factors are emblematic of an educational system that was aimed at upwardly mobile white men, for whom writing and rhetoric are in service to a newly specialized workforce during the nineteenth century. Yet, this history excludes how colleges, and specifically rhetoric and writing curriculums, might serve populations that did not have access to the white-male-dominated society. Not only do these histories exclude women, African Americans, and Indigenous peoples, these histories that celebrate the impact of Harvard and the "red brick explosion" are literally built on the backs of enslaved peoples and indentured servants who made the red bricks and the land that was recently forcefully taken from the Indigenous peoples that was "redistributed" through the Morrill Act for these universities (Lee and Ahtone 2020).

And yet, I have certainly felt the promise of the archive as a site of dreams, invention, and allure; however, there are constant reminders that the archives still remain a seat of colonial structures and powers. This became inherently clear as I began my own recovery work in rhetoric and composition, searching through the archives of the Cherokee Female Seminaries. These archives were still a product of 1830s research practices, which, perhaps not coincidentally, was the height of removal practices instituted in Andrew Jackson's America and a time of greatly felt and overt colonization of Indigenous peoples of that same America. And so, I return to the original problem of using only the archives as the source or recovery work: the scarcity of materials from the Cherokee seminaries due to hardships that befall the Cherokee peoples during a tumultuous nineteenth century. Beyond the seminaries' written histories, the materials located in the archives are tied to the political upheavals of the Cherokee Nation as well—upheavals that began before the establishment of the seminaries and continued long after. While the Cherokee people remained through years of removal, assimilation, and erasure, surviving even without a federally recognized government until 1975 when the commissioner of Indian Affairs approved the modern Cherokee Nation Constitution,[5] the dispersal of the Cherokee and their shared histories means that the ownership and physical locations of archival materials are scattered between several different governing bodies. Anyone who is familiar with archival work understands the grave impact this has on our ability to recover stories from the archives. Archives rely on the preserved ephemera—the textbooks, papers, journals, meeting notes, and so on. Little is left of the original seminaries for us in these archives. What is left has been processed and collected through the State of Oklahoma and outside of tribal ownership. Specifically, the archives I sought out were housed in forgotten floors of university libraries, maintained by the state, organized by archivists without any connection to the Cherokee people.

UNSEEING OUR DISCIPLINARY LANDSCAPES

While Harvard's shadow still looms largely in the histories of rhetoric and composition, considerable work has been done to find beginnings and reclaim disciplinary histories as diverse and multifaceted narratives that unseat Harvard as the center of educational reform and innovation in the nineteenth century. Scholars have begun locating overlooked nineteenth-century scholars and institutions whose archival materials may not be as robust, but the materials left still leave us stories to tell that offer a counter-narrative to the focus on current-traditionalism in the Northeast. David Gold and Jessica Enoch are two such scholars that challenge our located beginnings. Gold's *Rhetoric at the Margins* (Gold 2008) draws our

---

5. Today, the federal government recognizes three sovereign Cherokee governments: the modern-day Cherokee Nation, the Eastern Band of Cherokee Indians, and the United Keetoowah Band.

attention to the roots of education models found in the archives of colleges in Texas that served underrepresented students that uncover the ways that these underrepresented communities turned to local knowledge from the community to serve the students' needs. By focusing on the community and the students, models of education were framed around "community uplift and civic responsibility," which continued to encourage students to participate in their local communities. Even more, Gold argues, these local needs and local context changed the nature of writing histories for these populations in ways that Harvard's writing histories cannot address (Gold 2008, 17). In addition to Gold, Enoch's *Refiguring Rhetorical Education* examines the way nineteenth-century female teachers created new ways of teaching rhetoric and writing that recentered education around dismantling power structures of race, language, and culture to reshape pedagogy into a more progressive, student-centered approach (Enoch 2008, 7). While rhetoric and composition has been handed a history that has been inadvertently whitewashed through Harvard and the impact of current-traditionalism, Enoch's work showcases the ways that rhetoric and composition has always been a major part of progressive educational policies, even in the nineteenth century. While they are just two such scholars among many doing this kind of recovery work, both Gold and Enoch push the boundaries of our disciplinary origin stories to expose the cultural situatedness of our locations of writing and pedagogies entrenched in our histories. In addition to Gold and Enoch, Sarah Klotz's book, *Writing Their Bodies: Restoring Rhetorical Relations at the Carlisle Indian School* (Klotz 2021), provides a uniquely decolonial history of writing and pedagogy at the Carlisle Indian School as she uses decolonial archival methods to recover the writing practices of Indigenous students through the perspectives of the students themselves. Her recovery work centers early Indigenous literacy practices of student texts, which provides an overlooked yet highly important analysis of early Indigenous textual practices during the late nineteenth century, and because her work employs decolonial methodologies, it also does the work of decolonizing the ways that writing and rhetoric scholars attend to disciplinary histories. Even when limited to materials, our work is to push these boundaries and listen, just as Gold, Enoch, and Klotz do. The methods I use in challenging these narratives are the same archival methods used to establish claims to a disciplinary history told through the Harvard narrative. This is a deliberate move to explore the constructed nature of our histories and to engage with the important work that not only archival recovery does but also the stories that are uncovered—stories that often go undiscussed in limited scopes of patriarchal lineages of educational models.

Scholars such as Kitzhaber, Brereton, Berlin, Gold, Enoch, Klotz, Crowley, Hobbs, Graban, Mastrangelo, Ritter, and others have situated their work deep in the archives, envisioning and reenvisioning histories of rhetoric and composition scholarship and pedagogies. In order to challenge accepted narratives and see through the shadows, I focus on a location of composition pedagogy and history that runs chronologically alongside the development of the Harvard method of composition as discussed by Brereton, Berlin, and others. By revising the single origin stories of rhetoric and composition by examining the history of teaching and rhetorical curriculum at the Cherokee National Seminaries, I hope to actively listen to stories that are overlooked in our disciplinary histories—stories of women and BIPOC, and in turn, ultimately show that our disciplinary landscapes are not void of cultural influences that ask for vastly different approaches to composition pedagogies. The Cherokee National Seminaries as cultural locations give us a foundation to understand a model of teaching that on the surface could quickly be dismissed as another example of composition pedagogies that followed the Harvard tradition to our modern understandings of current-traditionalism. But ultimately, these locations tell a deeper narrative of Indigenous educational practices that fit a model of educational practices of the progressive movement of the late nineteenth century. My aim is to open up our bounded locations of writing, recovering what has been pruned away and looking toward this historical and cultural location of writing.

INDIGENIST LISTENING AND (RE)TELLINGS

To perform Indigenous revisionist history is to call out and resist colonized narratives, look back, look through, and look within as we shift our research from methodologies that are deeply embedded in colonialism. Through this reflective practice, research must be understood as relationship-building through ways of knowledge-making that are Indigenous. "Indigenist research," Shawn Wilson (Opaskwayak Cree) and Margaret Hughes (White Settler American) explain, is "about who we are, how we know and engage with Knowledge, what we do as researchers, and the ways we enact relational accountability" (Wilson and Hughes 2019, 7). When research is critically reimagined (Royster 2000) as indigenist, it invokes critically reflective actions that build relationships, which shifts the researcher's role to one of accountability and sustainability. In other words, the very process of relational research holds the researcher accountable toward the community in ways that sustain the community. It is always an active process that at its core develops meaningful research practices that create knowledge through "a process of strengthening or building our relationships—with community, with Place, with new ideas or insights" (Wilson and Hughes 2019, 12). As a researcher follows this path of relationship-building, they are held accountable to the moral impulses of indigenist research, which forwards Indigenous values of respecting and being accountable to all our relations (Wilson and Hughes 2019, 12). Indigenist methodologies and relational accountability are present even in the very heart of research: Inquiry. Rather than inquiry beginning with a data set or even a set of research questions, indigenist methodologies call for inquiry to begin with the self, reaffirming the importance of accountability. "Relational accountability points to the experience that when we recognize reality as relationships, we have to act differently," Wilson and Hughes explain, "At every stage, we have to ask ourselves, am I fulfilling my responsibilities to my relationships? Is this of benefit to the community? Am I being true to my values? Am I being true to the values and wishes of the communities with whom I'm working? Is this research approach enacting an ethics of care?" (Wilson and Hughes 2019, 13). Constantly invoking these reflective questions helps keep the researcher engaged and active within relationships while they also expand our understanding of the inquiry process. Rather than being driven by only the need to inquire about the content of research, the inquiry process is constantly filtered through self-inquiry, which actively centers the human back into research, challenging years of Enlightenment practices of removing the humanness of research.

I want to return to the story of that first time I stepped into the archives at Northeastern State University and the time the archivist used the Federal Educational Rights and Privacy Act (FERPA) to limit my access to the Cherokee Female Seminary archival artifacts, specifically the famous gradebook of Ann Florence Wilson. I have been telling this story for academic laughs for years at this point, landing on the punchline of "being FERPA'd," which almost always garners the same tenor of laughs as "dad jokes" in twenty-first-century parlance. Jokes aside, this moment has always stuck with me and, as I reflect now, was the start of my inquiry process to this entire book, I just didn't see it then. I'd like to use the excuse that I was a young grad student, fresh out of piles of theoretical texts of coursework. I'd like to say that I didn't know what I was doing, that I didn't frame my research questions rhetorically for the archivist. I'd even like to call her a colonizing gatekeeper. But all of those are just excuses, almost as cringe-worthy as my FERPA gaff. That moment in my research, when framed through reflective inquiry and Indigenous ways of knowing, was a call for relationship-building with the archives, but I wasn't yet ready.

Even though I was an Indigenous scholar, my scholarly ways of knowing were borrowed from colonizing methods that removed the human from archival research. I had done everything right—secured permission, followed protocols, set up appointments, worried about whether gloves were needed or not to handle fragile artifacts, and appeared with "legitimizing" credentials on university letterhead. But I did not take time to build a relationship with that document, with the Cherokee stories, or with the ancestors. Why was I FERPA'd? Was I entering the archives to give back to the community? Am I being true to my Cherokee culture when analyzing that gradebook? Am I being a responsible agent in that relationship? While FERPA protects current (and by default, living) students, it is not a stretch to see that by invoking FERPA, the archivist was gently reminding me of the very living nature of the stories created by archival artifacts and the material connection to ancestors, whether that was her intention or not. It's also a reminder that the ways we are taught research are colonized and do not acknowledge other ways of knowing, privileging Enlightenment and Eurocentric knowledges. I still tell this story anytime I'm asked to talk about my research, embellishing the details to land on the punchline, but now as I tell it, I am reminded of the importance of research and relationship-building. I'm reminded once again of origin stories, our relationships to them, and, even more importantly, the power of them when crafted through Eurocentric lenses.

Both decolonial and Indigenous methodologies have developed alongside each other, sharing and intersecting disciplinary spaces. Often, decolonial and Indigenous studies are used interchangeably and alongside each other in interdisciplinary fields such as Indigenous studies, rhetoric and composition, and social sciences. However, there is a recent trend observable in current publications that differentiates the two schools of thought through a development of specific Indigenous practices. These differences range from decolonial methodologies (such as Smith) that focus on the roles and relationships between the researcher and the participant, exposing power structures and Indigenous methodologies that are centered on specific ways of thinking (knowledge-making) through traditional Indigenous practices (used as methods). Typically, in Indigenous methodologies, the power dynamics of research are not brought out to the forefront but are implicit in their presence as researchers develop methods to navigate such power structures and hierarchies. I focus here on indigeneity as a framework for methodology, specifically turning toward material knowledge-making practices. Amidst this wave of decolonialism, scholars who were doing decolonial work also called for an "indigenizing of the Academy." Specifically, Devon Mihesuah, enrolled citizen of the Choctaw Nation and Indigenous historian, called on academics in Native American studies as well as those who work in other interdisciplinary spaces, to begin using more Indigenous theories rather than relying on non-Native intellectuals, such as Foucault, Said, and others, to build decolonial work, empowerment, and other activist work upon (Mihesuah 2006). In investigating the Indigenous dimensions of historiography, I use Chilisa's *Indigenous Research Methodologies* and Wilson's *Research Is Ceremony* to articulate Indigenous methodologies that relate to knowledge-making. Just as Smith and Deloria call out Eurocentric methods of research (Smith 2012; Deloria 1988), Chilisa outlines the distinction between Western approaches to research, and articulates Indigenous research that differs from Western notions of research and consists of four dimensions:

> (1) It targets a local phenomenon instead of using extant theory from the West to identify and define a research issue; (2) it is context-sensitive and creates locally relevant constructs, methods, and theories derived from local experience and indigenous knowledges; (3) it can be integrative, that is, combining Western and indigenous theories; and (4) in its most advanced form, its assumptions about what counts as reality, knowledge, and values in research are informed by an indigenous research paradigm. (Chilisa 2012, 13)

The work of Indigenous methodologies is two-fold: first, it seeks to *decolonize* to expose the colonial structures in research, and second, it works to *indigenize* research by replacing colonial conventions with approaches and methods that are culturally responsive (Chilisa 2012, 23–24). During this dual process, however, it remains paramount to not set up research binaries—an either/or—between Eurowestern approaches and decolonial approaches. Instead, I seek both/and from an Indigenous perspective. The reflective practice of interrogating and opening up research paradigms, Chilisa purports, is "a tapestry, a mosaic of balanced borrowing of less hegemonic Euro-Western knowledge and its democratic and social justice elements and combining it with the best of the democratic, liberatory, and social justice essentialized Indigenous knowledge and subgroups' knowledges" (Chilisa 2012, 25). Through these methodological moves, Indigenous research paradigms form a framework for knowledge-making practices that are attuned to cultural situatedness.

Indigenous research recognizes colonial structures in research from a decolonial framework and looks for ways to navigate these structures by building networked ways of knowing through the understanding that all things are related and relevant. Shawn Wilson, an Opaskwayak Cree scholar, purports, "If Indigenous ways of knowing have to be narrowed through one particular lens (which it certainly does not), then surely that lens would be relationality. All things are related and therefore relevant" (Wilson 2008, 58). Wilson critiques Eurocentric research and ways of knowing by explaining that the almost sacred belief in objectivity comes from the idea that in order to fully understand data, you must break it down into its smallest parts, separating everything it may be related to (56). Knowledge, therefore, becomes a "separate identity" (56) and intellect stems from the removal of emotions and motives (Wilson 2008, 55–56). To further the distinction between a Eurocentric approach to research and an Indigenous way, Wilson contends that Indigenous ontology is the idea that "reality *is* relationships or sets of relationships. Thus there is no one definite reality but rather different sets of relationships that make up an Indigenous ontology" (Wilson 2008, 73). This move to understand both Indigenous epistemology and ontology as relationally based also opens up practices of storytelling as epistemological, ontological, and relational as the researcher takes up the task of being Storyteller (Wilson 2008, 32). I argue that this theoretical and storied approach is a necessary framework, especially in the use of archival research. Archival research remains a contested research method due to the realities that archives are often removed from their Indigenous ecologies and placed within colonized networks, especially when those archives are compiled by researchers that either are not familiar with Indigenous worldviews or are not members of the affiliated tribes.

As we use archives to help us recover the histories of rhetoric and composition, we need to remember that the practice of "revising" history is more than just a creation of another narrative of disciplinary history. It's acknowledging the situatedness and materiality not only of accepted histories, but also of our own relationships with/in research practices that look back to these histories. Archives—those objects removed and colonized from their lived past—especially call us to seek out relationships between the object, the people, the time, and the place. While we can label such items on the outside of gray, archival boxes, it is our stories that theorize these relationships in an epistemological moment. My goal from the beginning of my research was not to assert one history's legitimacy over another, as competing origin stories often do, but rather to re-story our discipline so that it acknowledges multiple stories, voices, and histories as all accepted narratives. I am certainly not the first scholar to step into the archives with this goal in mind, and feminist historiographers in rhetoric and composition have relied of the theoretical frameworks of positionality to uncover the ways that our discipline has been shaped through students, teachers, and pedagogies that offer a counterpoint to the elite male-centric view of composition history (Glenn and Enoch 2010, 22). Rhetoric and composition's narratives centered on Harvard and other male-dominated teaching spaces, while limited, ultimately offer us a lens to talk back to and talk through. As David Gold explains, "we can no longer afford simple narratives of heroes and villains. It is not enough to simply point to the past for evidence of practices that align with our own constructions of what is progressive . . . we must examine how historical actors responded to their own contemporary exigencies, both micro and macro" (Gold 2012, 24). However, Jo-ann Archibald Q'um Q'um Xiiem, Jenny Bol Jun Lee-Morgan, and Jason De Santolo explain that "decolonizing research methods do not totally dismiss Western methodological approaches; they encourage us as Indigenous researchers to connect research to our own worldviews and to theorize based on our own cultural notions in order to engage in more meaningful and useful research for our people" (Archibald, Lee-Morgan, and De Santolo 2019, 6). Never is this more true than walking into the archives as a researcher—archives that are assembled through Enlightenment-era methods will exist, often under tension, in those assemblages that reinscribe colonialism. As an archivist, and especially an Indigenous archivist, you are subjected to the same colonialist structures that the archives are under. As Malea Powell, a mixed-blood of Indiana Miami, Eastern Shawnee, and Euroamerican ancestry, explains, "and here *I* am, an Indian talking about what it means to be an Indian in the archives, what it means to be the object looking back, the objectified engaged in the process of making knowledge about the processes that led to my objectification" (Powell 2008, 117). In a very real sense, there is no breaking away from colonialist impulses in archival research because the archives (and you) are already colonized. Every time during this process I stepped into the archives as "an Indian in the archives," I was aware of this tension and shadows within each box I carefully opened, even if I was unaware of what awaited inside.[6] This is a story, then, of indigenizing rhetoric and composition's histories and listening to the stories of the Cherokee National Seminaries that have been silenced in dusty archival boxes to guide us on our way. And so, as we remain still in the east, making relations through stories, let us take time to learn from teachers like Wolf and others on the ways that we can begin to seek out ways through all our relations to indigenize the archive.

---

6. While my work in the archives involved almost entirely paper ephemera, it's especially important to note here that many archives include the physical remains of Indigenous people, often stored in boxes and paper bags. So, while I found paper, many Indigenous scholars have found the literal remains of their ancestors on these same shelves. Archives, while to some are places of dreams and knowledge waiting to be shared, are for others literal places of nightmares and generational trauma.

2

WOLF WEARS (EUROCENTRIC) SHOES
Indigenizing the Archives

As approaches to education became more formalized in the eastern portions of the United States, these formalized changes in educational philosophies and rhetorical theories in nineteenth-century America occurred alongside the political upheavals and continued colonization of Native Americans through broken treaties, forced removals, assimilation, and cultural erasure. Situated at these intersections are the Cherokee National Seminaries, whose histories are entwined in the political history of the Cherokee Nation and federal and state governments. Now located in libraries, boxes, and files, the archives of both seminaries leave behind traces of stories; not only did both seminaries suffer devastating fires during their tenure, they also suffered from outside pressures through treaties enacted by the federal government and forced takeover by the state government. The ephemeral nature of paper documents associated with teaching practices—textbooks, catalogs, and student work—bear the marks of these damages. While those locations have been relegated to our written histories, the people and knowledges still remain within the material confines of archives and as part of the living stories. These living stories of the Cherokee become a point of ontological contact with Eurocentric research positionings in ᎧᎸᎩ (*kalvgv*, the east) as we continue along the Cherokee medicine wheel. As part of our ceremonial preparation to hear these stories, we begin with the encounters of the Cherokee National Seminaries and Indigenous metaphysics woven together with the Eurocentric impulses of archival research. This move to weave together what colonialism has caused helps us as researchers to navigate the ways that we can enter into a relational and metaphysical space with the archives as storytellers. This ontological shift as we make relations in ᎧᎸᎩ (*kalvgv*, the east) moves the role of the storyteller from the Eurocentric researcher to the Indigenous artifacts, asking us to listen and reflect on these encounters, who in turn asks us to shift from seeing only "what is" as material to acknowledging that the ideas and essences of "what is" is manifested through the relationships that we are in. So, as we journey in ᎧᎸE (*kalvgv*, the east), we begin with research stories and ontological framings to help us make relations with the storytellers in the archives.

For the Cherokee, the seminaries out in the prairies of northeastern Indian Territory stood as the central location of education and writing during the nineteenth century and also served as a focal point of a cultural location caught between traditional teachings and cultural assimilation during a time of great upheaval and erasure of Indigenous peoples and knowledges. Even in absence they remained present. Inspired by their dignity and sheer will to survive out in the prairies of Oklahoma, I decided that it was time to visit the archives of the Cherokee National Seminaries on a trip back home to Oklahoma during the summer of 2013. On this trip to Tahlequah, I spent the next few days buried in the archives of the library at Northeastern State University researching the histories of the Cherokee National Seminaries, determined that it would be easy to find my grandmothers this time around as a Professional Researcher. But like so many storytellers before them, my grandmothers had a subtle sense of humor. Instead of the imagined scrapbooks filled with old photographs, paraphernalia from school days, and little stories tucked in the margins written in the perfect penmanship of the nineteenth century that I had thought surely must exist, I found a very different collection. While I was looking for artifacts that I thought would bring me closer to their existence, what I found were legal documents, news articles, and promotional materials from the seminaries that were collected and organized in ways that decontextualized these artifacts from the Cherokee. Legal documents mirrored a colonized point of view that was forced assimilation to Eurocentric ideas of educational practices and reinforced a separate sphere educational model (Mihesuah 1998). News articles from larger print runs emphasized a similar "whiteness" that was also present in various promotional materials. In fact, on the surface of it all, you could just remove the word "Cherokee" in the titles and this didn't seem any different from other nineteenth-century seminary schools in the Northeast. But this wasn't the story I had heard. And it wasn't just unfamiliar to me—any Cherokee I knew and had talked to spoke only of the pride that our nation had for the seminaries and how our histories had always emphasized the importance of education as an integral aspect of their culture.

For me, the bookish nerd whose Cherokee identity grew from these proud stories of the importance of education, every history of the Cherokee celebrated these stories regarding education. It's nearly impossible to know Cherokee history without the stories of Sequoyah, who introduced writing through the development of the syllabary, stories of how my people transitioned from an oral society to a literate society seemingly overnight, the story of the creation of a Cherokee-owned newspaper (still in print today), and even more stories of the foundation of schools, owned and operated by tribal members during a time when the southeastern portions of the newly formed United States was very much considered the frontier. Not only is there an extreme sense of pride felt in every one of these stories but there is also the larger narrative of Cherokee survivance, our ability to survive and resist (Stromberg 2006), specifically because of our literacy practices and histories. All of these foundations of Cherokee identity and culture were obfuscated by those artifacts in the university archives it seemed, and I was caught between the tensions of familial stories of my grandmothers and institutional stories that they weren't a part of. Even now, I spend a lot of time asking why education belongs only to white people and their institutions. I stopped my research at this point to try and laugh at my own story that was turning into a sort of humorous tale of hide-and-seek.

In case I wasn't laughing along with my grandmothers enough during that first trip to the archives, the school materials that did remain, specifically the gradebook from the Cherokee Female Seminary, was kept silently away in an archival box, closed to my prying researcher eyes and protected by an archivist's interpretation and extension of the Family Educational Rights and Privacy Act of 1974.[1] The archivist at Northeastern State University explained that the descendants of those seminary students may not want their grandmothers' grades seen or published, you see, so I couldn't take a photograph that day. My grandmother and her grades must be smiling and laughing at my fall from researcher glory as I felt, perhaps slightly unfairly, FERPA'd. While I did leave that day with copious copies of various documents and scans of books written in the 1930s about the Cherokee Female Seminary's ties to Mount Holyoke in Connecticut, I realized that my research needed to take shape and grow over time. It's only now as I spend time reflecting on this story that this archivist may have, in her ways, been protecting my grandmothers and other Cherokee women, as she didn't know me, my story, or my intentions.

---

1. The Family Educational Rights and Privacy Act (FERPA) (20 U.S.C. § 1232g; 34 CFR Part 99) broadly protects the privacy of student records and is generally enforced when outside parties, such as parents, ask to view a college student's records with or without permission of the student. Access to these records is denied as long as the student is 18 or attends a school beyond high school. Being a college instructor, I was well versed in the applicability of FERPA at the time with current students and understood the sentiment of the archivist even if this situation was perhaps out of FERPA's purview.

When working in the archives, one of the easiest first missteps is to think about what the archives do not contain. The archival materials of the Cherokee National Seminaries are spread thin throughout several various institutional archives, with very few being in possession of the Cherokee Nation. Being familiar with archival projects in rhetoric and composition, I had walked into the archives expecting more materials. I expected to find textbooks, teaching documents, ephemera of previous students that had been donated, and programs of school performances in addition to informative yet sterile-feeling legal documents. On my first trip, I learned that the majority of artifacts in the archives were a handful of copies of course catalogs, a souvenir copy of a course catalog with a few pictures that was created after the seminaries had closed, blueprints of the original seminary buildings, a gradebook from the Cherokee Female Seminary, and a few copies of Cherokee government legal documents about the founding of the seminaries. I would be lying if I didn't say I was disappointed and considered that this project was a dead end (and certainly not substantial enough to fill the pages of a book). As I spent that night in a cabin on the shores of Lake Tenkiller, with my handful of notes and copies of materials I had acquired that day, all I could think about were the stories I had heard of the seminaries. I had to sit with these stories and these artifacts for a while before I realized what was immediately before me. The archives weren't empty like I had assumed. They were full of artifacts filled with stories. These stories were more than just stories about the seminaries, though. The artifacts spoke of Cherokee culture and ways of knowing and understanding the world, but my eyes and ears had been closed from the colonial approach I was taking to my research. "[Stories] can be good medicine," Daniel Heath Justice writes, "they can drive out poison, heal the spirit as well as the body, remind us of the greatness of where we came from as well as the greatness of who we're meant to be, so that we're not determined by the colonial narrative of deficiency" (Justice 2018, 5). These stories in the archive were indeed the medicine I needed to move from the positionality of colonialism in the archives to an Indigenous existence of knowledge-making, especially in the research process. The stories are also the medicine the archives need to resist the colonial structures in archival methods and the deficiency model in place when we do archival research. Justice explains that this sense of deficiency is "an externalization of settler colonial guilt and shame" (Justice 2018, 4). Archives are literally measured by boxes and feet, and nothing shouts deficiency like pulling a collection from the shelves only to find a few folders. The negative and very powerful story that was at work that day in the archives is that settler colonialism convinces us that Indigenous stories, like those of the seminaries, are not legitimate because of the *lack* of "accepted" evidence. What is at work in the colonized archive is how these colonial stories of research "[displace] our stories, the stories of complexity, hope, and possibility" (Justice 2018, 4). The first step into the archives of the Cherokee National Seminaries is understanding that these stories matter because they are medicine, as Justice reminds us, and to practice good medicine means to come into relation with those artifacts. But when confronted with the positivist foundations of archival research, the first question that we face is "What is valued as archival research and what artifacts are honored?" Depending on where you find your footing and your settling changes that answer.

WEARING WOLF'S SHOES: NATIVES IN THE ARCHIVE

Looking back, one of the key moments of exigence and my own bias in the archives came from a trip I took in 2012 to visit Cherokee, North Carolina with my graduate linguistics class. It was an early warm day in the mountains of the Smokies, and we headed out to meet Cherokee speaker Tom Belt, who was at that time the Western Carolina University Cherokee Language Program coordinator, in the mother town and spiritual heartland of the Cherokee, Kituwah (near present-day Bryson City, North Carolina). Because Kituwah was recently (re)acquired by the Eastern Band of Cherokee, the land is undeveloped and free of any kind of tourist markings. In the center is the mound of the ancient Cherokee Council House. Tom led us to the mound, entering it from the east and circling it counterclockwise, as all of our Cherokee ancestors would have done. In the middle are the ashes from the three fires brought by the Eastern Cherokee, the Cherokee Nation, and the Keetowah Cherokee, symbolizing our one spiritual fire. As we gathered, Tom told stories, and the one that has always remained with me is "Wolf Wears Shoes," perhaps because this story always makes me laugh while still deeply reflecting on my identity and position as a Cherokee scholar. The story, retold here by me as I remember it from Tom Belt, goes like this:

> Rabbit and Squirrel were taking a walk one day, chatting and sharing stories. Along came Beaver, excited to share what he had seen by the river, and after a little convincing, Rabbit and Squirrel followed Beaver to the riverbank. Noticing the commotion was Wolf, who decided he should also come along to witness this thing Beaver had found. Now, back then Wolf wasn't the ferocious predator that we know of him today. He wouldn't eat anyone back then, mostly because he was the kind of animal that thought he knew everything (and liked to let others know).

"Hey, y'all. What's all this commotion about?" Wolf said, in a sort of long drawn-out drawl.

Rabbit, who was always a bit of a trickster, told him that Beaver had found something and they were going to check it out.

"Well, I reckon I should go along since I'll probably know what it is," Wolf answered confidently.

They arrived at the riverbank, and Beaver pointed at the contraption he had found. Wolf started sniffing around, inspecting this thing they had found, scratching his chin deep in thought.

"Yup, I know what it is. This is a thing that the humans call 'shoooes.' They need 'em 'cause their feet are so soft. So they gotta put these on each foot so the hard ground doesn't hurt their tender feet. Yeah, these are definitely shoooes."

During this time, Rabbit had sat back listening to Wolf's analysis. Rabbit had known exactly what that contraption by the riverside was—it was a trap! He knew this because he had almost been caught in one before. He thought a bit about it and decided Wolf needed to be taught a lesson.

"Well, if this is what you say it is Wolf, how do humans wear these shoes?"

Wolf walked up to the trap and stuck his paw promptly in the trap. KRRRRIINNGG! The trap closed up on his paw, and boy did it hurt! "Yup, this is how they wear them."

Rabbit thought, "Hmmm, he still didn't learn his lesson, so let's try this again." Knowing where another trap lay hidden in the grass by the river, Rabbit ran up to it: "Wolf, I think I found another one of them shoooes is! You've got more paws, so let's see if we can find it!"

So, Wolf followed along, each step getting a bit more painful as he walked. "Here it is!" Rabbit yelled out. Wolf walked over and looked at it. Rabbit encouraged him along, "Well, aren't you gonna put it on?" Wolf picked up another paw and placed it a bit slower in the trap this time. KRRNG! The trap closed down on his paw and boy, did it hurt. "See, Rabbit, this is how they wear 'em" as he held back a yelp.

"Dang," Rabbit thought, "He still hasn't learned. Let's try this again." Like before, Rabbit led him to another trap, asking him to show them again since he had another paw that needed one of these human shoooes.

As Wolf walked to the next trap, he started limping and whimpering with each step, "Ow-ow-ow-ow. . . ." But as they approached the next trap, the same thing happened: KRRNG! "AAAAOOOOWWWWOOO . . ." Wolf howled this time, "Y-y—yup. This is how they wear them shoooees, alrigh—aaawwwooo . . ."

Still impressed that he didn't learn a lesson, Rabbit decided that they should try this one more time since he has one more paw. "OWWWWW-OWWWWW-OWWWW . . ." cried Wolf with each painful step as he walked over to the next, still pretty sure he was right about these human shoooes.

"Here it is! Here it is!" shouted Rabbit as Wolf cried his way over. "Put it on! Put it on!" Wolf very slowly lifted up his last paw and placed it gingerly over the trap . . .

"GET THEM OFF! GET THEM OFF! They hurt SO BAD," he cried out in pain. Beaver ran over and helped him out of the three traps on each leg. As he sat there, rubbing his swollen legs, he thought a bit, and then said, "You know. I've heard some of the humans say that their shoooes can be too small for their feet. I bet that's what's going on here. These shoooes are just too small for me and that's why they were hurtin' so bad."

Rabbit just doubled over and laughed and laughed, knowing that Wolf still didn't learn his lesson. And to this day, this is why Wolf is alone—everybody is tired of him pretending that he knows everything and won't listen to those who are trying to teach him even when it's painfully clear he is wrong.[2]

Wolf's story has stayed with me since that day in Kituwah, and perhaps for one of the simplest reasons there is. Looking back at the ways I had conducted research, I had been Wolf trying on shoe after shoe, howling with each step. Wolf shapes what I know about my past self and my relationship to Eurocentric knowledge, especially research methods. The first time I stepped into the archives at Northeastern State, I knew I had already committed a research faux pas. Whether it was the always lingering sense of imposter syndrome that often hitches a ride on the back of underrepresented academics or it was trying to plan a research trip while visiting family, I showed up that day having only given the archivist a few days' notice with a hastily sent email. Even with this early misstep, the archivist was eager to meet me and share the materials they had. Having worked as an archivist's intern in grad school, I confidently knew the procedures and immediately directed all of my attention toward current archival stances on the use of white gloves and cameras, how many boxes I could pull, and a healthy paranoia about keeping everything in the exact order it was initially presented to me. After a pleasant conversation about gloves and my excitement that I didn't have to wear them here, I quickly realized why. Because of the scarcity of archival artifacts, I actually wouldn't get to handle original documents. Instead, the archivist shared their vast knowledge of everything in the archives, their love and excitement of the seminaries and their histories, and stories of alums who visited every year. I took copious notes with each box that was brought into the little room they had set up for looking at the artifacts; however, my initial allure was shattered a little more as I asked if I could document Ann Florence Wilson's famous gradebook. Just like a crack caused by a wayward rock on a car windshield slowly grows, the mystique of the archive fell apart as the archivist explained to me that since the seminary still has descendants that meet every once in a while for

---

2. There is also a version of this story by the same title told by Sequoyah Guess in *Cherokee Stories of the Turtle Island Liars' Club* written by Christopher Teuton (Teuton 2012).

reunions, we needed to protect the women documented in the gradebook since grades were sensitive materials (even if the grades were from the mid-1800s). The entire time I spent researching, I became more concerned with rules, regulations, and procedures so that I wouldn't disrupt the aura or provenance of the archives. Even with the archivist acting as a helpful mediator, what I felt was the distance of a researcher in relation to the artifacts, now objectified as priceless and fragile ephemera. But even more so, I walked away that day feeling removed and even more distant from my past and my heritage than I ever have. Because, if I'm honest, while I was also there as a researcher, I was really there to connect to my ancestors and share my love of learning and education with them, only to find them tucked away on some forbidden page of a gradebook.

During that moment of distance and disappointment, I looked down and saw that I, too, was wearing Wolf's shoes. These shoes I had found were shaped by a solid foundation and experience with archival methods, but what I was given by wearing those researcher's shoes was a false and painful sense of confidence that I relied on to become that academic researcher I thought I longed to be. But with each step in those shoes, I felt like an imposter within my own culture. After I returned from that trip, worried that I came back empty-handed, the only way I knew to shed myself of these shoes was to go back to the stories I knew and begin there on my journey to uncover and learn how to listen and make knowledge with my ancestors. When analyzing institutional archival artifacts, such as blueprints and legal proceedings, stories such as "Wolf Wears Shoes" situate researchers as colonial settlers and uncover a theoretical and cultural positioning in the archives.

STORIES IN DUSTY BOXES

Part of what I experienced that first day in 2013 when I stepped into the archives echoes what Robert J. Connors and others articulate about historical research, archives, and our own personal experiences. He explains that our personal prejudices and biases as we enter the archives are just as present as the data the archives contain, even if some see this data as something that can be incorporated into archival research or overlooked (Connors 2016, 53). This doesn't come as any surprise to me—I knew that I was far from an objective researcher the moment I walked into those archives. I wanted to find the empirical evidence that supported the cultural knowledge I had received through my family and through the Cherokee stories I had heard. I had a personal attachment to those stories, and yet I felt the pull to be the scholar and the researcher that could toss that aside and "method" away that bias. Instead of convincing myself (and academic reviewers) that I remained an objective researcher when I walked into those archives, I decided to wrestle with this personal bias and investigate *why* and *from where* those biases were coming from, and I wanted to put that data in relation with the documents that had been preserved. As Connors argues, I decided that these prejudices and biases should be included in my research as data (Connors 2016, 54). After careful reflection, I realized that my bias stemmed from the stories I had been told my entire life about being Cherokee and the importance of the seminaries to Cherokee history. Beyond my family's history and connection with the Cherokee Female Seminary, I first experienced the history of the seminary through the ways that the Cherokee Nation presented the history of their educational institutions. Beyond the wider narratives of the Trail of Tears that almost everyone had heard of, my early observations of the ways that Cherokees tell their histories always centered on three figures: Sequoyah, John Ross, and the Cherokee Female Seminary. Our memorials celebrate them, our heritage sites are connected to them, and our reminders of how we have survived and are still here are woven through these histories. To say that the Cherokee pride themselves in their ability to become a Nation That Writes through the creation of a written syllabary, an ability to persevere through removal and struggle, and the undertakings it took to succeed in creating one of the earliest higher education institutions west of the Mississippi is no small matter. Through writing and creating a Cherokee syllabary, the Cherokee Nation has enacted their own rhetorical sovereignty, that is, "a guiding story in our pursuit of self-determination, the general strategy by which we aim to best recover our losses from the ravages of colonization: our lands, our languages, our cultures, our self-respect" (Lyons 2000, 449). In other words, the Cherokee Nation chooses to tell their stories in this way. My bias and prejudice that day in the archives was a reflection of the power of these stories, and as much as I tried to strip myself of those stories, I couldn't, and they become the data points that motivated my continued research.

Yet, while I encountered my own biases and dealt with them as I would of any other artifact tucked away in those dusty boxes, the whole notion of archival research is mired in colonial biases. I argue that treating this colonial prejudice as data in this case works both ways—not just from the researcher's own lived experiences, but from the artifacts being researched in archival studies. In the process of assessing, collecting, cataloging, and storing, these archival collections have their own inherent bias imposed on them by the archivist. In the process of trying to remove all bias, the archivist recontextualizes these materials through classification stemming from Eurocentric practices and organization embedded deep in archival work. Archival practices, and even the allure of archival "discovery," are prime examples of the ways that research practices are steeped in colonialism and Enlightenment-era thinking. Michel Duchein, former inspector general of the Archives de France, explains how the modern bases of archival science came about in the 1850s—a time in which men (typically) were compelled by classification systems that grounded much of the scientific work in chemistry, zoology, botany, and astronomy. This gave way to the principle of provenance, originally called *respect des fonds* in French, that maintains that documents that come from the same family, body, establishment, or individual form a "*fonds*" and are classified and arranged "out of respect for the original order" and not organized by how they are related as artifacts (Duchein 1992, 19). This collection method is still maintained and easily identifiable in any archive or special collection today. Look through any archival database and you will see collections named for donors and/or previous owners of the artifacts as the main title for that collection while the artifacts are described in the finding aids that accompany that collection. While digitization and online searching has made it easier to circumvent the *provenance* of a collection as researchers can enter search terms that pull data from the finding aids, the physicality of archival research—that is, the going to the collection, pulling of archival boxes, and handling materials—is still guided and restricted by *provenance*. As you research, you may only handle each collection separately so that the materials are not mixed, and even more so the subject you are researching may have related materials in several different collections that are scattered across locations, separated by miles, borders, and distances between the institutions that house these artifacts.

While these methods are often enforced to protect artifacts, the material practices of archival research lead researchers on a linear path of *provenance* as modern archival science does the work of maintaining a linear story of artifacts as they are potentially severed and kept separate from their cultural networks. However, as Mignolo argues, even if the methods of collection and preservation of artifacts maintains the coloniality of knowledge-making, the knowledge contained within these artifacts has not been colonized, so like him, I turn to decoloniality, which does "both the analytic task of unveiling the logic of coloniality and the prospective task of contributing to build a world in which many worlds will coexist" (Mignolo 2011, 54). In Mignolo's use of decoloniality, we do not need to turn to colonized ways of researching as the sole creation of all knowledge but rather we can see it as one way of knowledge-making that coexists even as it obfuscates other, non-Western knowledge-making practices. Ultimately, to not treat these lived experiences outside and inside the archives as data is to ignore a vital aspect of the archives' nature and being. In my specific research experience, the archival bias and data pointed to stories of colonization and assimilation, not just in the artifacts and what was represented but in the very existence of these archives not collected, assessed, or stored by the Cherokee. These archives along with several other collections concerning the Cherokee National Seminaries are housed outside of tribal ownership and control, always already existing in a colonized state.

ARCHIVAL LOCATIONS

So, I return to that question of what is valued and honored in the archives. Before I visited the archives of the seminaries in Tahlequah, I served as an archivist intern at a local historical society one summer. It was during this internship that I got the quick answer to the question of what is valued and honored in the archives of this local historical society. What was valued was anything that was assessed as *having* value by the archivist. We'd receive boxes field with a variety of ephemera, the hoarded files of a prominent professional whose materials were no longer in care of their family, a sword dug up from a local battlefield, and scrapbooks upon scrapbooks. After assessing and documenting, what didn't have archival value could produce monetary value for the historical society and was quietly listed on eBay. As someone who considers herself a bit of a professional hoarder of ephemera, like that one kindergarten painting of Easter eggs I made or that ticket from the first time she saw *Annie*, this was a bit of a shock to my system as I thought everything had a story and that if it had survived that long, it had a right to keep surviving and being honored. What kept going around in my mind is that for something that is considered fleeting from the time of its creation to be kept by someone else must mean that it holds value in and of itself. But I was told we were faced with limited space and limited funds, and so there was a limit to our archival value and that limit didn't make room for the personal value of others. This experience stayed with me as I endeavored on my own archival research, and I soon understood that the locations of our archives and the material conditions of those locations have a direct impact on what can be valued. What often occurs is that an archivist is left with the determination of what is kept and what is discarded based on outside forces and historical narratives of value.

Sometimes this is easy to determine, like a sword dug up from the Battle of Tippecanoe, and other times, especially in the fragility of everyday artifacts, that question becomes more precarious.

For those interested in pedagogical histories, the student-centered ephemera that has historical value can often be tossed aside as too ordinary by whoever possesses it, while what is seen as archivable often has some legitimatizing official documentation to it. While there may be some artifacts, like papers and books with marginalia and notes, what is typically kept and documented are official records, such as enrollment records, achievements, board meeting minutes, and some curriculum-based documents (Moon 2007, 2). Official documents can be useful when working on pedagogical recovery and certainly necessary for constructing a history, but the pieces of pedagogical pasts are a part of those everyday artifacts created by students and teachers and invaluable to recovery work. Yet, as I wish for those everyday artifacts to be stored alongside official documents, I'm quickly reminded of my own pedagogical traces—or rather, lack thereof. As a rhetoric and composition professor, I stress the importance of inquiry, reflection, process, and revision throughout my courses. Yet, if I were to think of what potential archive I am leaving behind or the traces of things my students have left behind, there is very little to show of that pedagogy. Yes, there are bullet points on my syllabi that might survive the years that have these listed as potential course goals, and I may have even included some means and outcomes. Yet, there is little rhetorical context, and even fewer student examples. Moreover, even this small, tangible trace is completely dependent on that syllabus not getting deleted as cloud storage runs thin. Our digital means have compounded a modern archival effort in some ways, as files can be so easily written over, deleted, or stored on a potentially inaccessible cloud when payment subsides. Unless we store and sustain massive files of previous students' work alongside the syllabi and random documents that may have some pedagogical ruminations in them, we have little to show of our teaching practices. Even if we do keep physical copies, those often end up in file cabinets in campus offices that may be discarded soon after we retire to make room for the next incoming professor. Let's not forget the lurking elephant in the room, either; the sustainability of the type of files and our ability to access them in the future. Even in the twenty years since I've been in college, the majority of my papers and notes from classes are locked away on some inaccessible Zip drive long since tossed because it wasn't useful anymore. Perhaps there are those of you out there who are better keepers of pedagogical practices than I, but when I look through the archives of nineteenth-century colleges, the lack of materials isn't something I'm going to question because of my own experiences as a student and as a professor.

While we recognize the value of what often is lost of pedagogical practices, historiographers have developed accepted methods of writing histories despite the lack of archives available. Albert Kitzhaber, frustrated with contemporary means of teaching composition compared to the progressive pedagogies he encountered while at Iowa State, turned to nineteenth-century textbooks as foundational documents to trace early influences of rhetoric on college courses in order to understand the common pedagogical practices of his time (Kitzhaber 1990, xx). James Berlin, facing a similar lack of materials, used the method of analyzing pedagogies by relying on rhetorics grounded in a noetic field; that is, "a closed system defining what can, and cannot, be known; the nature of the knower; the nature of the relationship between the knower, the known, and the audience; and the nature of language," to recover practices of writing instruction during the nineteenth century (Berlin 1984, 1–2). Meanwhile, John Brereton researched documents and reports from Harvard's archives to uncover the strong influence on composition studies that the Harvard methods of the late nineteenth century had on the field. While there are some archival collections that have a robust collection of handbooks, student papers, textbooks, and other materials from the same period (Carr, Carr, and Schultz 2005), others have had to turn to locations not often thought of as official, authenticated archives. Wendy Sharer, whose work revolves around family archives, recovers women's literary traditions and writings from scrapbooks, postcards, programs, and letters that she found from the time her grandmother participated in a variety of women's organizations (Sharer 2008, 47). Her work from these sources also asks us as a field to listen to these lived, emotionally connected, and familial experiences as valid and authentic research practices (Sharer 2008, 54). However, our preoccupation with physical and material evidence is still at work in these histories, as Freshwater explains, "In an age of simulacra, which is rapidly completing its transfer of the production and dissemination of information on to the computer screen, we still privilege the paper document of authentication" (Freshwater 2003, 732). The authority and legitimacy of physical evidence can hamper the ability to recover a history that so heavily relies on ephemera that may not have immediate value, which requires historiographers to utilize a different set of archives or interpret archival material not for content it contains but the practices it illustrates in order to open the archives up (Fierreia-Buckley 1999, 578). Yet, because of the *work* of composition, our archival materials are driven by the necessity to turn to the ephemeral and material. Our work is in the things produced (even left behind), and our interpretations are located in the practices located and nestled in the fibers of these papers.³

No matter where we locate our archives, like Wolf, we need to step back and recognize the colonial settler roles we take on as we "discover" an archive. It's easy to get swept up in the feeling of discovery of some uninterpreted, untold, and undocumented history that these primary artifacts hold on to. Even our humanistic approach to research lands us in the position of colonial settlers as we determine the means of historical narratives. The appeal of the archives grows from the roots of "a positivist methodology centered upon the painstaking accumulation of documentary evidence, followed by patient study and detailed comparative analysis" (Freshwater 2003, 730). Even the turn away from such positivist theory didn't impact the draw to the objects collected, assessed, and stored as archival evidence (Freshwater 2003, 731). Rhetoric and composition scholars have felt this allure and have been drawn to archival research through a similar legitimizing of the discipline's histories. Being drawn into the "Archive, the storehouse of data about the past," Connors eloquently states, "The Archive must be explored, analyzed, cross checked, deconstructed, reconstructed, made meaning of, be stripped, checked, and polished" (Connors 2016, 51). As I read and feel this same pull to the archive that Connors describes, I cannot ignore the colonizing language in this approach. I want to stress here that it is easy to fall into this sense of discovery among archival artifacts. Kelly Ritter, whose work recovers women's history in composition studies, explains that when we recover materials from the archives, we are tasked with a retelling through narrative impulses to recover these histories of composition studies, and this work is further complicated by "the sometimes-competing processes of discovery and interpretation" (Ritter 2016, 284). Archives also invite a certain intimacy and connection to the past that is often beguiling, and as Connors explains, "Here, for the composition historian, is the world of the written word, the picture, the table, the diagram, the voice on the tape. The Archive is where storage meets dreams, and the result is history" (Connors 2016, 51). Faced with the postpositivist

---

3. With the turn to digital documentation, our archives will slowly move from physical to digital, and with this, opens up a new means of archiving the work of composition. Groups such as the Digital Archives of Literacy Narratives (DAHL) are currently undertaking the important task of recording and archiving oral histories and literacy narratives. While we could argue the semantics of digital files and cloud storage being immaterial or still under the vestiges of materiality, I am excited about the work they are undertaking and only can dream of what an oral history of nineteenth-century writers would contain.

claim that research and history can only be known imperfectly through fictional biases, it stands to reason that the archive holds promises and dreams of finding legitimacies through an evidence-laden path of origins. More importantly, archives serve to emplace the researcher in the realities and materialities in an experienced and tangible past. Yet, we can often position ourselves as colonial settlers when we disassociate the meaning-making of archives from the being of and existences of those archives. For us to decolonize our work within archives, we first must unsettle our ways of knowing before we even open a box of artifacts.

THE RHETORICAL BEINGS OF ARCHIVES

Allure. Dust. Fever. Dreams. Trauma. Each of these exist alongside the archives and embed the reality of thingness and meaning-making in artifacts. Carolyn Steedman reiterates some of Connors's more fantastical views of archives as dreams, claiming that these dreams reside not in what is found but in the possibilities of what is not found yet. Even as the archive is meticulously curated and documented, "in actual Archives, though the bundles may be mountainous, there isn't in fact, very much there. The Archives is not potentially made up of *everything*, as in human memory; and it is not the fathomless and timeless place in which nothing goes away that is the unconscious" (Steedman 2002, 68). As a place of dreams, the researcher's imaginative sense tells them that there are holes, destroyed records, artifacts that were not deemed worthy enough to collect, and artifacts that just ended up lost. Even a culling of artifacts opens up the discourse for new interpretations and research based on the same collections (Steedman 2002, 68–69). Archives, through interpretive work done by historians, are able to leave the realm of "stuff" and enter into a place of human memory, and as we know, memory can be interrogated, situated, interpreted, and retold (Steedman 2002, 67). In this place that slips between the realities of stuff and the possibilities of memories, we find the ability to dream and invent (Bieseker 2006, 124). So, we return back to the role of archives in historical research: Archives serve as a place of both the written world through artifacts and the oral world through interpretation and representation. No wonder scholars in rhetoric and composition seek out the archives to define a disciplinary legacy as other scholars in other disciplines have also done. Because of this rhetorical nature of the archives, the archives are a productive and prolific space for scholars to dream and invent.

And yet, just as Wolf's shoes gave him the desire to dream and invent a sort of humanness, these dreams and inventions can cause real colonial harm. The textual and material nature of archives is often attractive to scholars because research can often lead to the feeling of treading on undiscovered or forgotten pasts in piles of documents unseen by researchers (Freshwater 2003, 733). The closeness and Benjamin sense of "aura" we feel toward the archive is heightened by our desire to create a past through text. That affect produced by the materiality of archives is what lures us in and asks us to sit with the archives and create a story from their threads to material pasts that we are now in close proximity to. However, as Kelly Ritter reminds us, there is a sense of forgetting that occurs in the archives. What is left from these close encounters is the *people* who produced those archives (Ritter 2016, 285). In discussing Neal Lerner and Linda Bergmann's work, Ritter contemplates how the archival affect of being in the same place as that history can impact our abilities to accurately represent those feelings through our writings about archival research. Just as Bergmann felt that her research verged on the edge of voyeurism, like "rummaging through the drawers of the parents of children for whom [she] baby sat in high school" (Bergmann qtd. In Ritter 2016, 285), the intimate affect of the archive can both hinder our ability to separate ourselves from storying *about* the archives or lead us to thoughtfully consider our human participants there with us in the archives, even if they have passed on from this world (Ritter 2016, 285). Whatever the case, the pull in the archives is felt on a very human level and is laced with a sense of intimacy, forbiddenness, and the drive to learn of something lost to the past. This pull we feel is rhetorical in nature and has a deep impact in the ways that we make meanings in and with archival materials. While I have also felt this deep pull into the archives, I also know that this pull and felt sense is akin to the ways that Manifest Destiny and colonialism in America pulled settlers into the "wild" and "untamed" spaces of land and dreams. In addition to Ritter's argument to remember the *people* of the archives, I also would like to add remembering the trauma that can be done when archives are romanticized through colonial inventions, often forgetting the people, the cultural landscapes, and the colonial sense of discovery and ownership of the stories and memories created by the settlers in the archives.

But whose memories are these? What happens to those researchers who enter the archives knowing that the cultural places of memory are being actively obscured through the colonial memories that Eurocentric colonial practices brought to the archives? The rhetorical makings of archival materials serve to remind us that our relationships with objects are never one-sided, with us observing from afar and viewing an object with no agency on their own. Rather, archives facilitate a connection to the past and to the histories they contain. Malea Powell pointedly reminds us that "history isn't a dead and remembered object; it is alive and it speaks to us" (Powell 2008, 121). Archival artifacts ask us to hear their stories, and we need to take responsibility and listen. We are invited and lured into an intimate, material relationship with the past through these objects, but with that allure needs to come the realization that these objects have been stripped of their language, their culture, and their relationships through the colonial process of identifying, assessing, collecting, describing, and sorting into dull, gray archival boxes often kept away from the public's eyes and ears. This colonizing process of removing and assessing artifacts creates our feelings of discovery and in part fuels the researcher's appeal to the archives. When we enter, still colonized in our practices and positionings, we can get swept away by the sense of authorship and the authority contained therein. In doing so, we lay claim to those stories and call them our own. We turn our eyes from the existence of ancestors to thinking that their being is not a part of that artifact we analyze.

For those, the trauma of entering an archive resonates not as archive space, but archive placelessness. As archive space creates new meaning and potentials of memories, it obscures the cultural tethers that artifacts grasp to. These tethers are pulled thin as new memories and histories write the archives. But for those cognizant of the cultural places of archives, the sense of placelessness can become an overwhelming affect of the archives. Edward Casey defines placelessness as emotional symptoms of "homesickness, disorientation, depression, desolation" that mirror the lack of having place. (Casey 2009, x). Indeed, as we hear Casey's words, the place of archives is one of *placelessness*. The artifacts are housed away, often behind institutional walls and with restricted access, and kept outside their place of origin. In instances such as the materials from the Cherokee National Seminaries, these artifacts went through the same placelessness as the Cherokee who were forced from their homes during the Removal. No matter what is added to the finding aid and descriptions and no matter our adherence to the notions of provenance, the artifacts are always out of place and out of time. Perhaps this is why we see potential in the archives. Our sense of wanting to place these artifacts so that we don't have to pay attention to the symptoms of placelessness and can replace them with histories is the progeny of academic dreams.

While scholars and philosophers talk of archival research as this moment of dreams and potential, for some these dreams, spurred by placelessness, quickly descend into nightmares. One of the deepest felt stories the archives are telling us is the colonial trauma in the archives and of those who step into the archives who relive their own cultural placelessness. Research, especially for Indigenous people, is that dirty word that has been tainted by the impact of colonialism in their personal and cultural lives (Smith 2012, 1). The archival space is the place where dreams of ancestors, left placeless through colonialism, are filtered through the traumas inscribed in the textual evidence so valued by history. In this archival space, Malea Powell searches the archives to find "documents and histories written *about* Native peoples by folks who had something to lose if Indians were seen as fully human" (Powell 2008, 116). She recognizes, as an "Indian in the archive," that "we are still in the midst of this war, still living through the paracolonial occupation and the damage done by documents, by words, has been at least as great as that done by weapons" (Powell 2008, 116). The trauma of the archive is that the archive was never meant to preserve the culture of Indigenous peoples. The trauma is that the archive reinscribes what folks want to think *about* Indigenous people. The Eurocentric potential for history is that of erasure or exploitation of Indigenous peoples. For the Eurocentric academic, our oral histories and stories are not valid because there is a sense that you cannot reflect if something lacks the physicality of text (Ong 2009, 14–15). Victor Villenueva reminds us, however, of the importance of memory and stories when we encounter exile and alienation in the archives. He prods us, "Exile. Alienation. What does one do when one becomes fully conscious of the alienation that arises from exile, of being radicalized, of knowing something ain't right and there ain't no puttin' it right but can't be no ignoring the wrong?" (Villanueva 2008, 84). What we do is remember to recover. Through this conscious effort and journey with the artifacts, we unsettle Eurocentric claims to our ancestors and remember that our stories are alive, just as our ancestors are in the archives. When we can't be *there*—there, in our cultural locations in the archives—we can reconnect with the lived sense of what is in the archives (Kirsch 2008, 22). To survive and resist, we must reconnect with what makes a space a *place* again. For that, we turn to what makes place for many—the land and the community. If the land is away, we connect to the community in the archives; that is, we too need to seek out our Charles Eastmans, like Malea Powell, and listen to our ancestors who are very much a part of those archives, even if it means first reliving their traumas together in that archival space. Storying together with the archives helps us repair those relations that colonialism seeks to sever. There is a place there, despite attempts to erase it.

(RE)SEARCHING FOR OUR STORIES AND (RE)MEMBERING IN THE ARCHIVES

Once again, I turn to Malea Powell, who guides us to remember that "we are obligated not just to our ancestors out of whose lives we 'make' that history but also to the places and spaces, and the living things therein, who remember them and—through them—remember us" (Powell 2008, 122). It's not just us and the artifacts in the archives that are making meaning. We are there with our ancestors, with the living artifacts and their stories, and we are there with the time and spaces that shaped those archives. Our stories about those archives aren't just products that are viewed outside of the archives, they are also storied *with* the archives and are now a part of that living being. The archives remember our stories, as those who come in after us will bring with them the pasts we have created. The weight of responsibility is the archives' deepest rhetorical agency. We must be attuned to it before we can do our part to decolonize it. Even with the deeply embedded structures of colonization and settler colonialism in the archives, what I find compelling, then, is the Indigenous Archives rhetoricity of *survivance*. That is, even if the archive colonizes artifacts in ways that obscure the present cultural locations of these artifacts, the Indigenous Archives survives in its indigeneity and resists this colonization through its survival. What we need to recognize, then, is that we are bound to listen and pay attention to the Indigenous Archives because it's not up to us to tell a story about these archives but to listen intently to the stories these archives are sharing.

So, why does the Indian go to the archives? Because our ancestors walked the same path, and being in that place puts us in relation with our ancestors, whose artifacts still hold on to their stories, resisting the colonization they are subjected to. While there is a strong case for Indigenous peoples making their own archives and an academic push to make this a reality (O'Neal 2015), many artifacts, especially those from the nineteenth century, are still kept outside of Indigenous sovereignty. Powell reflects on her time with Charles Eastman that day in the Newberry Library where her Miyammia ancestors walked, hunted, and gathered, by asking us, "What stories stand between thinkable and possible? How can we learn to tell them? What academic stories have each of us learned to let stand between us as borders, as canyons, as bridges, as homes? How can we learn to tell them through them? What are the consequences of 'writing back,' of thinking back, of taking back in all of this telling?" (Powell 2008, 123). This isn't a moment of white saviorism, where we can come in and "rescue" our ancestors. But it is a place of learning and wisdom so that in those archives, in spite of the trauma,

Figure 2.1. A photo from the late 1910s of my grandmothers: Jennie (Cowart) Williams, Allie Beth (Williams) Bishop, and Cynthia "Annie" (Williams) Armor (my great-great-great grandmother, who attended the Cherokee Female Seminary). Photo from the personal collection of Emily Legg.

we can learn the wisdom our ancestors are protecting for us. This is a place we must walk through, like the Apache who materially traveled through wisdom and self-reflection in places of learning (Basso, *Wisdom Sits in Places*), in order to understand the need to build relationships with the materiality and being of archives in order to hear their stories. Through this passage, *we can hear them tell us their value and how to honor them through stories.*

After leaving the archive space and setting aside my project for all of the other happenings of a graduate student heading out on the job market and trying to complete a dissertation, I eventually found one of my grandmothers when I wasn't even trying to look. Cynthia Anne Williams, my third great-grandmother (and grandmother of Lucille Nix) had been sitting on my bookshelves in my house the whole time, tucked away in a small section on the Cherokee Female Seminary in the book *Voices of Cherokee Women*. There was her name and her story, a reprint of an interview she gave shortly before her death in 1939 that was conducted by government workers as part of a Works Progress Administration oral narrative project led by Grant Foreman that was meant to "save" Oklahoma history, a mere thirty-seven years into its existence as a state. Telling her story as Annie Williams Armor (her married name), she began by explaining that even though we were Cherokee, we had remained in Georgia until 1882, almost fifty years after the Trail of Tears. Her father, Mat Williams, had gone on ahead to Indian Territory to establish a cattle ranch, just east of Muskogee. When she went with her mother and sister to live in Indian Territory, she explained that "even though we were Cherokee Indians, we were used to a quiet and secure existence, so the wild new country frightened my mother, and she preferred to live in town" (Armor 2013, 222). During their time in Indian Territory, Annie and her sister attended the Cherokee Female Seminary, but never graduated. After two years, Annie, her mother, and her sister, packed their belongings back up and returned to Georgia because her mother "decided that the West didn't provide the proper environment for the rearing of a family, especially for girls, as it was entirely too wild" (Armor 2013, 222). Annie eventually returned to Indian Territory in 1892, after her newly acquired husband secured a place out near Vinita. They were married again, according the Cherokee laws, in Vinita in 1893, so that my third-great grandfather could become a member of the Cherokee tribe (Armor 2013, 223) and, in turn, secured our family's place as citizens in the Cherokee Nation from then and through all time. Finally hearing her story in this unassuming book convinced me to broaden my archival search outside of Northeastern and away from the physical location of the Cherokee National Seminaries. Finding her original interview tucked away in the Western Histories Collection in Norman, Oklahoma, I finally heard my grandmothers more clearly. Our material histories and artifacts are as spread out and dispersed as our people, and you need to listen to our culture to hear them. But they still remain, ever and always, Cherokee.

PART 3

ᎤᏃᎸ: ᎤᎪᎲᎢ ᎥᏩᏔᎲᎢ

uyvtlv: ugohvi vgatahvi
North: Seeking Knowledge through Story

As we journey in ceremony through the Cherokee medicine wheel, we arrive in ᎤᏃᎸ (uyvtlv, the north), the place where we center all our relations on the knowledges we learn through stories. Even more, we spend time here to acknowledge and honor the ways that stories help us to continually seek knowledge as they live and breathe from storyteller to storytelling, making and maintaining relationships beyond the bounds of time and space. While here, open your mind and listen to the stories of our elders and ancestors as they share with us the balanced ways to seek knowledge, reflect on our practices, and ground the process of our knowledge-making by honoring the communities that maintain story as theory.

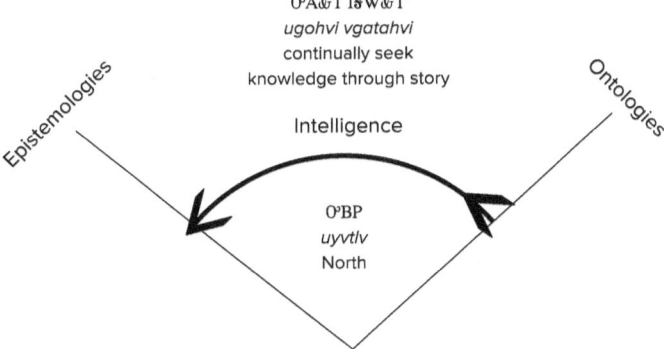

Figure 3.0. North: Seeking knowledge through story.

3
ARCHIVES OUT OF STORY
Severed Relations and Indigenous Worldviews

As I grew up rural and learned to drive around country roads, where clearly marked navigation was few and far between, directions often were passed from one person to another in the form of landmarks: "Head down the county line road until you see the co-op and turn north. From there, take the road until it turns from gravel to dirt until you pass a tree on your left. Your turn is right after that. Keep going until you see the metal gate just past the old Moffat homestead . . ." While there was a sense of aimlessness, there was direction and purpose with each meaningful landmark. Without the directions, the landmarks faded into the landscape; however, with direction, the landmarks created a new transition into the next segment of the journey. And so it is with following the medicine wheel into ᎤᏴᏢ (*uyvtlv*), the north, as we continually seek those storied landmarks that give shape to the journey to indigenize the archives. While the stories might seem like a long way around to find our way to the archives at the heart of this book, the stories we seek do the work along the journey to bring a Cherokee understanding to the archives. Without this work, the archives remain without story, severed from the traditions they sprang from. Take the time to do the work, to listen to the stories before you skip the landmarks and rush aimlessly to the end. In ᎤᏴᏢ (*uyvtlv*), we invite stories as our guides to knowledge-making, to prepare us to meet our ancestors in the archives in the next waypoint along the wheel. Whether it's "once upon a time" or "let us begin," here we pause for stories.

When I was younger, I had a book about constellations in the night sky, and when you opened the book without any light around, the constellations popped out from each page with glow-in-the-dark ink—the kind that, when you touched the page, you could feel the small bumps as you ran your fingers gingerly through the constellations. Between this book and my full-fledged enrollment in my elementary school's Young Astronauts club, I was convinced that I would one day find myself out in the far regions of space or at least a student of the night sky so that I

https://doi.org/10.7330/9781646425228.c003

could spend my time looking up at the stars or down on Earth. Clearly, that was not what ended up happening, but I'd like to think I still find myself navigating those constellations, even as I wander into the archives hidden from those night skies. Constellations have always been a navigational tool to help us find our way, acting as wayfinding methods. Yet, as we look up in the sky, we still think first of seeing the two-dimensional outline of a constellation, but the actual existence of constellations is a three-dimensional and a realized material space that not only gives us a sense of navigation but brings us into relation through our existence and habits of navigating that space. By drawing connections between praxis and wayfinding as rhetorical methodologies for research, we understand our work as continuously adjusting to the cultural and physical spaces where that work happens (Strantz 2015). In other words, wayfinding shifts our research frameworks from a two-dimensional linear perspective to a three-dimensional existence that puts us in relation with our research through constellating. Without the navigational wayfinding through constellative work and reflection, our research rests in static linearity, occasionally crossing and intersecting paths to form a new joint view. The Cultural Rhetorics Theory Lab explains that research as a "metaphor of intersection implies a linear arrangement in which a subject stands at the nexus of straight lines that only cross at one point. This linearity imposes ideas about causality or origins, both of which are generally also obscuring many of the other meaningful relationships between places, spaces, events, people, and communities. And it traps subjects who are literally held in place, skewered by multiple discourses" (Powell et al. 2014). It's the path laid out by these constellations and the ways we put ourselves in relation with them as wayfinding practices that lead us on the recovery path toward decoloniality, especially in archival research. Constellating methodologies are necessary means to attune our scholarly practices to the stories and histories of unrepresented voices that have been silenced through traditional Enlightenment practices of archival collection, documentation, and the preservation of Indigenous ontologies.

As I began my archival research at Northeastern State University back in 2013, I was caught in these intersections of coloniality, gender, indigeneity, and assimilation rigidly laid out in a linear path in the archives. In order to resituate myself and the artifacts in the archives that I was encountering, I needed to reframe my own knowledge-making through *constellating* and *relationship-building*. "A constellation, however, allows for all the meaning-making practices and their relationships to matter," Powell et al. explain. "It allows for multiply situated subjects to connect to multiple discourses at the same time, as well as for those relationships (among subjects, among discourses, among kinds of connections) to shift and change without holding a subject captive" (Powell et al. 2014). While I write about this moment as if it happened in the past, I want to take time here to explain that being caught in the two-dimensional intersections of Eurocentric research isn't a passing moment that, once we move past it, exists as just a footnote in our methodologies. The act of constellating is a continual and responsive act that demands active reflection and wayfinding. Much like the research ceremony of the Cherokee medicine wheel, constellating is not a path we journey on once but one we recall and reflect time and again, especially as we continue to grow and seek knowledge through living stories. To pass through it once is to deny the livingness and continuous ways that knowledge is made with all our relations. By (re)turning to constellating practices in archival research, scholars can decolonize archival practices and put artifacts and ephemera back into their cultural networks, peoples, and stories, even when institutional structures push back to keep them in linear order.

As I began to research the Cherokee National seminaries, I kept finding myself caught up in the tension of what I knew as a Cherokee, understood about relationships, and expected to find through accepted archival methods. Being caught, I was immobilized in my isolation that was amplified by the nature of archival research. Archival researchers often find themselves in a foreign place, left alone with generic gray boxes, perhaps being watched from afar by an overseeing archivist. This sterile environment, while perhaps ideal for scientific studies, is quintessential to a Eurocentric position of research that is solidified by the very language of "primary investigator" that research studies deploy. It's not unlike the notion that writers exist in isolation, being the sole progenitor of thoughts and text. Lone researchers and lone authors share space in that isolation, yet that isolation in composition has been replaced with process-driven pedagogies, and constellating research methodologies can find a similar path outside of that isolation through Indigenous-based ways of knowing. As Kristin Arola (Annishinaabe, Keweenaw Bay Indian Community Lake Superior Band of Chippewa) explains, "Turning to American Indian way of making can help refocus our attention to process-based pedagogies and can help shift away from a lone author and instead to an author who composes in relation to the world around her" (Arola 2018, 279). Listening to Arola's guidance to turn to Indigenous ways of making reminds me of a story, a quite famous one, told by Sequoyah Guess. He tells us how Turtle Island was formed by the collaborative composing of the animals living on the back of a great turtle in a vast sea along with a growing group of people. The Creator, seeing that the people kept falling off the turtle because their numbers had grown so large, called on the animals to help. First, the water beetle dove down to the bottom of that sea and brought back the tiniest speck of mud. That mud, once it met the air, began to expand. The people called on Suli, the buzzard, to go out over the mud to find dry land; Suli flew and flew, but he grew tired and flew lower to the ground to the point that the flap of his wings began to form valleys and mountains over the world. While the land was still drying, Suli returned to the people and cautioned them to wait still on the back of the turtle. While waiting, the people sent out Raven to survey the land to help them know when they could spread out over the land. While it took a while, Raven returned, carrying a branch in his hand. Together, the people ventured out over the land from the back of Turtle Island and found their place in the world that the Creator, animals, and they had formed together (Teuton 2012, 39–40). Just as the animals compose in relation with each other and in relation with the world around them, our writing and research practices are of and in relation with everything. Even if the tensions of the archives bring on a sense of isolation, we are in relation to those artifacts; the stories the artifacts tell; to the pasts, presents, and futures that are lying in wait. And I needed stories to remind me of that as I continued my archival journey to listen to my ancestors at the Cherokee National Seminaries.

SEVERED RELATIONS: ARCHIVES OUT OF STORY

While it may seem like a detour in the typical progression of sharing research findings, the understanding of the *hows* of Indigenous storywork is the first step to decolonize and indigenize the Cherokee National Seminaries archives so that those of us who take time to listen to the stories understands their place in Cherokee culture as well as the importance they have to the histories of composition and rhetoric. To open ourselves up to the stories in the Cherokee National Seminary archives, we need to decenter our own objectifications of what we are in the world and what stories are in relation to us and take that time in ᎤᏴᏢ (*uyvtlv*, the north) to honor those stories and make knowledge *with* those stories. Rather than making objects of study from archives and stories, I posit that we ground ourselves within the reflective practices of how stories and archives are operating and existing as part of our material realities. These reflective practices constitute a "practical rhetoric" (Sullivan and Porter 1997, 26) that serves as the foundational elements of Indigenous methodologies for archival research. For me to progress any more, I first need to step in relation with the methodologies that shape my archival research. Without this wayfinding practice, my research practices hold little meaning and step out of relation with the archives of the Cherokee seminaries, once again ushering in a colonial structure.

Yet what does it mean to be "in relation" with archives? How do I, a twenty-first-century Cherokee and academic, put myself in relation with artifacts and histories of nineteenth-century Cherokee? As we journey through ᏧᏴ (*uyvtlv*, the north), we recognize that seeking knowledge through story begins in reflective practice with the relations we made in the east, ᎧᎸᎬ (*kalvgv*). The practice of being in relation goes beyond an acknowledgment of causal relationships that exists. In Indigenous research, "in relation" isn't a question of causation or correlation. Being in relation is a reflective, active, and continual practice, beginning with ceremony and attunement to the communities around us and engaging in mindful community-building with everything (not just the people we interact with). As Winona LaDuke (Anishinaabekwe, Mississippi Band Anishinaabeg) explains, "Native American teachings describe the relations all around—animals, fish, trees, and rocks—as our brothers, sisters, uncles, and grandpas. Our relations to each other, our prayers whispered across generations to our relatives, are what bind our cultures together" (LaDuke 2015, 2). All our relations are the heart of Indigenous existence and ontology, and without that worldview, there is no Indigenous existence. "All our relations"—a phrase that LaDuke reminds us, holds together Indigenous cultures through the ways we experience the world around us, and "the protection, teachings, and gifts of our relatives have for generations preserved our families. These relations are honored in ceremony, song, story, and life that keep relations close—to buffalo, sturgeon, salmon, turtles, bears, wolves, and panthers" (LaDuke 2015, 2). Our communities do not end with humans; rather, they are sustained through our other-than-human cohabitants, that is, every human, animal, rock, tree, place, and even archival artifact are held in balanced relations together. While colonial practices of archival preservation may have severed the archives out of relation, the ceremony of storytelling in the archives once again realizes those severed ties. Through all our relations, even the archives can speak and engage in sustaining the community through an active and meaningful materialist positioning in Indigenous ontologies.

While this phrase is simple, "all our relations" invites us to unpack the meanings and layers developed in these three words, especially following the encounters Indigenous knowledge-making practices have in the north, ᎤᏴᏢ (*uyvtlv*), with Eurocentric epistemologies. Within Indigenous epistemologies, "all our relations" is a developing and sustained epistemological and ontological ecology that contextualizes our very material human, nonhuman, animal, machine, environmental, cultural, and temporal relations. Even more applicable in archival research, which has been stripped from its cultural context, placed out of time, and deprived of its stories, "all our relations" is also a moment of doing—an active stance. It does not refer to a static network or an isolated, closed-loop ecology that archives are placed within and in the confines of a finding aid. "All our relations" is grounded within an Indigenous sense of ecology that derives from a community that is less human-centric and more material in its nature, and in the abstract sense, is that basis of Indigenous metaphysics (Deloria 2001, 2). For Deloria (Standing Rock Sioux Tribe) and Wildcat (Yuchi member of the Muscogee Nation of Oklahoma), Indigenous metaphysics should be understood "as simply that set of first principles we must possess in order to make sense of the world in which we live" and from this set of first principles, we understand all our relations as "the realization that the world, and all its possible experiences, [constitute] a social reality, a fabric of life in which everything [has] the possibility of intimate knowing relationships because, ultimately, everything [is] related" (Deloria 2001, 2). From these principles, there is a blurring of the Eurocentric divisions between metaphysics, ontologies, and epistemologies. In Indigenous worldviews (or perhaps, if we put a Eurocentric spin on the word, "philosophies"), what the world is, what exists in the world, and how we know and understand the world is through the real, material relationships in that world—relationships that aren't defined through human-centric positions. Everything is related, and everything is an activating member of a community, with the agency to sustain that community.

The Cherokee have a word for this social reality: ᏍᎦᏚᎩ (*sgadug*). The ᏍᎦᏚᎩ (*sgadug*), according to Christopher Teuton (Cherokee Nation), is a community that sustains itself through stories that do the work of making meaning through relationships (Teuton 2012, 138–39). As another way to understand the characteristics of sustaining community, Jace Weaver explains what he terms the "wider community" that is best expressed through kinship terms. ᏍᎦᏚᎩ (*sgadug*), the "wider community," he writes, "includes all the created order. . . . No sharp distinction is drawn between the human and nonhuman persons that make up the community" (Weaver 1997, 39). Using the Lakota *mitakuye oyasin*, meaning "all my relations," Weaver explains that this phrase invites "the web of kinship extending to the animals, to the birds, to the fish, to the plants, at all animate and inanimate forms that can be seen or imagined. More than that, 'all my relations' is an encouragement for us to accept the responsibilities we have within this universal family by living in a harmonious and moral manner" (Weaver 1997, 39). He compares this worldview to the Eurocentric view Clifford Geertz establishes; that is, the individual is bounded within the universe as "a dynamic center of awareness, emotion, judgment, and action," meaning that the Eurocentric worldview is structured in a metonymic—a part-to-part—relationship. Indigenous worldviews, on the other hand, are in a synecdochic—a part-to-whole—relationship with the universe (Weaver 1997, 39). Part-to-part relationships are realized as one node acknowledges another and is maintained by the realization of that network; however, a part-to-to-whole relationship requires us to understand the ecology in a more holistic manner—one that reaches beyond our own realm of existential node. As a way to maintain and preserve these part-to-whole relationships, Indigenous people use stories that sustain all relations in a community, and these stories help all within that community realize their part and connection to the whole without centering on a specific part.

Stories and the act of storytelling are a living and situated practice and theory that create and maintain knowledge through and within ecologies and brings relationships into existence between humans, cultures, objects, technologies, animals, and lands. Because these experienced relationships are grounded in the action and process of doing and dwelling, they sustain and produce new synecdochic connections and knowledges that can recover histories filed away in dusty archival boxes. The role of stories and the storytellers in the synecdochic worldview, according to Weaver, is to act in a way that sustains the community through communal traditional stories that "belong to the People and define the People—the community—as a whole" (Weaver 1997, 42). These stories do not act as an imitation of the world, a mimesis, but rather create and sustain identities as well as maintain knowledges and epistemologies, even encompassing the idea that stories "have tremendous power to create community. Indeed, it may be that the People cannot have life outside of stories, their existence contingent upon the telling and hearing of communal stories" (Weaver 1997, 40). Weaver notes that stories exert an active force on the very fabric of Indigenous worldviews. He names this action a *communitism*, explaining that "*communitism*, or its adjectival form 'communitist,' is a neologism of my own devising. Its coining . . . is necessary because no other word from the

Latin roots *communis* or *communitas*—communitarian, communal, communist, and so on—carries the exact sense necessary. It is formed from a combination of the words 'community' and 'activism'" (Weaver 1997, 43). Weaver's framing of communitism as both *community* and *activism* highlights the participatory nature of actions within Indigenous communities and the doings of stories that work together and "seek creative ways in which to survive and persist as Natives in the midst of an alien culture that continues to dominate Native existence" (Weaver 1997, 162). When working in archival research and dealing with artifacts that have been colonized outside of their originating cultures and existence, Weaver's concept of *communitism* is useful in building an understanding of stories as producers of action and not just content since it connects the participants (including the archives) and agents within communities directly to the idea of action through activism.

Using this understanding and framework, storytelling, then, acts as a methodological framework that is *participatory* through creating and sustaining communities of human and nonhuman agents and centered on knowledge-making as an active force. Indeed, for Weaver, the role of contemporary storytellers in Indigenous cultures is to reaffirm the *survivance* of stories. He contends, "[Storytellers] are looking back and looking forward to new myths, creating in the process new, praxis-oriented view of identity and community" and, more importantly, they aren't just "'plastic medicine men' who peddle Native traditions—real and fictive—for material gain and recognition" (Weaver 1997, 164). For me and for the sake of my research, Weaver's understanding of the complex and force-felt nature of storytelling relationships built through participatory means act as the foundational framework to understand the way stories act and what they accomplish in our research methodologies that are necessary when treading the tensions between metonymic and synecdochic worldviews.

OF RHIZOMES AND EUROCENTRIC NETWORKS

One of the key aspects of the synecdochic relationships of Indigenous worldviews are by their nature a materialist relationship. Just as Weaver and LaDuke establish that all our relations are seen in kinship, the nature of Indigenous relationships is foundationally a materialist ontology constructed through gratitude for those relationships and maintained through reciprocity (Kimmerer 2013, 115). As Robin Wall Kimmerer (Potawatomi Nation) shares, "Each person, human or no, is bound to every other in a reciprocal relationship. Just as all beings have a duty to me, I have a duty to them. If an animal gives its life to feed me, I am in turn bound to support its life. If I receive a stream's gift of pure water, then I am responsible for returning a gift in kind" (Kimmerer 2013, 115). For my archival work, I am responsible to the archives and bound to the same reciprocal relationships. If the artifacts in the archives have stories to share, I am bound to listen, learn, and continue the storywork those artifacts have maintained (Archibald 2008). Kimmerer frames that reciprocity to material relations is inherently tied to responsibility, and it is that responsibility we feel to the whole of the ecology that makes us pause and recognize those relationships (Kimmerer 2013, 152). For me, when working with archival artifacts, I have also felt that sense of pause before this project, asking myself, How do I reciprocate and act responsibly toward these artifacts? How do I maintain this relationship in gratitude? Kimmerer contends with similar questions in her own writing process, beginning by acknowledging the trees that gave up their life for her work. While contemplating a blank sheet of paper, she explains that "writing is an act of reciprocity with the world; it is what I can give back in return for everything that has been given to me" (Kimmerer 2013, 152). The sense of writing she feels is no different than the relationships of the archives and myself as a researcher. My responsibility to the artifacts is a responsibility to the whole of the story of Cherokee culture and knowledge-making. The stories I write are held in relation through the stories I've been told.

In the synecdochic relationships of Indigenous worldviews, storytelling acts as the thread to ancestors, places, and times between the lived experiences of the community as the stories are told again and again. These stories are not only a nugget of information that is passed on but a living participatory practice that creates relationships between all relations and brings those relationships into an active existence. To emphasize a point, the importance of stories and storytelling is not on who the author of that story is or even what the story is about; rather, it is the *telling* of the story that gives it meaning and knowledge. Thomas King (Cherokee Nation), in his book *The Truth about Stories: A Native Narrative*, quotes Okanagan storytelling Jeanne Armstrong, who explains the position of the storyteller in relation to the story: "Through my language I understand that I am being spoken to, I'm not the one speaking. The words are coming from many tongues and mouths of Okanagan people and the land around them. I am a listener to the language's stories, and when my words form I am merely retelling the same stories in different patterns" (King 2005, 2). King, who is a storyteller himself, reframes this as "the truth about stories is that that's all we are" (King 2005, 2).

These stories shape and create our existences, realities, and material relations in the ways we participate through storytelling—not as authors but as persons and relations embodied through stories. This materialist relationship has always already been a part of Indigenous worldviews and relationship-building that is sustained through these participatory ontologies and epistemologies. Cherokee storyteller Marilou Awiakta explains how America is seeking wholeness because it is out of relation and focused on the individual American dream, and the only way this may be possible is to go back to all of her roots through these storied encounters: "The Native American Story—and the holistic mode of thought it embodies—spring from the original root in our homeland. The story is designed to move among the strands of life's web, both within the individual and within the community, to restore balance and harmony" (Awiakta 1994, 155). This "going back" serves as a distinct moment in which worldviews collide between fragmented, disassociated knowledges to an ecological model of knowledge-making. To her, the story and its "ancient ways offer a helpful pattern in making new connections among our different people and academic disciplines" (Awiakta 1994, 155). Even in Eurocentric philosophies, there is an observable shift to ecological thought and existence, and this shift has made its way through rhetoric and composition as well with scholars such as Laurie Gries, Marilyn Cooper, Thomas Rickert, Diane Davis, Jeff Rice, Byron Hawk, and others writing about and observing the materialist threads inherent in rhetoric and writing. The turn to a materialist orientation is not a new voyage of philosophical discovery, however, as Indigenous peoples' worldviews (and therefore philosophies) have always been oriented to our material relations.

Given the trajectory of Eurocentric thinking, from the enlightened individual to the isolated modernist, the turn away from human-centric positionings is, in many ways, a turn away from the individual and back to the societal that acknowledges the relations around us. In my own indigenist positionings, I see this as a (re)turn to Indigenous ontologies as well as a moment of healing the philosophical ends of theory by (re)turning to the material world around us who has never stopped sharing her stories and has only asked us to listen. As Deloria explains, "American society is unconsciously going Indian. Mood, attitudes, and values are changing. People are becoming more aware of their isolation even while they continue to worship the rugged individualist who needs no one. The self-sufficient man is casting about for a community to call his own" (Deloria 2007, 11). While Deloria is focused specifically on the American social, the same shift and searching for community can be felt in recent materialist-driven theories in rhetoric and composition. Whereas Indigenous worldviews have always been ecological, Eurocentric worldviews are turning to ecologies and networks to recontextualize the role of the individual in relation to a human and nonhuman society. However, there are still key differences between the two worldviews that need to be unpacked. Put simply, according to Deloria, "[changing thought patterns] is an extremely difficult transition for any society to make" (Deloria 2007, 15), and indeed, the traces of a metonymic worldview in Eurocentric philosophies is hard to erase. In Lyotard's declaration that the individual exists not as an island but in a complex postmodern relation (Lyotard 1984, 15), power structures and dynamics shift from a hierarchical frame. Here is where the individual's place in Eurocentric worldviews shifts to a more ecological framework, evolving through Toulmin's comparison of early Enlightenment philosophies that imposed rigid hierarchies, standardization, and uniformity to twentieth-century philosophies that situated the individual in ecologies, differences, and adaptability (Toulmin 1992, 194). Just as Deloria describes, Eurocentric relationships start resembling an ecological state similar to various nodes of a network when they are joined together. This shift brings about a rise in materialist ontological metaphors, resembling the material and organic world around us, rather than the abstractions and objectifications of scientific thought.

A popular and apt metaphor of rhizomes stemming from the works of Deleuze and Guattari becomes a productive thought experiment to understand the subtle tensions between the metonymic and synecdochic relationships, especially when put in conversation with Indigenous ontologies. For Deleuze and Guattari, the rhizomatic network accounts for several agents but also the social contexts and power dynamics that act as nodes within that network as well. Deleuze and Guattari specifically focus on the rhizome as nonhierarchical compared to a root-tree relationship. (Deleuze and Guattari 1987). Both grounded in the natural world and focused on connected/networked relationships that may be or may seem unnatural, the rhizomatic system focuses on the lack of a clear beginning and end to the rhizome. It is propagated and grows, acting as an assemblage of nodes. Yet, as a metaphor drawn out from the natural world, a rhizome sprout can be cut away and become another set of rhizomes, distinct and separate from the previous rhizomatic system it grew from. I am reminded of this each time I am out in the flower garden. In the fall, as my plants begin to grow dormant, the rhizomatic bulbs of my perennials are asking to be divided as their network is growing beyond the nutrients available in that one place. These bulbs do not thrive without division; they struggle for resources, taking from each other. They will return the next year, but often with fewer and smaller flowers as they crowd each other out. Each part is acting on its own rather than on the whole. But as I do the work to divide these networks, the individual bulbs that are planted elsewhere and thrive in their own environment and network. In this sense, the rhizomatic system is emergent from the node of the rhizome plant. I bring this up to showcase the subtle differences between the traces of the metonymic (part-to-part) relationship that rhizomes and networks inhabit. While rhizomes may act synecdochic (part-to-whole) when seen in the network, once they are cut away we see the metonymic relationship as the whole remains unchanged and the part begins a new whole when propagated elsewhere. While the tension between these opposing worldviews can be felt, weaving together conversations between theory in a Eurocentric sense and stories-as-theory in an Indigenous sense serves as ultimately productive spaces as these theories play up and out against each other. In Indigenous cultures and for the peoples practicing within those cultures, ecologies are experienced in a very literal sense. They aren't emergent or bounded in the same ways as networks and assemblages, and the experiences that happen in these ecologies are carried across temporal boundaries. While these differences between worldviews are important to note, these worldviews still share a space to bring each into conversation with one another.

THE MATERIALIST STORIES WE TELL: WHEN ANT MEETS SPIDER MEETS GRANDMOTHER WATER SPIDER

A clearer distinction between a Eurocentric approach to ecologies and an Indigenous approach can be highlighted using Ingold's discussion of Latour's actor-network theory (ANT) in his story "When ANT Meets SPIDER." In this story, SPIDER is curious about ANT's function as an individual in the colony, and more specifically, what this colony consists of. Full of puns, ANT explains that the act-ant does not exist as an individual agent, but instead, its agency is distributed throughout the network (Ingold 2008). While SPIDER accepts that the colony is a network of act-ants (emphasis on the *act*), he still wonders about the role of non-ants in this colony. When asked if non-ants have social lives, ANT retorts, "Absolutely. *Anything* can belong to the network, whether ant or non-ant. It is precisely this point that I take issue with my colleagues. They seem to think there is something about being an ant—some essential anthood—that sets them apart from other creatures, in a separate world of *anture* as distinct from the material world of nature in which the existence of all creatures is confined" (Ingold 2008, 210). What ANT is proposing is not just a system based on connectability and relationality (although both are inherent in the system), but a network that also treats nonhuman actants as exhibiting equal active roles in that network as human actants. This posthuman system is defined through these distributed actants, which *do something* in the network (Latour 2007, 128). Another way to frame actor-network theory is to focus on the push/pull relationships between actants. When one actant impacts the network, there is a reaction (even an unexpected reaction) that occurs in other actants (Latour 2007, 129). In this way, a network doesn't hold a thingness but rather becomes a snapshot of actions at that time that action is occurring. Returning to Ingold's narrative, ANT claims that this is no different than SPIDER's web and therefore should be easy to understand. However, SPIDER counters, "The lines of my web are not at all like those of your network. In your world there are just bits and pieces of diverse kinds that are brought together or assembled so as to make things happen. Every 'relation' in the network then is a connection *between* one thing and another. As such, the relation has no material presence" (Ingold 2008, 210). SPIDER's critique of the nonmateriality of ANT turns the conversation to the importance of materiality in these networks. While ANT makes no material distinction between human and nonhuman, SPIDER points out that "our concept of agency must make allowance for the real complexity of living organisms, as opposed to inert matter" (Ingold 2008, 94). For SPIDER, these connections and relationships are built in *experience* and *real-world* complexities and do not reduce to a nonmaterial abstraction. For him (SPIDER and Ingold), the ability to adapt to the perceived environment requires skill and attunement that is developed within the organism and the environment (Ingold 2008, 214). In this web of experiences, knowledge-making resides in that growth and adaptation. It's not just a snapshot of any given moment but has a real, material temporality of growth. In other words, the web and the ecology is all the snapshots all at once. Ingold's SPIDER (skilled practice involves developmentally embodied responsiveness) theory more fully relates to the ecological functions of participatory relationships and the ways that knowledge-making occurs in these relationships. The temporality and growth in Ingold's social theory helps situate the *whole* of ecologies. While Latour's ANT and Deleuze and Guattari's rhizomes function as networks, these networks are emergent—that is, they exist at a particular time in a particular place. An ecology has no solid points or nodes and encompasses an entirety of what can be seen as an ecosystem that includes knowledges and experiences of pasts, presents, and futures. Knowledges and existences are not bifurcated like a rhizome but instead exist in plurality as other knowledges and existences. Yet, Eurocentric SPIDERs are still living under the shadows of "I think, therefore I am," which lets in the individuality of nodes and networks in social relationships, shifting to a "we know, therefore we embody together." Ingold's SPIDER, while grasping at synecdochic meanings, still only senses them in the abstract, as the response to embodiment—the response being both the knowing and existing.

However, spiders and ants are a bit different in Indigenous worldviews and as they serve as a different sort of teacher, we should listen to Ulisi Ama Kanonesgi, Grandmother Water Spider. The knowledges she takes with her are contextualized not just through embodied relationships but also the past, present, and future experiences. There is no beginning and end of a response to agents. It's cyclical, just as the basket she weaves for her back. In Indigenous worldviews, ecologies are not mere abstractions or metaphors. Indigenous metaphysics is based in the literal, biological ecologies and the experiences that have been passed down, felt presently, and will continue beyond that person's existence. Just as a spider's web feels the vibrations of the fly that lands on it, those vibrations affect the spider who is attuned to those movements, and also to the leaves to which the web is attached. The leaves, then, are connected to the trees that also blow in the breezes, and those trees are connected to the ground that they happened to be placed in. Now, because of the spider's experience in the world, she will know whether the fly or the leaves create the vibrations, but she may also be aware of the effect that the ecosystem around her plays into this moment as well. This is what is meant by *all our relations*. The fly on the web doesn't just bring its present state, it brings with it the experiences and knowledges of its ancestors, just as the spider's instincts are also passed down through evolutionary traits. Daniel Wildcat, a Yuchi member of the Muscogee Nation of Oklahoma and codirector of the Haskell Environmental Research Studies Center, puts it this way: "The incredible gulf between Western and Indigenous metaphysics is best summed up as follows: in the Western context, metaphysics became a study for philosophers; in indigenous communities metaphysics would be understood as the basis for living well—attentively, respectfully, and responsibly—in this world" (Wildcat 2001b, 52). These experiences and knowledges are grounded in *being* and *dwelling*, and they are not emergent and nonmaterial. Wildcat also explains that "we, human beings, in all our rich diversity, are intimately connected and related to, in fact, dependent on, the other living beings, land, air, and water of the earth's biosphere. Our continued existence as part of the biology of the planet is inextricably bound up with the existence and welfare of other living beings and places of the earth: beings and places, understood as persons possessing power, not objects" (Wildcat 2001a, 12–13). It is these relationships that sustain communities that are not just human-centric but all-encompassing of every agent in these ecologies: animals, plants, place, time, environments—everything that is experienced. Within Indigenous ontologies, the material is not just the human and nonhuman actants, and it is not just the embodied responsiveness. It is experienced and ontological relationships that produce knowledge-making systems.

WHAT IS WOVEN IN OUR BEING: GRANDMOTHER WATER SPIDER'S SENSES OF ALL OUR RELATIONS

In her Indigenous worldview, Grandmother Water Spider understands what ANT and SPIDER are still learning. She was there a very long time ago, in the beginning, when there was no fire and the world was cold.

> The Thunders sent down their lightning and put fire into the bottom of a hollow sycamore tree that grew in the middle of an island. Now the animals knew the fire existed there because they could see the smoke coming out of the top of that sycamore tree. But they could not get to the fire because of the water that surrounded the island. So, they decided to hold a council to decide what to do.
>
> During the council, every animal that could fly or swim was anxious to go after the fire. So, they began to volunteer. One by one they tried, beginning with Raven. Raven, who was large and strong, flew high above the water and over the sycamore tree. But as he tried to figure out what to do next, the heat scorched all of his feather black. This frightened him, so he returned without the fire. Other birds volunteered, including the hoot owl and the horned owl. But each faced similar problems as the heat from the smoke burned their eyes and the ashes that floated through the wind left rings around their eyes. No one brought home the fire.
>
> Now at this point, no more birds would venture over to the island, so the snakes tried because they could swim through the water and dart quickly through the flame. However, the smoke burned their nostrils and the flames seared their bodies. Even the great large snake, who climbed the tree could not retrieve the fire.
>
> It was time for another council, for the world was still dark and cold and without fire. But at this point, the birds, snakes, and even the four-footed animals all had some excuse for not getting the fire. You see, they were afraid to venture back over to the burning sycamore. Until at last, Kananeski Ama'i'yehi, the Water Spider, said she would go. Now, you may

know of this water spider because she is the water spider that can run across the top of the water or dive down to the bottom, so she had no problem getting to the island. But the animals asked how she might bring back the fire. Water Spider said that she would be able to manage that just fine. And so, she began to spin a thread from her body. She then wove this thread into a small basket which she placed on her back. She crossed over the water and through the grass to the burning Sycamore. She took one small coal of fire and placed it into her woven basket, and came back across the water with it. Ever since, we have had fire and the Water Spider keeps weaving her baskets.

Embodied in Ulisi Ama Kanonesgi's (Grandmother Water Spider) story are experiences that are grounded in action, doing, and dwelling; for Grandmother Water Spider and the council of animals, they sustain and produce new connections and knowledges in balance with one another. Much more than a metaphor for networked knowledge-making or networks of social existence, Indigenous stories are *actions* and *doings* and are not meant to be dislocated as individual objects of study. They are a spider's web, balanced on the back of Grandmother, holding knowledge of fire and responding to the whole of the ecology. Marilou Awiakta explains, "The story is designed to move among the strands of life's web both within the individual and within the community, to restore balance and harmony. Its ancient ways offer a helpful pattern in making new connections among our different people and academic disciplines" (Awiakta 1994, 155). She clarifies how this is different from a Eurocentric model of existence that "reasons from the outside in, from a collection of facts to a conclusion" and continues with the web metaphor to distinguish how knowledge is made in "being" (Awiakta 1994, 155). She contends, "From there we spin strands of thought outward and in ever-widening circles to a parameter of understanding, where the story itself can be told. In short, we will follow the pattern of the Native American story and weave a web where we can be still and *know* that in the belly of the story is life for us all" (Awiakta 1994, 155). These experienced ecologies are balanced with the knowledge-making properties of stories within those ecologies, making a more complex model for ontological relationships. It is these relationships that consist of a research methodological praxis that asks us as scholars to respond, adapt, and continually develop rhetorical methodologies based on the experiences and local knowledges that we have. While there is distinct merit to Latour's, Ingold's, and other Eurocentric philosophers' groundings in materialist relationships as researchers look toward methodologies that respond to material agents, I argue that the traces of a metonymic (part-to-part) foundational worldview still inhibits our ability to experience the holistic environment necessary when seeking out a reflective intercultural work that places the scholar as a part-to-whole relationship with all of the participants (human and nonhuman) that are embodied in their work.

What Grandmother Water Spider knows through the weaving of her basket is that these relationships are held together in the balance left by collapsing distinctions between ontological and epistemological experiences. This balance is contextualized within Indigenous concepts of ecologies and "all our relations." Vine Deloria Jr. makes the comparison between Einstein's theory of relativity and an Indigenous understanding of relativity. He explains, "Space, time, and matter, Einstein argued, are concepts whose measurement should be in relationship to the context in which they are to be used. That is to say, these ideas are not part of the eternal structure of the universe in and of themselves but are how we describe this universe, and therefore as we do have experiences, we can use these ideas and that have substance as long as we remember that we are part of the process of gathering information" (Deloria et al. 1999, 32). This ecology based on relationships between human and nonhuman agents is only able to be experienced through those networks and is made sense of through the same experiences. It is a lived/living practice.

Tim Ingold explains this understanding of a *sentient ecology* based on the epistemologies of the hunter-gatherers of the Taimyr regions of northern Siberia, whose concept of ecology draws parallels between other Indigenous worldviews. He shares that the knowledge from these ecologies is not a standardized, formal knowledge. Rather, these knowledges are felt in the cultural practices and relations within that person's environment (Ingold 2011, 25). The Cherokee call this balancing ecology SGAƟ', *duyuk'ta*, which is a balancing force sustained in these knowledges based on experiences within a very real ecology and is maintained through storytelling that reveals these immersive ecological relationships. Because of the immersive nature of ecologies in Indigenous worldviews, a community emerges through these relationships, a community held together in balance through "respect. Reciprocity. All our relations" (Kimmerer 2013, 153). For Kimmerer, these three community-sustaining actions are the three rows of the beginnings of a basket, and each row brings a strength to the ribs, as "order and stability emerge from the chaos" (Kimmerer 2013, 152). From my own experience as a basket weaver and through the lessons of Grandmother Water Spider, the beginnings of basket weaving are what holds the basket together and gives the basket its shape. Kimmerer explains that whatever we name these rows, "the three rows represent recognition that our lives depend on one another, human needs being only one row in the basket that must hold us all. In relationship, the separate splints become a whole basket, sturdy and resilient enough to carry us into the future" (Kimmerer 2013, 153). These first three passes of weaving are the hardest and the most important, and in Cherokee baskets, create the shape of Grandmother Water Spider to remind us of how Indigenous experiences and knowings are balanced to create and sustain communities. Nothing of our being is outside of the communities it sustains.

GRANDMOTHER WATER SPIDER'S BASKET: DUYUK'TA AS ONTOLOGICAL AND EPISTEMOLOGICAL REPOSITIONING

Each time we hear Grandmother Water Spider's story of basket weaving and fire gathering, the story serves as a living reminder of the ways Cherokee survive as Cherokee, even though they are spread out in all directions in unfamiliar places. Just as the animals were in the dark and Grandmother Water Spider used her knowledge of weaving to bring fire back to the council. Her basket is held together in the ways the ribs create balance, and the fire within is new knowledge to sustain the lives of the animals. The ontological and epistemological work this story does is that it teaches the Cherokee ways to navigate and balance their knowledge within the world around them, always practicing SGAOʼ (*duyuk'ta*). For the Cherokee and other Indigenous peoples, stories, along with other traditions such as ceremonies, crafts, and songs, work to keep individuals and their culture in balance. These traditions urge them to practice *duyuk'ta*, meaning "placing importance on the good of the whole more than the individual; having freedom but taking responsibility for yourself; staying close to earth and all our relations" (Duncan and Arch 1998, 25). Much like Grandmother Water Spider, the Haudenosaunee creation story of Sky Woman, Lisa Brooks (Abenaki) explains, is the Indigenous practice of participatory thinking that sustains relationships in ways that keep culture and society in balance. In the story, animals work together to bring up a handful of dirt from the depths of the water after seeing Sky Woman. Each tries unsuccessfully to bring up the dirt: the small rat gives up his life to bring a small handful of dirt to the turtle's back. Because of his work, the geese are able to fly up to Sky Woman, who releases a seed she has carried from the Sky World into the dirt of the turtle's back. From this seed, the Earth is born (Brooks 2008, 238). Brooks emphasizes that "the thinking that results in the creation is cooperative, drawing on the insights and abilities of all the members of the community to solve the problem at hand" (Brooks 2008, 238). This story shares several aspects with Grandmother Water Spider's story in which animals work together as a community and in council to try to harness fire, which they knew was powerful.

Brooks further explains that through these stories "human *participation* is highly valued because it attempts to work in concert with the activity of creation, as opposed to acts motivated only by individualistic desire and will" (Brooks 2008, 240). For Brooks, these stories that stress the importance of holding council and deliberation focus on the community and how activities will affect others (Brooks 2008, 238). For her, as scholars, we are a part of "a long indigenous intellectual tradition" of participatory thinking, relationality, and action (Brooks 2008, 240–41). Brooks's statement echoes Deloria's, who maintains that "Indigenous re-search methods and methodologies are as old as our ceremonies and our nations. They are with us and have always been with us. Our Indigenous cultures are rich with ways of gathering, discovering, and uncovering knowledge. They are as near as our dreams and as close as our relationships" (Deloria 1997, 182). Our methodologies, as such, should be framed through these aspects, and also actively participate in the communal and relational existences and knowings. Researchers are weaving together the theoretical worlds of storytelling with the actions and deliberations that stories invite and the relations they uncover and sustain. In order to understand the theoretical worlds of storytelling, it is equally as important to understand Indigenous worldviews that are deeply expressed, not just through stories but all aspects of understanding one's place within the world—our Indigenous place.

Recognizing an Indigenous worldview goes beyond acknowledgment, however. To understand the synecdochic worldview, you need to continually practice and embody it as it goes beyond words, frameworks, and lenses. There is a felt repositioning in this embodiment that creates a fundamental shift in thinking and being. Someone once asked me what I meant by "Indigenous," and for a moment I was caught up in the classifying actions of the English language, trying to explain that Indigenous can mean different geographic and geopolitical locations while bringing incredibly diverse groups of peoples from all over the world under its umbrella. Or perhaps, like Merriam Webster reminds us, Indigenous refers to something of a particular place, a Native and nothing more. But I was simply caught up in the language, and I stumbled in those words. Yet I reminded myself what every Indigenous person knows: We were always here and We are still here, the before-1491s and the after-1492s, still honoring our lands and languages. "Indigenous" is not a classifier, a word added to another to enhance meaning. It's a storying; an animate actionable bringing-together and being-of existence not bound by time or language. *Anehiyai*, for the Cherokee. The storying of place is not merely a coincidence, a happenstance of being there; it's the being of a "place creates the relationships and guides life-forms on interconnected trails on the land, now as ever before" (Larsen, Johnson, and Wildcat 2017, 28). Our prayers are to the four directions, our arts are representations of the cosmos, our houses of ceremony are models of the greater universe. Our metaphysics *is* the physical world, and we are of that world, beings woven in the fabrics and not the center (Deloria 2003, 152–53). The threads alongside our being are the animals, plants, rocks, trees, air, birds, and flowers, and all of creation being of that place are what makes the web of Indigenous knowledges, and the relationships and kindships of the knowledges are what is found in each of the four directions—east, north, west, and south (Absolon 2020, 76). This rooting within Indigenous knowledges that shifts us and our being into an ever ongoing coexistence through more-than-human relationships (Larsen, Johnson, and Wildcat 2017, 21) and the stories we tell and the ceremonies we keep bring us back in balance in these places, even when we have been removed. Because of the materiality and world positioning of Indigenous archives, our research and our worldviews must be shifted into ᏍᎦᏊ (*duyuk'ta*, balance) or we will always be out of story and out of relation with archives.

In other words, we need to recognize the community we are participating with, and honor that the archives are just as much a part of that community as any other human participant. At the heart of that community is ᏍᎦᏊ (*duyuk'ta*). This balance, ᏍᎦᏊ (*duyuk'ta*), as Qwo-Li Driskill (Cherokee Two-Spirit), explains, is "central to Cherokee values and community. In addition to 'truth' and 'justice,' ᏍᎦᏊ is used to translate the following English words: honest, outright, and right" (Driskill 2016, 15). The right way—that is, the ᏍᎦᏊ (*duyuk'ta*) way—within relationships is represented in the Belt That Would Not Burn, a Cherokee wampum with a woman and man on either side as representations of the Cherokee people, connected by a beaded path of life. The wampum belt, once thought lost, has been teaching the Cherokee how to walk the path of harmony and balance, which has always been the guide of negotiating ways to survive. "The ideal place to be," according to Kimberly Wieser (mixed-blood, southeast Native ancestry), an Indigenous scholar in Native American studies and environmental studies, "is in the middle, to be centered in one's ontology, so that one lives in the awareness of one's connection to all being, to the material, all part of the Mother

Earth and Creator Spirit" (Wieser 2017, 29). Ultimately, the ontological foundation of SGAΘᏮ (*duyuk'ta*) in Cherokee culture "advocates for both balance and cultural groundedness" (Wieser 2017, 190), and like living stories, the wampum belt has refused to burn. Lloyd Sequoyah told this story in 1978 during a case between the Eastern Band of Cherokee (EBCI) and the Tennessee Valley Authority, who had plans to flood the old Cherokee capitol of Echota. He reminded the courts and the Cherokee people that as long as the wampum belt, representing *duyuk'ta*, survives, the Cherokee people survive. Even when the belt burst into flames and the Cherokee thought this meant the end of them as a people, the belt remained intact—every bead, thread, and deerskin backing (Duncan and Arch 1998, 15–16). The Cherokee knew then, and know now, that if they continue to follow the balanced path of *duyuk'ta*, they will survive and that they are still here.

THE BASKETS WE WEAVE AND THE STORIES WE TELL

SGAΘᏮ (*duyuk'ta*) is ceremony enacted through story and embedded throughout Cherokee culture. While I have discussed the theoretical foundations of SGAΘᏮ (*duyuk'ta*), it is as much story and theory as it is material, especially as we follow the ceremony of the Cherokee medicine wheel. SGAΘᏮ (*duyuk'ta*), especially in traditional Cherokee basket weaving, is both present in the making and in the results. Like Qwo-Li Driskill, I look to these Cherokee cultural practices, specifically, Cherokee double-weaving basketry, to guide my constellating framework and to theorize with SGAΘᏮ (*duyuk'ta*). As a practice, Cherokee double-weaving creates double-walled baskets, which are baskets that have an interior and exterior wall that are created from one set of ribs and several runners. Before you even begin weaving, you must prepare the reeds by gathering them, stripping them, and then soaking them in water until they are pliable. This is the first step in relationship-making in the northern quadrant of the Cherokee medicine wheel—building an understanding. After soaking, you need to stay close to the water because eventually the reeds will dry as you work with them and need maintaining, as all relationships do. You begin with the ribs—four for each direction—and stabilize them with the first runner by weaving counterclockwise around the ribs. This is ceremony. The first runner creates the initial balance that acknowledges all four directions and keeps everything in place. Only when you have this balance can you move forward with the next runners, weaving in and out of the ribs. Much like following the pathways of the Cherokee medicine wheel,

Driskill explains, "Such a weaving, then, moves beyond a concept of intersectional politics. Though intersections do take place in double-weaving, the weaving process also creates something else: a story much more complex and durable than its original and isolated splints, a story both unique and rooted in an ancient and enduring form" (Driskill 2010, 74). When we turn to a model of Cherokee basket weaving, we embody an intercultural praxis; that is, a critical and reflexive practice rooted in the linking and networking of intercultural work and scholarship. But rather than think of intercultural work as merely a lens, a story, or an academic object through which we situate our understandings, we are taking part of an intercultural action—the doings of intercultural work and how that creates and sustains transdisciplinary scholarship that seeks out ways to think through borders and to weave together knowledge-making practices. Specifically, Cherokee double-weaving teaches us that knowledge-making is created and balanced between the flexible and responsive agents that serve as the ribs of a basket. Each of these agents or ribs are contextualized and woven through and with other active agents in the kairotic moment of storytelling: culture, experiences, relations, and knowledge. These act as our reeds and runners as all our relations are woven together for form and strength. Once we weave up the ribs, in traditional Cherokee basket weaving, the ribs are bent down to form the outer wall. So instead of defining borders, we weave together the inside and outside, beginning from the inside and to the outside so that everything is held together, creating muscle memory and even leaving fine splinters felt much later. This is the storytelling, and through this storytelling, knowledge-making is held in the basket and becomes balanced between the flexible and responsive agents of the ribs of a basket: the storyteller and listener as well as the story and environment. After my years of basket weaving, which I will admit still needs work and is in constant reflection, no basket I have made has ever looked the same as my own embodiment has become just as much of a basket-shaper as my hands and materials. Some of my baskets have been tightly woven and evenly shaped, yet small. Others, like the first one I made, was large yet full of holes and didn't quite resemble the basket I had intended (I lovingly named this one the "dissertation"). Yet in each one, I can look in, see Grandmother Water Spider, and feel materially connected to the knowledge and stories I constellated in that making.

If basket weaving teaches us how to develop a constellating practice in our research, storytelling acts as the theoretical impulse in our methodology that breaks the linearity and isolation of Eurocentric research practices, especially in archival work. Storytelling provides the theoretical footing that guides researchers to re-tool dominant methods of knowledge-making that exist within colonial, top-down structures and practices inherent in archival work. In this way, stories are the theory-making thread that situates us in specific ontologies by showing us the way (methodology) rather than telling us a certain way (set of methods). As Lee Maracle (Stó:lō Nation), First Nations author and theorist, contends, "among European scholars there is an alienated notion which maintains that theory is separate from story, and thus a different set of words are required to 'prove' an idea rather than to 'show' one. . . . Doing requires some form of social interaction and thus, *story* is the most persuasive and sensible way to present the accumulated thoughts and values of a people . . . there is a story in every line of theory" (Maracle 2015, 162). When seen as theory-making, the act of storytelling constellates the researcher, artifacts, and cultural situatedness by way of relationality that is the foundation of Indigenous epistemologies and ontologies. The focus on constellating through story breaks the researcher out of the linearity of objectivity that seeks to pull about the data from the researcher and break down parts into identifiable objects, classified separately (Wilson 2008, 56). Indigenous methodologies of storytelling work to bring the researcher and artifacts back into relation with one another in ways that recover the cultural existence of both. Shawn Wilson (Opaskwayak Cree), First Nations scholar and methodologist, explains this relationality in this way: "If [I]ndigenous ways of knowing have to be narrowed through one particular lens (which it certainly does not), then surely that lens would be relationality. All things are related and therefore relevant" (Wilson 2008, 58). Because of the theoretical work of storytelling, Cherokee stories of balance can recover relationships of ephemera so that it is constellated with Cherokee knowledge-making and epistemologies.

Always a part of storytelling and theory-work is the ᏍᎦᏚᎩ (*sgadug*, community), that it brings together and sustains. During the course of my research on the Cherokee seminaries, I learned how to weave Cherokee double-walled baskets from Cherokee scholars Qwo-Li Driskill and Angela Haas. For several cultural rhetorics conferences, we would meet up, bringing reeds and buckets from Oregon, Illinois, Indiana, and Ohio to Michigan State University, and we would host workshops on weaving double-walled baskets. Always with a language lesson as part of our practices, groups of cultural rhetoric scholars would sit together in circles, sharing buckets and stories, and begin their careful weaving. Centering the ribs is always the toughest part, and even those of us who have done this several times before often struggled. But as the ribs held, our baskets began to take shapes. We began weaving the interior walls, slowly and after a few rounds, more quickly making our way halfway up the ribs, now held even more tightly. We reached the point where we felt like it was time to turn the ribs down on the outside of our wall. We began the process again, weaving down this time, each of us growing more confident as our fingers began to remember the movements and slowly turning to prunes from the water we shared. Once we reached the bottom, we carefully finished off our baskets by tucking the ends back in. No basket was ever the same. Some were tightly woven, some were small and egg-shaped, others were flared and opened. Yet, all of them were imbued with the life of the stories we were telling and sharing. They were our baskets, our embodied cultural theory work, and these baskets stay with us as our minds think back to those workshops and our fingers recall the tensions, work, and memories we gained. Little did I realize then that these moments of basket weaving with my ᏍᎦᏚᎩ (*sgadug*, community) were the start of the ways and practices that shape how I understood archival research as balanced within the Cherokee ceremony of the medicine wheel. Looking to those baskets, I see now the theoretical, spiritual, and physical resemblance of the medicine wheel, and I honor each of those memories and (re)storyings each time I look back at my baskets, however misshapen I feel they might be. I'm always grateful for these moments as a scholar, and thinking back to those workshops continually shapes and reshapes the way I approach my own methodological practices.

In the figure of storytelling methodology, knowledge-making is balanced between the flexible and responsive agents: the storyteller and listener as well as the story and environment. Each of these agents are contextualized through and with other active agents in the *kairotic* moment of storytelling: culture, experiences, relations, and knowledge. While some may see this as a rewriting of the rhetorical triangle, it also represents a basket and Indigenous methods of basket-making. Purposefully in practice to mirror the Cherokee medicine wheel, the four directions of knowledge-making (also adapted from Cherokee teachings) represent the ribs of a basket, which act as the structure of a basket but can only be held together through the canes that are woven counterclockwise around them. Together, these actions work to give form and content to knowledge-making and represent the *praxis* of storytelling.

Knowledge-making in Indigenous cultures is centered within storytelling, which is positioned as central to meaning-making at the same time as it is balanced, collaborative, and situated. Storytelling acts as knowledge-making praxis where the story, participants, environment,

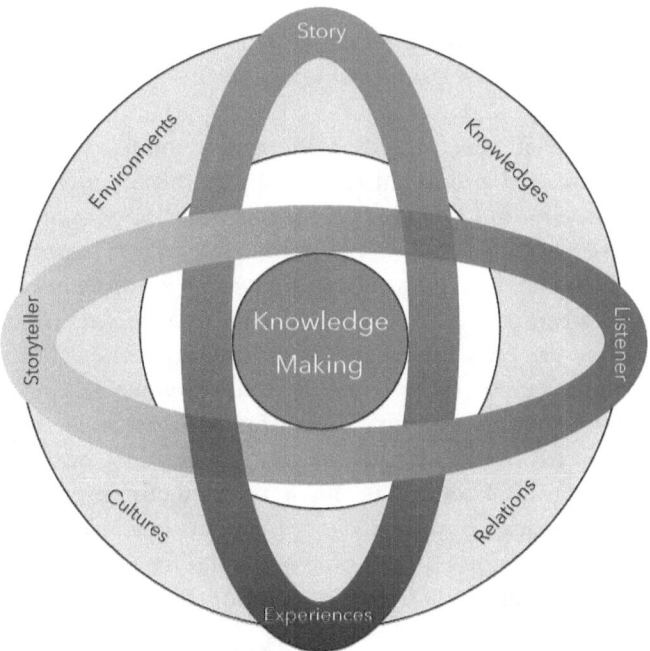

Figure 3.1.
Knowledge-Making Praxis.

time, and place are active agents in the creation of a way of knowing, understanding, and relating. Because of this knowledge-making force in storytelling, Indigenous beliefs are centered on stories. This is why stories matter to Indigenous people—stories act as the thread to ancestors, places, and times between the lived experiences of the community as the stories are told again and again (see Ingold for a contemporary reading of life through lines). It's not a nugget of information that is passed on but a living practice that creates relationships between all relations. This Indigenous practice of seeing all relationships within storytelling creates agency to re-tool dominant methods in existing colonial structures. So, the processes unfolding through storytelling are not just a way of doing things (e.g., we don't just *tell* a story). Stories aren't just static tools; they are productive forces that live and respond to outside changes and are networked with other active forces. When we apply storytelling methodologies to archival work, as researchers we are actively required to listen to the stories of the artifacts rather than imposing knowledge on them. These artifacts bridge contemporary experiences as part of the archives with the past knowledges that they have maintained through local knowledge of time and place, and we need to pay attention to the ways in which they tell their stories. These stories are in the mediums they present themselves, in that we are privy to the knowledges they hold, and these stories are always ecology-based, which draws porous boundaries around what is considered the artifact because its relations are ecologically networked in ways that help it create knowledge. An artifact never stands alone and remains removed from its human and other-than-human relations, and these networked artifacts create stories with multiple agents that share authority in order to sustain and survive, though not always in predictable ways. Cherokee stories, to offer an instance, now reference white people and recent historical events, such as removal narratives. While this may be (mis)seen as a way to undermine the "traditional" story and undercut the validity of the tale by labeling it a myth, the tribal elders and storytellers explain that the story is responsive and relational, meaning that the knowledges made in these stories are shared not just among participants but also across temporal boundaries. They are, in this sense, reflective practices. In this way, Indigenous research treats all story elements as active forces (i.e., methods, participants, stories, technologies), building a network of agents and knowledge-making practices that respond to the European linear-based methods.

While this may seem like the long way, through both the east and the north, around to think of archival methodologies, the long way around puts us back into relationships with the archives and their cultural locations so that we may make knowledge with them (and not *about* them). Just like a double-walled basket, we've made our way up through the interior wall, and now we've reached the point where we must bend the ribs down and weave our outer walls to be in good ceremony and good balance in our methodological praxis. As Awiakta reminds us, "weaving begins at the center.... From the simplest basket to the most complex of the double woven ones, this principle is the same: *The ribs must be centered and held in balance.* In a sense, they are the fixed bearings that guide the rhythm of the weaving" (Awiakta 1994, 35). *Duyuk'ta* is difficult to begin, but once it is centered, our weavings and knowledge-making hold it in place as long as we follow the paths to keep everything centered. As with the study of Indigenous rhetorics and meaning-making practices such as basket weaving, Malea Powell writes, "we study the *how* of that meaning making.... We study *how* those practices constitute things like texts and baskets. We study *how* those things carry culture—both the traditional practices around which tribal cultures cohere and pantribal Indigenous practices that create our web of Native relations" (Powell 2014, 471). In other words, it's not the *what* of stories or the *what* of baskets, it's the *how* of storytelling and weaving and *how* storytelling and weaving constitute a reflective, responsive, theoried, intercultural praxis. As we return and learn from Grandmother Water Spider, who spun the basket that carried the fire, I ask that we, too, work to weave our baskets of intercultural praxis, to practice storytelling as knowledge-making, and to strengthen our scholarship by the communities that sustain us. Our pathways to archival methodology need to be a place of *duyuk'ta* and story so that we can coexist with those archives and put ourselves back in relation with them. Through the orality of stories, whether written or spoken, Indigenous ontologies and epistemologies are collapsed into an ecological relationship held in the basket of Grandmother Water Spider. It's both the knowledge of the first light and the existence of that light held in the bowels of her basket. Collapsing ontologies and epistemologies doesn't end in destruction; just as the fire was brought to the community, this balancing of being and knowing is brought into Indigenous ecologies that sustain communities as a whole. This results in a repositioning of knowing and existing held in balance through all our relations and maintained through storytelling. When archival artifacts such as those related to the Cherokee National Seminaries are brought back into relationship with Cherokee culture through the orality of stories, they are repositioned to be in balance with knowledge-making. This repositioning shifts the archive's ability to tell its stories rather than us telling the archives its own stories. It's time we begin to listen.

4

STORYING DUYUK'TA TOGETHER
Indigenous Storytelling as Rhetorical Methodology

As I initially conducted archival research, I was struck by how much colonization of research I encountered and I was even more taken aback by how uncomfortable my own role was easily taking the position of settler colonial in the archives. It was always my hope to recover Cherokee pedagogies and nineteenth-century writing, but on what authority did I have to construct the stories that would be seen as recovery work? I felt alone in the archives, where even my education and training felt unaligned with the cultural practices and participatory knowledge-making that I had learned through my culture and scholarly elders. In this sense, the past of Cherokee nationhood felt too separate from the present of Cherokee culture. I was alone in the archives until I listened and understood that I wasn't. The more time I spent with the artifacts and writings of nineteenth-century Cherokee that were tucked away in the archives, the more I learned to listen and attune my research to the stories the archives told, and not the stories I hoped to create. My ancestors were always in the archives with me, but it took time for me to be ready to hear them. By taking the necessary time to pause in the north and seek knowledge through storytelling, I soon realized that a constellation—a path among these stories—began to develop into the methodology grounded in this storied knowledge that needed to guide my research. Here, through stories, we begin to see the application of these stories on both the epistemological and ontological levels of developing relations.

As I continued to ground my own knowledge-making in the wayfinding stories of the north, my research took me down the path of better understanding the rhetorical nature of Indigenous storytelling, specifically how the rhetorics of storytelling situate the relationally knowledge-making process with human and other-than-human participants. Seeing the ways that Cherokee writers and tribal leaders used writing as a means of survival and resistance during the nineteenth century helped me understand that I needed to decolonize my own research practices and fully commit to indigenizing my own knowledge-making with the archives and with my ancestors. Only then did I see that I was no longer looking for what stories and recovery work were in these archives. Instead, I began to see how the archives were telling stories. The *whats* and *hows* of storytelling are one of the key shifts from Eurocentric relationships with stories to Indigenous relationships within stories. Because of the complicated and colonized state of the history of the Cherokee National Seminaries, the archival research and historiography of this time in Cherokee history calls for an indigenized methodological approach to archival research that specifically invokes Cherokee practices of *duyuk'ta*. Without that balance, the archives and ourselves as researchers are out of balance, unable to hear or listen to the stories of Cherokee cultural practices. Specifically, to practice *duyuk'ta* in archival research, I trace current work on Indigenous methodologies (Archibald 2008; Wilson 2008; Smith 2012) and explore what it means to indigenize our research methods through storytelling ontologies. Storytelling as a knowledge-making praxis develops a networked way of knowing so that we may re-tool dominant methods of research that exist within colonial structures and top-down knowledge-making practices. This process of indigenizing our archival research methodologies uncovers a path through traditional Cherokee stories that opens up the archives so that we can listen to the recovered histories of the Cherokee National Seminaries.

Notions of what makes a methodology and how it is defined shifts across research studies, and, depending on who you ask and in what discipline that person works in, you may encounter several different understandings of what methodology might be. While the general concept of methodology may be thought of as a theoretical framework, I find this definition unsatisfying as it places bounds and limits on *how* a methodology acts as a wayfinding force in knowledge-making. This idea that methodology as a framework also fails to respond to the rhetorical practices of research and makes methodology the governing and policing body of a set of methods that fails to respond to participants, data, and circumstances. Rather, in Indigenous research and especially in Indigenous archival research, the participants, both human and nonhuman, are responsive and ecologically tethered. As researchers, we need to understand methodology as also being responsive and ecologically tethered to our research. In order to move characteristics of static methodologies into characteristics that are responsive and flexible, I turn to Sullivan and Porter for a more robust application of the concept of methodology that asks researchers to reframe the understanding of methodology through feminist approaches in research as a *praxis*

(Sullivan and Porter 1997, 64–68). "Research as critical practice [praxis] requires that we continuously apply multiple concepts," Sullivan and Porter contend, "not just in order to retest with a variety of methods or add triangulation of theory, method, or gate, but to bring in different epistemologies (or different sorts of warrants) to bear on the same situations" (Sullivan and Porter 1997, 74). This rhetorically aware and ecologically responsive understanding of methodological praxis is necessary when doing decolonial and Indigenous research. The static variants of methodology can be a colonizing force, not only to our research, but also to the researcher, peoples, cultures, and objects of study. However, when we shift our research impulses and methodologies to methodological praxis, we seek out research methods that are balanced and attuned to the cultures, histories, and power structures. Praxis, therefore, gives us critical impulse to respond to the recent calls for decolonizing and indigenizing our research through ways that are responsive, reflexive, and relational. By listening and spending time with stories, we see the ways that stories guide us to be responsive, reflexive, and relational, distributing knowledge throughout networked communities that situate both the storyteller, listener, environment, and technologies (Haas 2007, 2012; Stromberg 2006; Wilson 2008) as active participants in the knowledge-making process.

MATERIAL STORIES UNDER RHETORICAL STUDY

When scholars are in the business of doing nineteenth-century archival research, they are in the business of print and materiality. The static nature of print and the materiality of artifacts lures us into an analytical framework of a *thing* that can be studied. We are both in communion with the artifacts in the archives and also in a self-perceived power over the archives as our research agendas position us as investigators and discoverers of stories and histories. What happens is that our research methodologies are driven by the textual impulses to read and report. The analogy I see here is that we often mistake ourselves as saviors of the stories and settlers in the archives. However, my aim in laying the framework for a storytelling methodology in archival research is to shift our positions from ones of tellers to ones of listeners. The archives we encounter are not subjects of study; it's time we start thinking of them as participants and teachers in knowledge-making. So, when Thomas King (Cherokee Nation) writes "the truth about stories is that's all we are," he constructs a deceptively simple sentence that captures the important role of stories as an unassuming presence of stories in our daily lives (King 2005, 2). Our very existence is understood through stories as they shape our memories that construct the very core of our being. We relate to our families, friends, and acquaintances through the stories we share with them and remember about them. We digest complex human relationships by reading stories, no matter how historic, fantastical, or dystopian they may be. Every night as parents read stories to their children, they are passing along more than early literacies, they are immersing their children in the ways we construct the world around us and the ways we understand ourselves and our relationship to that world. It's in this deep and complex sense of stories that King introduces us to the ubiquitous power of storytelling in Indigenous cultures (King 2005, 2). As King shares stories that are at once deeply personal and relatable in addition to exposing the trauma, politics, and community of a modern Indigenous existence, his storytelling becomes more than just a plot-driven narrative, couched in wit and memorable characters. His writing draws attention to the complex truth of stories and the way he engages in storytelling actively performs the ways that storytelling operates as a lens that builds a deeper understanding of who we are, how we are, where we are, and what we are. These stories are *all* we are while at once we are both speaker and listener connected to the world around us (King 2005, 2). Storytelling immediately invokes responsive participations and produces meaning through the exchange of stories, and so the sharing and listening of stories is the deepest way we create while we seek knowledge.

In what he calls his "Native Narrative," King clarifies changes between an Indigenous storytelling event as it compares with Eurocentric approaches to the moment of storytelling: "In the Native story, I tried to recreate an oral storytelling voice and craft the story in terms of a performance for a general audience" (King 2005, 22). For him, the "oral storytelling voice" captures the "exuberance of the story but diminishes its authority" as a means to draw agents together and highlight the values of Indigenous storytelling, especially compared to the Eurocentric storytelling mode (King 2005, 22–23). After telling two different creation stories, an Indigenous story of animals working together with humans to build the land on the back of a turtle and the Christian story of Adam and Eve tempted to break the one rule that God has laid out before them, King uses this moment of comparative storytelling to draw a distinction between an Indigenous storytelling act and the Eurocentric act. While the Indigenous act, lacking in authorial voice, brings together the speaker and listener as one, the Eurocentric storytelling mode relies on a "sober voice" creating a "sense veracity" and authority (King 2005, 23).

The cultural values placed on each of these events offers us a theoretical window to understand the roles that storytelling plays in our relationship to the world around us. For the Eurocentric lens, stories (re)create the authorial voice to disseminate knowledge from a source of knowing to those needing to learn, while the Indigenous stories provide a means of knowledge-making that relies not on the authority of the story but on the *act* of storytelling and those networks it creates. Stories and storytelling are that pathway, but the ways that stories are analyzed as text/object in Eurocentric circles denies the relationship-making practices of Indigenous stories and storytelling. It is in this place of distinction, between the Eurocentric mode of study and the Indigenous mode of rhetorical practice, that I start to build up the ways that storytelling, as an Indigenous means, acts as a knowledge-making methodology, built on rhetorical participatory moments.

Indigenous rhetoricians and scholars Lisa King (Delaware), Rose Gubele, and Joyce Rain Anderson argue, "Story and rhetoric, then, go hand in hand. Indigenous stories (theorizing, speaking, writing, and making) are the rhetorical turns that reorient the framework that so long has pointed back toward the Greco-Roman tradition, even as Euro-American epistemologies have received and given that tradition a new birth. Indigenous rhetorics are the memories, the memoria, so to speak, of this land, its original logos and the means through which relationships among all communities on the land can be restored" (King, Gubele, and Anderson 2015, 9). By invoking specific Indigenous rhetorics, these Indigenous scholars shift the ownership of rhetoric and rhetorical terms from Greco-Roman origins to having distinct Indigenous cultural practices that are grounded in the ecologies of storytelling. The differences felt between Indigenous understandings of stories and storytelling and Eurocentric views of stories can be seen through the approaches to stories in various disciplines. The study of narrative, stories, folklore, and oral traditions is certainly nothing new or on the margins of academic practices. However, approaches to studying storytelling are varied, grounded in various disciplines, with each emphasizing different tenets that distinguish the role and act of storytelling as a specific human and cultural activity.

While I could venture into all of the vast schools of literary theory and their various disciplines that engage with narrative, I stop here to highlight a key aspect of literary theory: The narrative is treated as the *object* of study. Theorists are focused on the content, the forms of the content, the classifiable terms, and even the turn to the signifiable and unsignifiable. The story remains the same: it is the Text. The Thing.

While there is certainly value in these forms of study, the text has been amputated from the *act* of storytelling due in part to print culture and replicability of texts through a printed and accessible medium. Marilou Awiakta, Cherokee storyteller, explains that the Eurocentric dynamic regarding stories is one of detachment. She contends, "Without the [story's] cultural context, the story sickens. Forced into the 'boxes' of Western thought, it may die. . . . Usually, the Western story (especially if a white male writes it) has organic unity with the thought construct from which it arises" (Awiakta 1994, 164). She continues that these familiar forms—novel, short story, myth, fable, folklore, and so on—can each be divided and classified, reduced to content and conflict-driven narratives (Awiakta 1994, 164–65). These detachments help to create order, form, and thingness. While those oft-cited literary theorists help us approach an understanding of storytelling, they all still regard stories as either something to study, something to analyze, or something with hidden meanings and mystical properties.

In these instances of objectified storied things, the story has been separated from the act of storytelling, even to the point of arguing that, now that the author is dead, long live the Text (Barthes 1987). As a response, Deloria, in what he calls "the communication gap," remarks on how stories, in their material form through print, have been colonized through the history of Eurocentric approaches to the medium/text. "Western civilization has always depended upon the ability to symbolize, categorize, specialize, and divide according to function," Deloria explains (Deloria 2007, 19). In this way, not only does the text become the message but this act of dividing by form and function also becomes an act of Eurocentric approaches to both communication and knowledge-making through segregated disciplines. While there is certainly value in pursuing an analysis of our stories as the message, there also is value in turning away from our forms and classifications and studying our stories as speech acts, which invoke a participatory nature. My point here is not to say that these lenses of analysis are not useful or needed (because they certainly are); what I am purporting is Eurocentric literary theories colonize Indigenous storytelling through objectification and undermine the rhetorical nature of storytelling to the point that drawing direct comparisons between Indigenous storytelling and Eurocentric literary theories obfuscates knowledge-making work that Indigenous storytelling accomplishes (Archibald 2008, 17). Deloria calls us to question the Eurocentric relationship of message and medium, to stop being rational observers of our events and texts and instead seek out and understand our knowledges as part of a system that contends that "all things are related" (Deloria 2007, 25). Specifically, Deloria calls for ecological thinking that prompts us to turn back to the text, not as the sole object of study but as the embodied communication act that exists in a networked state of story, speaker, location, time, audience, and all other relations that participate as a part of that moment.

Beginning in ceremony and traveling with the stories has prepared us to now *listen* to the archives as storytellers in ways that respect the relations we have with both the material and immaterial properties of archives and archival research. In addition to preparing for archival research through the more "typical" means of waiting for boxes and folders to be pulled, asking if gloves are required (and making sure you wear them when told), double checking that you only brought pencils to take notes, making sure to ask if photos are allowed (and honing your notetaking and memory skills if not), and all of the other little acts of preparation that go into archival work before any sort of analysis can begin, we need to prepare both ontologically and epistemologically for stories the archives tell. As I reflect on writing this book, perhaps this is why I felt it necessary to deviate from academically traditional means of sharing my research. The knowledge-making and storywork that I journeyed through is a journey and story meant to be shared. It's a story that is necessary for the colonial encounters we face when preparing for archival work with Indigenous artifacts, especially as those artifacts remain print-based but still hold on to traces of storytelling orality with all our relations.

STORYING CHANGE: THE RHETORICAL (RE)POSITIONINGS OF STORYTELLING

For my own work in the archives, I needed a methodology that not only acknowledged the Indigenous ecologies present in archives, but that sought out ways to re-indigenize my methods. Since my work also intersects with revisionist histories, the storytelling as methodology helps guide my approach and situates me within a knowledge-making praxis that draws on action, lived past and present experiences, and material relations and reciprocity and uncovers the connections that have always been there through all our relations. Stories as knowledge-making practices create a living thread and leave meaningful traces between the teller and the listener that operates through all our relations. This is true for human participants in storytelling, yet it is equally true for the relationships between archive and researcher. Along this networked continuum in the archive, the story does not act as thing but creates a movement and repositioning of knowledge between the members of this storytelling frame. Telling and listening exists as a participatory practice. While the teller creates the narrative frame and begins the story, the listener enters into that frame and brings along their own understandings and context to make the story relevant to their own frames as well. This narrative place, while discursive in nature, is also crafted through the ecologies in which it is situated. These ecologies encompass the environments, technologies, passersby, time, and place—all of which become agents in this storytelling continuum. To simplify, think about the last time you told a story. What prompted you to enter this storytelling frame? What spurred the story's exigence? While there are plenty of times when we premeditate the story we want to share, there are just as many that are spontaneous moments of story-making, making a storytelling methodology one that sustains the community by fluctuating and responding to the needs of that community. In research, the responsiveness of storytelling methodology gives us a space to (re)acquaint our own positionings with the participants, including archival artifacts. Doing so keeps us in continual praxis in our knowledge-makings.

A story is never the same, even when written down in the material technology of writing, ink, and paper. Like the quantum physics conundrum of "once something is observed, it's changed and can't be observed," stories are unobservable because they are in relation with every acting agent, whether human or nonhuman. Even when written, stories change and make different relations and knowledge based on who is writing them and who is reading/hearing them, because those agents are also in relation within their ecologies. In these participatory relationships, stories, storytellers, and listeners all work together to build knowledges; that is, they sustain traditional knowledges and create new knowledges that are carried through traditional knowledges. During these ecological encounters, Lee Maracle explains the dynamics of storied practices:

> We are listening—our imaginations fully engaged—to what is said, what is not said, and what is connected to what is not said. The words spoken by other direct the listener to imagine and think. Rememberers attend to the words spoken with care, so that the oratory can be repeated later. They commit to recalling without judgment every word spoken. The speakers use words sparingly with poetic force, vision, and poignancy, so the rememberers will have an easy time of recall. Once the first round of deliberations is up, we imagine the story that will encourage us to look again to peel back each layer and gain deeper understanding. (Maracle 2015, 232–33)

The relationships between each agent are carried through to the next encounters, each learning, adapting, and contributing to that new encounter. Stories that live, breathe, adapt, shift, and change as part of Indigenous worldviews are participatory practices in addition to active agents within ecological networks. Stories are both the material and etheric, and this dual existence becomes the making of knowledge.

In research, methodologies are the guiding principles of interdependence, and our methodologies must reflect practices and knowledge-making that are ethically and responsibly conducted. I argue that methodologies need to be understood as more than just frameworks for analyzing data, but as reflective practices that put us in relation with our participants broadly defined as human and other than human agents. When we consider archival methodologies, especially working with Indigenous archives, our first methodological practice should be in ceremony so that we acknowledge that our knowledge-making is interdependent on the archives, just as the future of the archives is interdependent on the histories we write as those histories become a part of the archives for others who might access them. Storytelling, then, is the practice of relationship-building, and together, all of those in storytelling work interdependently with each other to make knowledge. In this way, they can be enacted to produce a means of knowledge-making that serves to weave together the participants, the timeliness, the environment, the place—all relations in an ecology of participation. Deloria argues, "Nontribals can measure the distance to the moon with unerring accuracy, but the moon remains an impersonal object to them without personal relationships that would support or illuminate their innermost feelings" (Deloria 2007, 12). In Indigenous stories, every entity—human, nonhuman, place, and event—is deeply embedded in personal and ecological relationships. In these entanglements of storytellers and listeners, the knowledge that is created is not just in the passive motion of moving between agents of storytelling. Instead, knowledge is shifted from a thing that is produced independently and individually to a thing that is both produced in participation with agents and the thing that maintains those networks. Being of the world and knowledge-making within that world requires stories to keep that world in balance as *duyuk'ta*. Once we assert our position as primary researcher, we are no longer "of" the world and we use that claim to distance ourselves along with our attempts at staying objective to try to maintain those hierarchical systems. But when we are of the world, our balance in that world is through relationships formed by storytelling praxis. In this way, we are never outside of stories, and as Thomas King explains, once you hear a story, it's a part of you. "But don't say in the years to come that you would have lived your life differently if only you had heard this story. You've heard it now" (King 2005, 29). This change that occurs is the change of knowledge-making that is sustained through storytelling that doesn't result in differences. You are still you when you gain that knowledge, but you are changed through that knowledge. The diffractive and agential realism of storytelling is the lifeforce and the knowledge-making praxis that causes our shifts in positionality while we are still a part of the world (Barad 2007). This is how we can be in relation with stories and make knowledge with storytelling.

As I continued to pursue archival research and seek out more artifacts from the Cherokee National Seminaries, I came across many stumbling blocks, especially as I had to widen my search to archival sources outside of Cherokee lands in northeastern Oklahoma. Even when I found a newspaper here or a letter there, these artifacts were often one of the only documents in their collection. They were both out of place and out of time. The placelessness of the artifact was directly connected to the simple fact that these artifacts, like the Cherokee who created them, faced removal and colonization. However, like the Cherokee people, the artifacts are always already part of ecologies from whence they came. These artifacts have and are still agents that are dwelling in those systems even as they assume new roles in their archival environs. The ecology of stories is deeply connected to the material places and lands where those stories reside in addition to the inhabitants of that land, especially the other-than-human dwellers. These ecologies give stories local knowledge through these relationships that is more than just the knowledge of the place; instead, it is "tacit knowledge embodied in life experience and reproduced in everyday behaviour and speech" (Cruikshank 2005, 9). In these places of local knowledge, a connection between the past and contemporary experiences of those places helps Indigenous peoples to understand and retain cultural values that have been oppressed and pushed for Eurocentric worldviews. I find this framework especially important when researching archives. The artifacts, while out of their cultural places, are both produced by and resisting the local knowledge of archives. Archives impose colonial knowledge, yet the artifacts maintain local knowledge of their own places when we, as researchers, seek out the ecological relationships of those artifacts and listen to the stories they are telling. In doing so, we see the artifact as more than just a document or text, but as a storytelling bridge that crosses the boundaries between historical and contemporary experiences.

While turning to local knowledge of contemporary Cherokees gave the archives a sense of place in a placeless existence, I found that these archives were under a colonized veil of timelessness as well, decontextualized from their histories and culture. In order to recontextualize them and to listen to them, storytelling provides the means to reconnect those material objects with their previous materialities. Since stories are not vessels of knowledge but rather makers of knowledge, stories act as material agents in the knowledge-making process. Because of their agency, they make change in the world through the ways they embody time as part of that relational lived practice. Rifkin continues that one of the living dynamics of stories is their temporal sovereignty as well; that is, "acknowledging the significance and effects of the forms of temporal relation [stories] both reflect and bear" (Rifkin 2017, 36). As evidence of this, Chris Teuton tells the following story that occurred while working on his book *Cherokee Stories of the Turtle Island Liars' Club*: While trying to record one of the stories by the elders, the background noise made the recording unusable, as it drowned out the storyteller's voice. When Teuton returned to the elder to ask if he would either rerecord the story or allow the use of other technologies to clean up the noise, the elder told him that that wasn't necessary. He explained that the story, although recorded, was simply not meant to be heard and passed on as knowledge in this case. Also, in this case the technology played an active role in determining that the time was not appropriate for the retelling and that this story's knowledge was not meant to be gained at this specific moment (Teuton 2012). In this rhetorical moment of storytelling, the text/content is realigned with the humanistic impulses of relation and kinship that moves stories away from being content-driven into being storytelling acts. While the content still can be analyzed, classified, and sorted through various forms of "story," the interrelationships between the narrative and act help us understand the ways our stories and our events respond as a networked state with time and place being agents of storytelling alongside the storyteller.

This ability to retain temporal sovereignty through each retelling demonstrates stories' abilities to make cumulative knowledge over time, gathering up experiences, sharing them at the appropriate time and place, and giving knowledge to those that are listening. However, there is a subtle yet distinct difference between what is typically taught as kairos and how timeliness is understood in Indigenous worldviews. Whereas kairos, as traditionally taught in rhetorical studies, is time determinant—that is, it is centered on the opportune time of the moment—Cherokee rhetorics of storytelling is time relational. In other words, Cherokee rhetorics of storytelling invoke the ways stories are in relation with specific times and places. When I think specifically of Cherokee time-relational rhetorics in storytelling, I recall the stories shared when meeting with Tom Belt, Cherokee language scholar, storyteller, and elder at Kituwah, the Cherokee spiritual homeland in North Carolina. We spent a good portion of the day walking around the grounds of Kituwah, meeting where the council house stood on the mound that still exists, and I learned about our ancestors and their connection to this specific place. Although I carry the knowledge from those stories with me and thus can retell those knowledges in this book, the specific stories conveyed to me at Kituwah were meant for that specific time and place. Rather than time determining the "spark" of storytelling, the stories are in relation with specific times and places. They are not emergent and they already exist; however, they are only told at those times (which are often cyclical, such as seasons or times of the day) and in specific places. Without the specific time and place, Tom Belt would not have shared these stories. Cherokee stories are always in relation with time and place, often with certain stories only being told during certain seasons, events, and gatherings. "For Native storytellers, there is generally a proper place and time to tell a story," explains Thomas King, a novelist of Cherokee descent. He continues, "Some stories can be told any time. Some are only told in the winter when snow is on the ground or during certain ceremonies or at specific moments in a season" (King 2005, 153). The time to tell stories depends on the relationships between location, participant, nature, and specific moments, such as being in the archives.

Stories not only teach us how to interact with the world around us but explain how we are drawn together and depend on these relationships. In Cherokee, the relationship between Selu (Corn Mother), Kana'ti (the Hunter), and their interactions with the plants and animals around them, put Cherokee values on gender balance into a dynamic relationship with the world around them. In this story, Selu produces corn and beans from her body to sustain her family while Kana'ti goes out each day to bring back a deer to add to the daily sustenance. These ecological relationships drawn between stories are also enacted in daily life. As a way to draw relationships between Selu, Kana'ti, and contemporary relationships, Cherokee wedding practices call for the groom's mother to bring venison to the ceremony, while the bride's mother provides corn and beans. As a white blanket is drawn around the bride and groom after they receive these gifts, their lives are drawn as one. Without stories, these ecology-based relationships are unclear and the meaning is lost. When separated from this knowledge-making praxis, the stories can be seen as categorical, each encounter asking for a different type of story. However, I argue that we should resist the urge to categorize these stories as a way to pull them apart from this complex network of action. When collected in print, Cherokee stories are often categorized by similar types and elements—animal stories, creation stories, Little People[1] stories, monster stories, and others. However, these categories serve only to identify the characters and plots in these stories and are disingenuous to the *doings* of stories. Rather than treating each story as its own object, which I admit has power in other venues, I seek an understanding of how these stories are enacted and networked through oral impulses in storytelling.

HOLDING THE CENTER: LANGUAGE AND PRINT AS THE RIBS OF STORYTELLING PRAXIS

While many Cherokee stories are now shared in print with no author but perhaps with the name of the storyteller, the heart of the story is always in the tellings and spoken sharings of those stories. During the years of the seminaries, the use of the Cherokee language was even more prevalent than today. Therefore, it isn't far in the memories of any Cherokee that these stories, shared in English, still have their origins and spirit within the Cherokee language. Cherokee culture is deeply embedded and syntactically rooted to its spoken language, and even today, the Cherokee language is incredibly important and serves as a sacred connection to Cherokee culture, values, and beliefs. Tom Belt, Cherokee language instructor whose first language is Cherokee, explains that "we were told that the old people would say that the language was given to us by the creator. It is a gift. If it has been given in such a manner then it becomes a sacred thing." Belt explains that the language you speak shapes the way you think and understand the world. "It is the way we reach into each other's hearts," he contends, "to lose that, they said, to stop speaking that language, is to stop that kind of understanding of the world." Even the structure of Cherokee shapes the speaker's relationship to the world. Belt points out that Western European languages that are noun-based, like English, put the emphasis on the individual, making them the center of the universe. Cherokee, however, is a verb-based language that

---

1. Little People—or as the Cherokee call them, Yunwi Usdi—are small humanoid creatures that live in the mountains and in tunnels. Sometimes known as Moon People because they only come out at night, Little People are typically quite benevolent and help the Cherokee that live among them, such as helping lost children find their way home or helping with the garden. However, they can also be very mischievous and use their magical powers to harm those who disrespect them, teaching us to remain in good relation with them. Because of the magical nature of these beings, I have always been taught that you can only tell stories of the Little People at certain times so that we don't disrespect or upset them.

recognizes the actions of others in the world first and then brings it back to the individual. To him, and to the Cherokee who are continuously working on language revitalization, Cherokee culture will continue from generation to generation and "we will always be Cherokee. It's the being that's most important" ("Tom Belt: Cherokee Language Teacher" 2011). By speaking the language, the Cherokee people are practicing Cherokee culture in one of the most sacred ways—the Cherokee language. It's important to note that stories with their origins in the Cherokee language are by their linguistic features different from stories told in English. As a medium, the Cherokee language differs ontologically and epistemologically from English because it is verb-based, with case endings that are relationally based on the physicality of the objects, the direction the speaker stands, the distance between speaker and object, and even the relationships between the speaker and listener. Sometimes this means that you can have four to five different prefixes or suffixes on verbs, and each of these prefixes and suffixes changes the inherent meaning of a sentence. (Duncan and Arch 1998; Holmes and Sharp 1989). What this generally means is that many puns and most wordplay are lost during translation. A good example of this type of wordplay can be seen in the English sentence "Pass me the gravy." The verb, "pass," has shape markers in Cherokee, meaning that the shape of the object affects the case of the verb. So, in Cherokee, if you wanted to subtly insult the chef by calling their gravy lumpy, you would ask, "*Asu:sdi deskv:'si*," which literally translates as "Gravy it-solid-hand-me," instead of the polite "*Asu:sdi desginehv:si*," of "Gravy it-liquid-hand-me" (Holmes and Sharp 1989, 23). Just as the subtly of the joke is lost when it is translated into English, the humor inherent in this Cherokee wordplay and in stories is lost when a story is translated into another language. For Cherokee storytellers, they know that telling a story in Cherokee will construct a different kind of story and engage the listeners in different ways. Telling a story in Cherokee also means that the language, serving as a rhetorical medium, acts as a network between human participants and objects, surroundings, technologies, locations, and distances.

While orality is at the core of storytelling, Cherokee stories often are shared and distributed to a wider audience through print. Gerald Vizenor, Minnesota Chippewa Tribe, White Earth Reservation, tells us that "the immanent pleasures of an aural performance are unbodied in translation; the tribal experiences that were heard in stories, and natural variations on stories, are transformed in publications that are seen as cultural information" (Vizenor 1993, x). One of the clearest examples of this transference between oral and print is James Mooney's *Myths of the Cherokees*, printed in 1900 yet still immensely popular and still currently in print over one hundred years later. Mooney was an American ethnographer and lived several years with the Cherokee. At that time, just as the seminaries were being forced to close, the tribe saw the inherent value of collecting and printing their stories as cultural artifacts in part due to the federal policies of dissolving tribal governments. When visiting Kituwah, Tom Belt explained to me that Mooney's collection of Cherokee folklore and sacred formulas often left out key cultural values because the Cherokee storytellers that Mooney recorded knew that the audience would be outside of the tribe and that some teachings and practices are meant only for tribal members. On the surface, not much of the story has changed. But those familiar with the stories will immediately know what is missing and will be able to fill in the rest of the details with their own intimate knowledge when speaking and sharing the story to other Cherokee. The tribal members and storytellers knew that the medium and the intended audience was not focused on the practice and experience of storytelling but on the preservation through printed word. While tribal members often direct printed collections of stories, currently the same practice of adjusting, withholding, and adapting stories for print continues. These storytellers took advantage of the fact that printed words remain the same on the printed page as long as the same edition is produced. This feature of printed stories can be used as a power disruption in that information can be changed or withheld in order to maintain sovereignty over the stories and the embodied teachings and relationship within. In this way, this slippage of meaning and omissions of cultural details acts as a protection and means to react against colonial power structures. Protecting stories from colonization through these rhetorically strategic maneuvers ultimately serves the good of the community and provides an ethical means of survival against forced erasure. Yet, because of this printed collection, the stories from Mooney's collection both survive and resist colonization, especially as it was carried out during the nineteenth century.

These stories are a continual act of survivance, an active and dynamic negotiation of survival and resistance (Powell 2002; Stromberg 2006). Indigenous stories embody survivance through the practice of storytelling and languages that maintain culture (Vizenor 1993, viii). When we tell stories, cultural teachings and practices are encoded into stories that act as vessels between ancestors and contemporary experiences. As stories are passed from generation to generation, each instance of the story connects memory, experience, and teaching and brings each speaker and listener into the world "as part of an ancient continuance story composed of innumerable bundles of other stories" (Silko 2012, xix). This continuing thread is at once resistance and survival—survivance. Weaver contends, "Native survival in the face of internal colonialism and the revitalization of Native traditions attests to the truth of Said's repeated theme that this is always *something being the reach of dominating systems*, no matter how totally they saturate society, and this is the part of the oppressed that the oppressor cannot touch that makes change possible" (Weaver 1997, 11–12). Just as stories tie the past to the present as cultural survivance, so too do they adapt and bring in historical encounters, without changing the cultural and traditional impulse of the story, ultimately tying together human and other-than-human relationships, past and present (Trafzer 1993, 21). Many Cherokee stories will now reference white people, specific locations post-removal in Oklahoma, contemporary technologies such as guns (instead of bows), and so on. This does not mean that these stories are any less of a thread, but it shows an adaptation to continue, bringing in all experiences as part of the continuous story.

Even in the archives, the importance of language and oratory specifically plays a major role in survivance through stories. Just like the survivance of the Cherokee through removal, assimilation, and erasure, stories are living, constantly adapting to circumstance and context, finding ways to still be Cherokee and teaching Cherokee how to navigate the world even when appearing in writing and in the documents and ephemera of archival boxes that seem to be a stagnant window into the past. "The stories may change slightly, but the nucleus of their message remains," Cherokee storyteller Sequoyah Guess, and Cherokee scholar Chris Teuton write. "The stories shared in this book change a little with each storyteller, each telling. By the time you have read them here, they have already changed; they are living things" (Teuton 2012, 4). Spoken stories enact rhetorical survivance as lived practices, passed from generation to generation, and adapting to contemporary situations. The traditions of the past are inherently bound in the traditions and knowledges of contemporary experiences. Not only are the stories surviving and bridging past and present, but they are actively resisting the colonial powers that bound notions of "Native" and "indigeneity" to the distant past, one that remains comfortable and conquered by Eurocentric ideas of progress and civilization (Weaver 1997, 19–21). These moments of survivance are deeply felt in stories and celebrated as stories continue from one storyteller to the next, developing traditions of storytellers that are the protectors of culture and the disruptors of power. Storytelling, whether in print or spoken, is the shift from a Eurocentric view of orality (and the effervescence of it) to the materiality of realized relationships.

This materiality of all our relations in the archives is realized through the orality of stories, which invokes the participatory nature of gratitude, responsibility, and reciprocity; that is, storytelling is a *living* and *reflective* practice that exists both as material and oral in Indigenous worldviews. Stories were always meant to be vessels of knowledge that were fluid and "loose" and shifted meaning and roles, and this caused anxiety around the writing of stories because these writings can take on an "air of authority" (Teuton 2012, 4). When speaking, subtle changes in context such as the direction the speaker is facing, the time of day, the audience, or the animate and inanimate objects of the stories change the way the story is told, whether it is shared or not, and how the speaker retells the story (Duncan and Arch 1998, 17); these rhetorical practices are always a part of storytelling for the Cherokee. Orality is the life-breath of storytelling, yet the Cherokee were facing a Eurocentric society driven by the impulse of writing and literacy. Cherokee survivance is in the realization of strength that comes when we understand the kinships between the two and the power of their rhetorical sovereignty.

Sequoyah's syllabary, developed only twenty years prior to the seminaries in 1821, provided the necessary means for Cherokee orality to shapeshift into written language without losing their inherent oral rhetoricity. Cherokee stories, preserved through the Cherokee language and written down, shift us away from the oral/literate binaries that rhetoric and composition still tussle with. Rather, Cherokee rhetorics of storytelling move orality and literacy back into relation with one another and in a network of rhetorical practices that all contribute to the practice of knowledge-making through the means of survivance. Jo-ann Archibald (Stó:lō First Nation), whose influential writings on Indigenous storywork, explains, "The mystery, magic, and truth/respect/trust relationship between speaker/storyteller and listener/reader may be brought to life on the printed page if the principles of the oral tradition are used" (Archibald 2008, 20). There is no split between the ways that knowledge is made and the relationships that form between storyteller and listener if that story is written or spoken. Our divisions between orality and literacy are only complicated when we view them through Eurocentric lenses, and when we situate them and ourselves in Indigenous knowledge-making praxis, the etheric rhetorics of orality are preserved. Writing doesn't change that, and that preserved orality is Indigenous survivance. Joshua Nelson, Cherokee Nation citizen and Cherokee scholar, shares that it is important to remember that storytelling, as part of an oral tradition, is meant to be a living force whose goal is to document change (Nelson 2014, XII). The slippage in tellings, the changes from storyteller to storyteller, and the additions and revisions over time are necessary to the life of stories. Because of these shifts, storytelling doesn't operate to make facts or add permanency to content, it's there to keep us in balance through reflective practices and knowledge-making.

Cherokee storytellers will often begin by explaining that this is how they heard the story, and, much like LaVar Burton, you don't have to take their word for it. As a rhetorical force, storytelling goes beyond a retelling of types of stories and operates as *gagoga*. While the literal translation of *gagoga* in Cherokee means "s/he is lying," Cherokee storytellers explain that "lying" accurately captures the living nature of stories as they are told from one storyteller to the next. When a storyteller begins a story, he or she is not concerned with the validity of the tale's content but instead of the ways it connects knowledges past and present. At the same time, the storyteller is also not seeking to transfer specific knowledges to the listeners. Rather, the how and why of the story enact a moment of knowledge-making that may or may not be received, meaning that storytelling in Cherokee is not a top-down, content-driven event but rather an encounter with cumulative knowledges. While the literal translation of *gagoga* implies deception, the Cherokee play with the slippage between lying and storytelling, knowing that the stories capture the knowledge in Cherokee teachings but the events and characters in the story can't be verified, especially ancient stories of talking animals and roaming monsters (Teuton 2008). Christopher Teuton, a Cherokee scholar working closely with the Turtle Island Liars' Club of Cherokee storytellers further explains that "lying invokes a cultural process of interpreting contemporary experience in relation to the cultural truths traditional stories express" (Teuton 2012, 137). Understanding storytelling as lying helps us understand the changing nature of these stories as they not only vary from storyteller to storyteller but also bring in more contemporary experiences, including ancient stories that refer to modern technologies, such as guns, or colonial encounters with white people within creation stories. Once again, this does not invalidate the story as false or even as a contemporary re-telling. The story is a living force, emphasizing the networks between the past, present, and future states of knowledge. In this way, storytelling as *gagoga* maintains the practice of *duyuk'ta*, keeping the contemporary experiences in balance with Cherokee cultural frameworks, such as teachings on gender, roles in society, relations to land and animals, individuals and community practices, and so on.

Even Cherokee stories grounded in orality when presented as print-based stories contain both a record of permanence and a loss of authorship (and authority). Vizenor explains that the language game of what is seen in print and not heard in stories leads to different stories and reminds us that "the printed word has no evolution in tribal literatures; the word is there, in trees, water, air, and printed on paper where it has been at all times" (Vizenor 1993, x). This new role creates a space to preserve and retain cultural practices for distinct audiences and those privy to the whole of the story, as presented in oral-based situations. What this does is provide a means to not only disrupt institutional power and Eurocentric claims on print and literacy but also provide a space for this slippage in authority in storytelling that emphasizes a polycentric worldview that requires multiple mythologies. Because of the Indigenous worldview of "all our relations," stories need to enact a practice that acknowledges multiple mythologies, and to do so requires that these stories not assert one universal Truth or author, but instead employ a shared and slippery authorship that leads to a multiplicity of understandings and truths. Weaver explains, "Ultimately reality, which we see through a glass darkly, is like a child's kaleidoscope. How it is perceived depends on how the cylinder is held, even though the bits of glass that form the picture are unchanging" (Weaver 1997, 33). Stories, like this kaleidoscope, are also composed of the same features, but depending on the storied practice and encounter, the meanings of the stories invite a slippage of truths. Returning to the metaphor of the kaleidoscope, he continues, "The task must be to learn as much as one can not only about the given pattern but about the individual bits of glass, so that when the cylinder is shaken we can know something about the new image when it forms" (Weaver 1997, 33). In understanding the ways that slippage in authority works, it's important to highlight Weaver's statement here. The story is not meant to be an obfuscation of truths resulting in a lack of reality but instead understood as a multiplicity of truths that result in a newer, layered understanding of those truths. Each time a story is told, it can and should produce a different knowledge based on how those truths are parsed through that specific moment. In this way, the stories remain communal—not just to the culture and community but as enacted in a network of participatory knowledge-making. It is exactly the participatory nature of storytelling that brings archival artifacts back into the community, not as objects of study but as teachers and ancestors that have their own stories to share. In part, these artifacts, when positioned as active participants in storytelling methodology, begin their work to once again sustain the communities they have been removed from. Without stories, we easily fall back into the research paradigm of primary researcher telling a story of a removed artifact rather than participating with that artifact to play our roles as researchers in sustaining communities alongside the artifacts.

BUILDING THE "HOW": PRAXIS THROUGH
PROCESSES OF INDIGENOUS STORYTELLING

By centering archival methodologies in Indigenous theories and rhetorics of storytelling, I posit that these research moments are the realization of these interdependent participatory networks in the archives—an understanding of *all our relations* in the archives. By situating stories within Indigenous views of ecologies, we turn to research practices that are outside the traces of Eurocentric understandings of stories so that we look to stories not as objects of study but as the knowledge-making force that brings the researcher and archives together in cultural understanding. Knowledge-making is networked through the storytellers, the listeners, the stories, and the environment. Just as ecologies are realized in a literal sense for Indigenous worldviews, so are environments. Environments are specific, geographical locations[2] that are in a symbiotic and biologic relationship with all of the inhabitants of that physical space. Again, this is drawn from the Indigenous worldview of "all our relations," as Deloria explains, "if we greatly expand our understanding of the sense of being relatives, we discover that plants, birds, and animals often gave specific information to the people. . . . Here is a bird-human relationship that involves information about the plant and its use" (Deloria et al. 1999, 37). Knowledge-making is formed in these environments through posthuman relationships that are occurring naturally (and even technologically) in those environments. In this understanding, a *gagoga* is a Cherokee way of knowing that recognizes the entire community as knowledge-makers/producers and storytelling as knowledge-making is not placed within one individual/agent who passes the knowledge down to others (Teuton 2012). *Gagoga* also emphasized the communal authorial voice of stories, which also maintains *duyuk'ta*. If there is no author, the story has no central power, no hierarchy, and no place of origin. It has always been a decentered story and it will live on past any current generations as stories as long as it continues to be told, slippages to content and all. Instead, it is knowledge that exists in a networked state with the community inhabiting the roles of knowledge producers of all our relations—human and other-than-human. Explaining ways of reading American Indian literature through

---

2. Lisa Brooks, in her book *The Common Pot*, explains the importance of physical geographies in Indigenous stories through Keith Basso's concept of place-making. She also builds on Deloria's point that geography in stories (specifically creation stories) is much more important than the chronological events of that story. In this understanding, the physical place plays a powerful role in stories as the specific locations of knowledges. Since everything is networked through relationships, place is an active and literal agent within these ecologies and environments. (Brooks 2008, xxiii)

the application of oral practices, such as storytelling, Teuton contends, "The act of returning with new knowledge and fresh interpretations creates new terrain upon which the community may continue to grow. Knowledge is sought and valued in relation to the collective harmony and survival of the community as a whole" (Teuton 2008, 197). This knowledge, which stems from the balance of listening and telling within a community is the power of the story. Knowledge is produced within a network created by the community of both the listeners and the storytellers. This network serves to create a participatory culture that sustains community relationships—a community that extends between human, nonhuman, place, and time.

A static story replicates but does not make or network new understandings; however, by deploying a storytelling methodology, we can expand the ecologies of explanation in ways that help us uncover the posthuman frameworks in our research, and especially in archival research that is necessarily driven by nonhuman agents alongside human interventions. Storytelling acts in Indigenous cultures as a central tenet of knowledge-making practice; the story, participants, environment, time, and place all participate as active agents in the creation of ways of knowing, understanding, and relating. Hastings Shade, a Cherokee storyteller from the Turtle Island Liars' Club, was talking to Chris Teuton one day about learning by doing, specifically on the role traditional crafts have in teaching. He explained how the elders used to talk to him about learning, saying "'*Nijadolihvi jadetlosgwasdi. Tla yidetlosgwasdi.*' 'If you want to learn you're goin' to learn. If you don't want to learn you won't learn.' And if you learn, it's going to be yours. And if you don't learn it, that knowledge belongs to someone else" (Teuton 2012, 141). This is the way it is with stories. Stories are there to tell and to hear, and if you are willing to listen, you will take that knowledge with you. Stories are not meant as objects to be set aside, owned, or taken control of. They exist as a knowledge-making praxis that sustains the community of all relations (human and nonhuman, material and nonmaterial) together. Most importantly, stories are the *how*; they are how we learn, how we create balance, and how we make knowledge.

Stories are the knowledge-makers, and when we are brought into that storytelling model in relation with all that is a part of that model, our knowledges and worldviews are shaped and formed *if we choose to listen*. This is a weighty task and a powerful methodology because of the ability stories have to enact knowledge. Knowing this, it's important to keep Thomas King's words close at hand: "So you have to be careful with the stories you tell. And you have to watch out for the stories you are told" (King 2005, 10). This isn't just the case for Indigenous stories, either. Stories of colonialism are embedded in our research practices and shroud an Indigenous worldview of "all our relations" that seeks to sustain ecologies that acknowledge our human/nonhuman and our material/nonmaterial agents. In other words, stories are theory and these theories aren't the sole property of Western thought and philosophies. Because Indigenous peoples' understanding of relationships is built through experiences, these experiences are transferred through a knowledge-making praxis that is cumulative and participatory, and not separated into disciplines, philosophies, or expertise. Deloria argues, "If the student keeps the methodology of trying to relate bits of information to all elements in the scenario, that is to say, to regard information about plants as relevant to the birds and animals who use them and the location where they are found, there is no question that a great deal of important knowledge will be achieved . . . eventually the student will discover that he or she is the possessor of a knowledge much broader, deeper, and more comprehensive than what is being taught in the classroom" (Deloria et al. 1999, 39). The broad, deep, and comprehensive knowledge produced through storytelling in these participatory ecologies is why I see storytelling methodology as an incredibly productive mode of research and inquiry. Storytelling methodology seeks to uncloud deep relationships and structures through a participatory act between storyteller and listener, even if either of these roles is filled by a human or other-than-human. These stories we share develop our theoried worlds, weaving together agents in diverse, intercultural worldviews and develop meaningful relationships that seek to sustain our communities. As we share our stories and weave our baskets, let us remember that storytelling is not a tool that crafts the story as an object or artifact. It's not a means to an end. It is a living and situated practice that disseminates knowledge within ecologies between humans, cultures, objects, technologies, animals, lands, and so on. By retooling our dominant ways of knowing here in the north, we can begin the work started by decolonial methodologies of revealing and contesting power structures and move into an Indigenous and intercultural framework of navigating these structures in order to understand the complex rhetorical ecologies that situate participants, materials, environments, technologies, and cultural practices together. This journey now has prepared us to enter the west, to listen, and to understand, and we are prepared with the knowledge to understand the stories the Cherokee National Seminary archives have been telling all along.

PART 4

ᏧᏕᎵᎬ: ᎤᏍᏆᏂᎪᏛ ᎠᎦᏙᎲᏍᏗ

wudeligv: usquanigodv agadohvsdi
West: Keeping the Wisdom

ᏧᏕᎵᎬ (wudeligv), the west, the place where the sun sets. And yet, our ceremony does not end here. Although the setting sun signals, for some, the end of the day, for other relations, the setting sun brings about the nocturnal life world. ᏧᏕᎵᎬ (wudeligv) is a place of transfer, from a world run by the sun to another run by the moon. For the Cherokee, this is a place where we move from making knowledge to keeping the wisdom with those who have transferred from the place we understand as "living" to the honored places of passing, to join with all our ancestral relations. Here, in ceremony, we are asked to work industriously with our ancestors to continue the living knowledge and keep the wisdom of those seven generations back and seven generations in the future. Here, in ᏧᏕᎵᎬ (wudeligv), we look back to look forward.

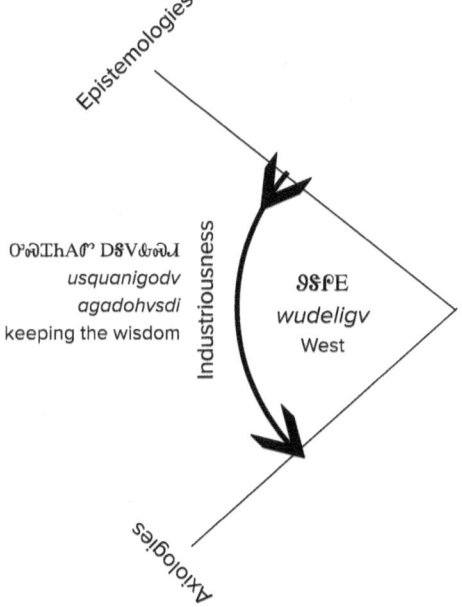

Figure 5.0. West: Keeping the wisdom.

5
STORIES EMERGING FROM DUSTY BOXES
Finding Duyuk'ta at the Cherokee National Seminaries

The Cherokee National Seminaries are often portrayed in history books as being caught between the world of the full bloods and the mixed bloods, tradition and assimilation. To a great degree, the narratives of what happened in the continual contact between these worlds plays out as assimilation overtaking tradition for the sake of Cherokee progress as the Cherokee Nation from back East morphed into one of the Five Civilized Tribes of Oklahoma. However, this progression-to-whiteness narrative obfuscates and simplifies the survivance of the Cherokee people. As Joshua Nelson, a Cherokee Nation citizen, argues, "The story of mixed-bloods adopting white dispositions and betraying traditional interests for the sake of profit has become so ensconced that it can be taken as a factual rather than as a historical construct to be integrated" (Nelson 2014, 28). The subjection to assimilation of the Cherokee people is a scapegoat and easy to digest. It's easy for colonizers to see some sort of conquest as the Cherokee people adapted white education systems to do the work of erasing their own culture, and it's a straightforward narrative for those who have been colonized to find a way to explain their own generational trauma and the ways that generational trauma has impacted their families and communities (and continues to impact them as well). Yet, this narrative is a result of binary knowledge systems, where there are two extremes on each end of a linear path. For the Cherokee, the binary that has subjected their stories since contact is the binary between tradition and progress. And in the tensions between tradition and progress is an uncomfortable coding of assimilation.

That uncomfortable feeling is not a new one and happens more than it doesn't when we frame the world in systems of binaries. Those spaces between are often occupied by what others might not want to confront yet (re)claimed by those who find themselves caught in two worlds. When researching the Cherokee National Seminaries, I often found my work floating in that third space of existence and being caught up in the

https://doi.org/10.7330/9781646425228.c005

narratives of assimilation. On the surface of research, it's easy to read the changes in Cherokee society at the beginning of the nineteenth century as being driven by assimilation. They adapted a centralized government, established a writing system, and created a school system built on the models of elite white society. Even when doing genealogy research, many of the resources that document Cherokee list their race as "white" and their tribe as "Cherokee." Cherokee culture was defined through the question of race by those on the outside, and as anthropologist Circe Strum argues, "Running throughout much of the scholarly literature is the assumption that the racial ancestry of Cherokees correlates not just with their class standing but with certain social values. Full-bloods are often understood as cultural conservatives, as bearers of 'tradition,' whereas mixed-bloods are expected to be oriented toward progress and change" (Nelson 2014, 149). The easy question to ask at that point in researching was "Is this assimilation?" And yet, while researching with Cherokee stories, language, and culture in the center of my methodology, the question of assimilation kept steering me away from the Cherokee voices in the artifacts I continued to spend time with. The more time I spent with archival artifacts, my questions shifted to "Who is telling the story of assimilation and where is it coming from?" Not once did I hear a Cherokee person tell me that we had assimilated and had been erased as a culture. In fact, the message was just the opposite: the Cherokee people are thriving and we are still here just as we always have been. Who benefits, then, from a successful narrative of assimilation if the erasure of Indigenous peoples isn't successful?

In spite of the massacres and federally sponsored genocide of Indigenous peoples, our stories and bodies were woven into the fabric of America's founding and its exceptionalism. As Deloria reminds us, "The white man had been forced to deal with the Indian in treaties and agreements. It was difficult, therefore, to completely overlook the historical antecedents such as Thanksgiving, the plight of the early Pilgrims, and the desperate straits from which various Indian tribes had often rescued the whites" (Deloria 1988, 172). In many ways, the stories that put Indigenous peoples in the service of the American dream kept us visible even when we were the undesirable original occupants of the Americas. Because stories are the keepers and life-givers of culture and identities, the new occupiers found another strategy that explained away the massacres and genocide and kept Indigenous peoples still in the service of the progressive narratives of a new nation. Deloria continues, "Laws passed by congress had but one goal—the Anglo-Saxonization of the Indian. The antelope had to become a white man" (Deloria 1988,

172), and its success depended on the erasure of Indigenous people through the stories told about them and not by them. I found myself confronting these kinds of narratives in my research, and one of the misconceptions I've wrestled with is how we think back and write about traditions and traditional cultural practices *with* the nineteenth-century Cherokee rather than *about* the nineteenth-century Cherokee.

Our ways of talking about traditions are linked to the ways we think about assimilation, especially when writing about nineteenth-century Cherokee. When we link tradition to assimilation, the assumptions inherent in this linkage frame tradition as meaning something pre-contact and assimilation is that de-linking of traditions that occurs post-contact. As these words become embedded in scholarship and narratives of history, traditions are often seen as an object that gets lost, taken away, and removed through contact. Traditions then have the guise of being stable and enduring—if they are able to survive. When reading the histories of the nineteenth-century Cherokee, the survival of traditions becomes harder and harder to imagine. However, Cherokee culture and what is often called tradition is held in its stories and language and practices. They are living and ever evolving as they are passed from person to person. Traditions are not objects that can disappear as our ancestors walk on; rather, they are actions and practices made living through the bodies of the Cherokee that survive. From body to body, the stories and practices subtly adapt and shift to its new contexts.

As we understand 9SfE (*wudeligv*), the west, as a place of transfer and transition, what this means is that our ancestors are always already teaching us lessons. Our ancestors are also with us as we make knowledge, not just through their words in what has been written but in the stories we hear and in the ways that their experiences are coded into our very being through kinship. The direction west is not about looking to the past but learning with the past as it is living in the present. When we do this, we can uncover and listen more deeply to the wisdom of our elders in all our relations. I am reminded here of basket weaving once more. While the motion of and principles of basket weaving remain the same, each basket weaver brings a set of new hands, new muscle memories, new materials and dyes, new tensions and shapes, and, ultimately, we end up with an array of new baskets and practices. However, because the stories are told and the practice-as-theory of weaving remains the same, we can all look at our diverse baskets and see the shape of Grandmother Water Spider at the center of the ribs and runners. We are still connected to the stories that maintain Cherokee culture and traditions. From this framework of understanding, I hope to disrupt the binary of traditions as objects and assimilations as the practice of removing these objects through storytelling. The practice of storytelling is so deeply central to Cherokee ways and knowledge-making that the careful rhetorical navigation of these federal policies by the Cherokee became difficult to overlook the more I worked with these archives. From the founding of the seminaries to the careful construction of balance and *duyuk'ta* in the pedagogies and purpose of the seminaries, the Cherokee Nation spoke to the prevailing stories of assimilation while crafting their own stories of sovereignty and resistance for their own people through their own established educational policies. To honor the continuation of Cherokee culture through these rhetorical navigations, I refrain from using the word "traditions" and instead will replace it with "practices" to evoke the ongoingness of Cherokee culture that reaches as far into the past as it does into the present and future. When we begin here with the Cherokee Nation's response to assimilation policies through their own navigation of these difficult times, we are able to situate and constellate ourselves with the Cherokee of the nineteenth century, ultimately giving us a space to critically reimagine (Royster and Kirsch 2012) the ways the Cherokee used education and writing as their own sovereign methods of resistance.

CONSTRUCTING SEMINARIES AND BALANCING GENDER ROLES: A FOUNDING IN BALANCE

While the Cherokee Nation established both of the seminaries through the same act and conceived of both on equal footing, subsequent joint acts explain in detail exactly how the Cherokee Nation provided for both seminaries as well as how these provisions would be carried out. One of the many important aspects of this act is that it does not distinguish between the two seminaries, not once providing different goals, means, or outcomes for either school. Each section of this act refers directly to both schools under the same heading rather than separating out different provisions for each. Even the pay for instructors, male and female, was equal. (Cherokee Advocate 1847) From the inception of the seminaries, the Cherokee never intended them to be two separate schools; rather, the seminaries were always thought of and carried out as one system of school divided into two buildings to house each gender of students. While the separation of the seminaries seems to be based on gender, it is much more nuanced than categorizing humans via biological sex. Theda Perdue, who has written extensively on Cherokee gender, has this to say about the ways that Cherokee understood gender (not biological sex) in the context of society: "The Cherokee understood what it meant to be a woman or a man even when the individuals confounded that understanding, but because gender did not shape their organization of the world, they were able to incorporate individuals who defied gender into their social organization." (Perdue 1999, 39–40). She also further explains that the Cherokee language is not gender based and there are no separate verb cases to denote gender. Rather, classification of male or female is based on the roles that individuals took on in society, typically influenced by the story of Selu and Kana'ti. For the sake of this book, one should read "male" and "female" as meaning a person who operates in Cherokee society as either a man or a woman.

Yet, even the separate buildings for each of the seminaries were constructed from the same set of blueprints. This blueprint (there is only one) is kept in the archives at Northeastern State University and makes no references to any differences for the male building or the female building. The blueprint is only labeled as "Cherokee Seminary." The buildings, while at different locations, were exactly the same and any further improvements done to one building were completed on the other, carried out through various acts by the tribal council. These joint changes are documented through various newspapers reporting on the seminaries during the nineteenth century. One specific case refers to an outbreak of measles during the early 1880s at the female seminary. The *Cherokee Advocate*, the newspaper of the Cherokee Nation during this time, reported on the measles outbreak and made a case to the tribal council to create the position of a medical superintendent for each institution. The piece, written for the newspaper on November 30, 1883, begins by evoking the love of the seminaries by the people and that this love should be given to the institutions from the government especially because of the current prosperity of the Cherokee government. The author then shifts the tone of their piece to direct the reader to the amount of sickness that has befallen both seminaries, resulting in at least one girl in each dormitory room having a case of the measles and suggesting that while the male seminary has not had as many cases, an outbreak could occur as well. The author ends the piece by calling for an increased pay of the physicians, supplied materials, and coordination between the seminaries as well as other institutions run by the Cherokee government.

The tribal council acted and both of the student catalogs from the late 1880s from the male and female seminaries boast of a medical superintendent and modern facilities to serve the students at each seminary. The balanced approach to creating and maintaining the seminary may seem like a nod to efficient government matters; however, in keeping

Figure 5.1. Men standing in front of Cherokee Male Seminary in the early 1900s. Photo by Robertson Studio, McGrath-Benedict Collection, Courtesy of the Oklahoma Historical Society.

with Cherokee practices of *duyuk'ta* (balance), the approach to operating the seminaries mirrored Cherokee teachings and practices. *Duyuk'ta* practices both survive and resist assimilation through their adaptation and application in a nineteenth-century world. While a single blueprint and joint acts could be overlooked, they are the material manifestation of practices from that time, resisting assimilation through their means of upholding *duyuk'ta* from pre-contact times. These stories from within the archive speak to one another and to us as we begin the process of meaning-making through our reading and listening to the Cherokee context of archives. Without the knowledge of Indigenous meanings and practices, these stories become moments of happenstance and are lost to our histories. Because we situate this history within a Cherokee indigeneity and not through a Eurocentric lens, we can start to construct a decolonized history of educational institutions in these seminaries. Because of the evidence of Cherokee practices of *duyuk'ta* in the establishment as well as construction of the seminaries, we can read comparisons across both seminaries, not as gendered differences but as balances maintained throughout.

Throughout Cherokee society, past and present, practices of *duyuk'ta* have been transposed into Cherokee societal structure through

Stories Emerging from Dusty Boxes   139

Figure 5.2. The graduating class of 1875 standing in front of the Cherokee Female Seminary. Photo by L. C. Handy, Grant Foreman Collection, Courtesy of the Oklahoma Historical Society.

traditional stories, such as the story of Selu and Kana'ti. The story goes that long ago a hunter, Kana'ti, and his wife, Selu, lived with their son. Now, another, Wild Boy, who called himself a brother and had sprung out of the blood from the game that Kana'ti would bring home every night, also joined them in their home. These boys were curious and followed Kana'ti one day to see where he got his game since he seemed to bring it home every day without fail. The boys followed and saw him open a cave door and one deer would run out. This was the deer he brought home. Seeing this, the boys snuck off and wanted to catch the game for themselves. Opening the cave, they let all of the game escape at once. Knowing this, Kana'ti scolded the boys, telling them they would now have to work for their game since he would not be able to bring it home every night. Selu, knowing the boys were hungry since there was no meat, told them to wait as she went out to the storeroom. She came back with baskets full of corn and beans. She continued to do this every night so the boys would have food. Again, being curious, they decided to follow her out to the storeroom to see where the corn and beans came from. They hid and watched as she rubbed her hands all over her body. Corn and beans came from her body and into the basket. Theda Perdue, historian of the Cherokee, explains, "The myth of Kana'ti and Selu provided the Cherokees with an explanation for why men and women in their society lived the way they did, occupying separate categories that opposed and balanced each other" (Perdue 1999, 17). Just as the ribs of the basket go off in opposite directions, gender roles within Cherokee society create that structure of balance—not balanced through hierarchy in the Eurocentric sense but rather through the structure of relational balance and harmony. Men were in charge of providing the game, just as Kana'ti does, and women's role was tied to the land that they cultivated, owned, and produced corn and beans to also provide for the family (17–18). This structure kept the Cherokee family, as well as the society, working together, balancing each other on equal footing. And the story of Selu and Kana'ti maintains this balance each time it is told and each time it is listened to. As Awiakta tells, "Perhaps one reason versions of this story are still often told is that they so well express Cherokee philosophy of harmony, which begins in the tangible world with Mother Earth. Selu and Kana'ti model this harmony between genders" (Awiakta 1994, 23). This harmony of gender is not just enacted in stories but is also carried out through Cherokee societal culture. Qwo-Li Driskill explains the Cherokee practice of *duyuk'ta* is a performance of balance in Cherokee song and dance, where the men sing and the women shell-shake, and is illustrated in the physical placements of men and women's bodies during the stomp dance (Driskill 2016, 62). This structure kept the Cherokee family and community working together, balancing each other just as the stories taught us to do and the dances help us perform and practice (Driskill 2016, 63). By weaving the telling and the listening of this story with the establishment of the Cherokee National Seminaries, the reciprocal respect between the genders becomes part of that living knowledge that is obscured through the colonialization of the Cherokee during the nineteenth century.

As the cult of true womanhood became dominant in American society during this time, perpetuations of separate spheres of gender and society are often read onto the seminaries, as they were separated into male and female institutions. This colonial reading has the greatest impact on the ways we understand the purpose of the Cherokee Female Seminary. Because of Eurocentric ideas of separate spheres in society, we are told to listen to the story of the seminaries as a narrative of the marginalization of Indigenous women and their place in Cherokee society. Indeed, as women they faced the confines of imposed separate-sphere roles, a colonization of their bodies as powerful, and subjugation to an imposed patriarchal system from European contact. As Indigenous peoples, they faced marginalization, assimilation, and forced removal from their land and their culture through federal policies aimed at erasure. Before contact, the Cherokee women held equitable social status in their towns and councils as Carolyn Johnston explains, "When the European encountered the Cherokees in the sixteenth and seventeenth centuries, they were shocked to find that women had so much sexual freedom and held considerable political, economic, and domestic power. To them, Cherokee women represented sexual danger" (Johnston 2003, 11). The survival of the tribe depended on the Cherokee women who brought forth food from the Earth season after season, just as Selu did, and the role of men leaving the town to hunt for game and bring it back to the community, just as Kana'ti did. With this role as owners and producers of the land, Cherokee women held positions, roles, and behaviors that European women, and even some European men, did not (Johnston 2003, 11). However, as intermarriage increased between the tribe and Europeans, these patriarchal ways slowly uprooted the role of women in the Cherokee societies. Even as early as 1750, European patriarchy replaced the social and economic roles of women. Kay Givens McGowan explains, "Native women who had enjoyed positions of leadership and equality were now experiencing the double jeopardy of being both discriminated against as a woman and treated unjustly as Natives by the newly arrived Euro-Americans" (McGowan 2006, 58). Cherokee society was balanced through a clan system of matrilineal kinship. When married, a man would leave his clan and join the clan of the woman he was joined to. All of their children would then belong to the matriarch's clan. If she had sons, they would leave and join the clan of their wives while the matriarch's daughters would continue the clan line. Just like Selu, they remained rooted to the land and the ground for their clan to prosper and the men moved between clans to introduce new members to clans. In this system, it was the women who decided who they would marry and when. When a Cherokee woman wanted a divorce, she would remove the man's belongings from their shared house, placing them outside, signaling the separation. The man would then leave the clan. Yet, as contact with colonists and settlers increased and intermarriage became common, the tensions between matrilineal kinship order and patriarchal practices and descent caused Cherokee society to wrestle with precontact practices and those being brought into the tribe.

My own family ancestors dealt with these tensions in the 1770s as my ancestral line begins with the intermarriage of William Shorey Sr., a white interpreter, with Ghi-goo-ie, a member of the Bird Clan. Their son, William Shorey Jr., also married Cherokee women and upon his passing in 1809, he supposedly dedicated a will to his grandnephew, John Ross,[1] and left his possessions to all of his children and relatives, including his sister. However, his eldest daughter and my ancestor, Elizabeth Bessey Shorey, claims that this oral will must have been made when he was drunk and she took charge of her sisters. This case went before tribal council and ultimately it ruled in favor of the other descendants of Shorey. Theda Perdue explains that this case "demonstrates the difficulty of interpreting a specific inheritance exclusively along the lines of one system or the other" (Perdue 1999, 141) and that his will is in accordance with a matrilineal descent and Elizabeth's requests follow a matrilineal kinship system. However, the difficulty in the case comes from the multiple wives William Shorey Jr. had. In a clan system, his property and daughters would have remained with his eldest daughter's clan, verifying Elizabeth's case. This erosion of the clan system during this time shows the effect that Eurocentric notions of familial relationships had on a kinship system, where everything was kept in balance based on kin and not blood relations (Perdue 1999, 141). These tensions were still at work even after the creation of the seminaries, and Cherokee were still working through ways to adapt their cultural practices with the changing society around them.

Yet, even in my family, the sense of belonging to the Cherokee Nation still had vestiges of the Cherokee clan system. When my third great-grandmother, Cynthia Anne Williams, who attended the female seminary for few years in the early 1880s, married her husband, a white man from Chicago, in Tennessee in 1884, she decided that they also needed to be married a second time in the Cherokee Nation, now located in Indian Territory. This second marriage, albeit to the same man, meant that her husband could have all of the benefits of any member of the Cherokee Nation (Armor 2013), which maintains the matrilineal progression of citizenship for the Cherokee. While this may seem like a slight detour through my family history, what I would like to emphasize is that the role of gender in Cherokee society during the nineteenth century was complex as traditional clan kinships systems eroded yet still remained a part of Cherokee culture. Women still functioned in society as matriarchs and brought men into the tribe as full members through marriage even through the end of the nineteenth century. However, the story of gender roles and societal balance being erased by contact is the story that continues to exist and because of this prevailing narrative, the stories of Selu that are told within the Cherokee society are whitewashed

---

1. John Ross is most known for being the chief during removal and also oversaw the creation of the seminaries.

out of Cherokee history. This story of erasure is the work of colonization, attempting to obscure what the story of Selu and Kana'ti is telling, and it has tried to erase the complexities of the ways that Cherokee culture still remained practiced, albeit in different contexts during a tumultuous time in Cherokee history. Joshua Nelson addresses the complexities of Cherokee women who have been seen as succumbing to the cult of true womanhood by various scholars who have perpetuated this version of history. He argues that because of the binaries we set up in history regarding separate-sphere domestic roles divided along the lines of strict gender roles, historians tend to view "assimilation and resistance as the only options available" (Nelson 2014, 92) for Cherokee women. Rather, he argues that Cherokee women should be understood as leaders in the ways that they educated themselves and spoke to the political and social concerns impacting their community. More importantly, they were capable and motivated to determine what was useful to them and their communities, not as some appeasement to outside, white influence (Nelson 2014, 92–93). When we frame Cherokee history and the roles that Cherokee took in their society through colonizer stories of assimilation, we perpetuate a version of history that serves to support the success, and not the resistance to, Eurocentric dominance. Cherokee society, and especially Cherokee women who are subjected to colonizing and patriarchalizing power structures and stories, deserve the positioning of their histories with their own cultural stories as theoretical lenses. When we draw connections between Selu and Kana'ti, which would have been a story often told in Cherokee households and gatherings, and the seminaries as specifically Cherokee institutions of education, the rich history that maintains Cherokee sovereignty unfolds and guides us to a better understanding of the knowledges of paths of survivance these nineteenth-century Cherokee share.

A PUBLIC EDUCATION FOR THE CHEROKEE, BY THE CHEROKEE: THE SURVIVANCE OF CHEROKEE WOMEN, KINSHIP, AND SOCIETAL ROLES THROUGH EDUCATION

As we can now see, the creation of both seminaries needs to be understood through the lens of Selu and Kana'ti, rather from a colonialist lens of assimilation. While it is true that the seminary students were schooled in separate buildings, it doesn't mean that they were separate or operated as producers of separate-sphere societies in Cherokee culture. M. Amada Moulder explores the early impacts of assimilation and acculturation of education on the Cherokee Nation. However, rather than presenting a story of abandoned tradition, she maintains that Cherokee women, through education, practiced gender balance as well as reinforced community ties. Moulder explains, "[Cherokee women] used the outsider tools of a patriarchal society to retain power as women . . . Cherokee women took these tools [of education] and indigenized them. That is, they used English-language literacy for Cherokee political purposes and to preserve Cherokee communal values" (Moulder 2011, 77). The establishment of both the male and female seminary can be read as a separate-sphere structure when we come from the understanding of hierarchical relationships in Eurocentric worldviews; however, the mirroring of curriculum, shared pedagogies, and emphasis on balance in relationship with others tell a different story. These might have been two separate buildings, but the practice of *duyuk'ta* is carried out in the administration and education of Cherokee students rather than imitating Eurocentric impulses in education. As evidence of the survivance of Cherokee cultural practices by way of the Cherokee Female Seminary, the pillars of the old seminary building that burned down are still the cultural heart of Cherokee heritage in Oklahoma. Park Hill, near the Cherokee capital of Tahlequah, is the original plot of land that the Cherokee government set aside for the seminaries. The pillars from the old seminary are preserved right outside of the entrance to the Cherokee Heritage Center, which serves as a museum dedicated to the Trail of Tears, an art gallery, and a genealogical research center for Cherokee. Additionally, the cultural center is home to two historical villages, created by the Cherokee, to represent Cherokee life, practices, and culture. Diligwa is a recreation of a 1770s Cherokee town with typical Cherokee houses, a council house, and a stickball field. Visitors can interact with Cherokee tribal members who do historical reenactments of various Cherokee crafts and practices. In addition to the older village, there is also Adams Corner, which is a replica of a Cherokee town in Indian Territory during the 1890s. This town has several craft and mercantile buildings in addition to residences that showcase the kinds of houses that Cherokee lived in during this turbulent time. There is also a school and a church on the premises and a farm nearby with livestock and gardens. When walking through the extensive grounds of the cultural center, the pillars of the Cherokee seminary stand out in the middle of it all and the foundation of the building is outlined in stone. When you are there, you never get a sense of the passage and erasure of Cherokee practices and society. Rather, all three buildings and villages operate jointly to showcase the cultural survivance of Cherokee life. Even if context and lands change, Park Hill still remains the place that

Figure 5.3. The Cherokee Heritage Center with the pillars from the old female seminary still standing in 2021. Photo by Emily Legg.

Cherokee travel to. In doing so, much like the ways Kana'ti and his sons are nourished by Selu, Cherokee are sustained through this cultural preservation. In many ways, the Cherokee Female Seminary is still keeping tradition alive and serving as the cultural heart of Cherokee society in Oklahoma.

To understand the weavings of Cherokee culture with educational institutions, it's helpful to start at the beginning of the seminaries and their ties to schools on the East Coast that served as models for the Cherokee national school system during the early 1800s. The connections of the seminaries to Mount Holyoke go well beyond just their founding. In the years leading up to the opening of the seminaries and during the years that the seminaries were closed, Cherokee women traveled to Massachusetts to attend Mount Holyoke in South Hadley and many came back to be teachers in Indian Territory (Fry 1988, 40–44). The Cherokee tribal government also sought graduates of Mount Holyoke to serve as principals at the female seminary. Upon the arrival of Ann Florence Wilson in 1875, four of the previous seven principals of the female seminary were graduates of Mount Holyoke. While the connections to Mount Holyoke ran deep, the Cherokee seminaries stood out on their own right as an institution with their own cultural practices and prestige. According to Lola Garrett Bowers and Kathleen Garrett, who penned the biography of Ann Florence Wilson, one of the longest serving principals of the female seminary, the seminaries were "not a tradition measure by Old World standards, but one to be proud of by the New World yardstick. When the seminary had been established in 1851, Harvard attained the hoary age of 200-odd years, but West Point was only 50 years old. Mount Holyoke College was only 14 and Vassar, Smith and Wellesley yet to be" (Fry 1988, 56). Bowers and Garrett continue, "Education with the Cherokees was almost an obsession," and "through a succession of Mount Holyoke College students, graduates, and teachers, Mount Holyoke's own high standards of scholarship and deportment flourished in the Cherokee Nation" (Fry 1988, 57). The high values and standards at the Cherokee seminaries were set by the tribal government, who was willing to pay teachers high salaries for the time (Whitmore 1953), and funded the seminaries without any federal government assistance. Instead, the money for the seminaries as well as all of the Cherokee public schools came from the interest the Cherokee received on the sale of lands to the federal government (Starr 1921, 231). Because the Cherokee could fund the entire school system on their own in addition to minimal funds from boarders at the schools, the Cherokee could have complete sovereignty over their education, making sure that the education that their citizens received would support and uplift the Cherokee community. In the treaty from 1835 that called for a Cherokee school system, the tribal government added a section stating that no missionary schools or other establishments were allowed to be created without first gaining permission from the tribal council, and they must be focused on developing Cherokee national interests and meeting community needs (Starr 1921, 225). The Cherokee also included a section in their constitution that gave the tribal government the right to oversee all aspects of education, from the establishment of school, the promotion of education, and the "diffusion of general intelligence among the people" (225). The Cherokee held complete sovereignty over their school system without any interference or reports done by the federal government until 1898 (Starr 1921, 229). The high standards set by the tribal government and carried out through recruiting and supporting teachers well made the seminaries well known as rigorous and outstanding models of education west of the Mississippi during this time, and it was all for the Cherokee and by the Cherokee.

In the years right after the official founding of the seminaries, members of the Cherokee governing body traveled to the Northeast to seek out schools that could serve as a model for what would become Cherokee-serving educational institutions. In 1850, a year before the seminaries opened, David Vann, the Cherokee Nation's treasurer, and William Potter Ross, who had been educated at Princeton and was the nephew of the current chief John Ross, traveled to Massachusetts, looking for teachers for the seminaries (Agnew n.d.). On this trip, they hired Thomas Van Horn, a graduate of the Newton Theological Seminary, and Oswald Woodford, a graduate of Yale. While visiting Mount Holyoke, Vann and Ross were impressed with Mount Holyoke's seminary model as well as its students. They hired two of Mount Holyoke's students, Ellen Whitmore and Sarah Worcester, as the first teachers of the female seminary. During their visit to Mount Holyoke, Vann and Ross also studied the seminary education model, and adapted it to serve Cherokee purposes. With fresh teachers now in place and an educational model to follow, students began arriving at the female seminary in Park Hill, while the male seminary would open its doors to applicants a year later. Applicants to both schools were required to be members of the Cherokee Nation as well as have the literacy skills needed to pass entrance exams that included English language proficiency in spelling, reading, arithmetic, grammar, and geography. Ellen Whitmore explains the excitement of these first days at the Cherokee Female Seminary, writing in her journal:

> Wednesday, April 30th: Eight girls have arrived. I find it difficult to maintain a calm and undisturbed demeanor.
>
> Thursday, May 1st: The first day of our examinations is past—it has been wearisome and exciting. We have examined 13 and tomorrow will be busy.
>
> Friday, May 2nd: Another day has fled. I have examined all who have applied except one—she will be here in the morning. (Whitmore 1953, 18)

The curriculum and education model was based strictly on Mount Holyoke and designed for both Cherokee seminaries by Mary Chapin, a principal at Mount Holyoke at the time (Mihesuah 1998, 27–31). Whitmore, once again writing in her journal, explains how teaching duties were split between her and Sarah Worcester on the first day of classes held at the female seminary, explaining the preparations the day before: "Services in the school room commenced at 11 o'clock. [Chief John Ross] and family were here. Monday, May 12th we commenced recitations, found the young ladies interested and lessons learned well! I told them they must arise and retire promptly, they must not 'enter rooms' or make 'communications.' I have taken history, one class in grammar, two in arithmetic and the reading. Sarah has the writing, botany, one class in grammar, one in arithmetic and singing" (Whitmore 1953, 18). These early writings from the journal of Ellen Whitmore give us a firsthand account of the earliest of days at the seminary and capture the excitement, newness, and eagerness of everyone involved. They knew that the present they were living would be remembered as stories passed on for generations.

While the curriculum was rigorous, Mount Holyoke's model extended beyond instruction and established a socially conscious educational structure that addressed problems of financial access to education that many families faced, especially after removal. Lisa Mastrangelo, who has done extensive historical work on rhetoric and composition curriculum at Mount Holyoke, explains, "Working under different social constraints than their male counterparts and often utilizing different modes of pedagogy, women, especially at the Seven Sisters Colleges, made an often unacknowledged contribution to the history of rhetoric." She continues, "Active pedagogy and student-centered discourse can be seen throughout the models" (Mastrangelo 1999, 47). Mount Holyoke created a uniquely student-centered approach in all aspects of curriculum design that was heavily influenced by the school founder, Mary Lyon, and this appealed to the Cherokee. Lyon, who founded Mount Holyoke in 1837, wanted a school that all women could attend regardless of educational or socioeconomic background, insisting that they not call the school a college, a word that she felt was pretentious and had a "wholesome aversion" to (Locke-Stow 1887, 149). One unique, and often contested, method of education was the inclusion of daily chores and household duties as part of the women's responsibility as students at the seminary. This requirement was not to enforce a domestic sphere within education or to promote subjugation to men. Rather, it kept the cost of tuition low so that more students would be able to attend the seminary and receive a higher education that wasn't bound by socioeconomic constraints. According to the Mount Holyoke Catalogue (Mount Holyoke Seminary 1867):

> All the members of the school aid to some extent in the domestic work of the family. The portion of time thus occupied—about one hour a day—is so small that it does not retard their progress in study, but rather facilitates it by its invigorating influence. Yet it is no part of the design of this Seminary to teach young ladies domestic work. This branch of education is exceedingly important, but a literary institution is not the place to gain it. Home is the proper place for the daughters of our country to be taught on this subject, and the mother is the appropriate teacher.

This focus on an egalitarian approach through domestic responsibilities to one another was one of several ways that Mary Lyon encouraged a more democratic space and relationship-building not just between students but also faculty. If we contextualize the political upheavals of the Cherokee Nation, we can see why such an educational model such as Mount Holyoke's appealed to a struggling tribal nation. Boarders paid a nominal boarding fee subsidized by funds from the Cherokee government that provided board, laundry, lodging, lights, fuel, textbooks, and supplies. Boarders were expected to provide their own comforts, blankets, linens, and toilet accessories (Starr 1921, 231). However, If any family was unable to pay the boarding fee, the Cherokee government paid for every expense (tuition, room, and board) for up to fifty students (Starr 1921, 231), making Cherokee education accessible to every student regardless of means. As the tribal government planned, education would not only improve individuals within the Cherokee Nation but improve the community overall, as it was forced into a new territory without the resources and governmental system they had before. With educational strategies shaped by Eurocentric models and pedagogies, the Cherokee Nation could speak back to a larger public and implement governmental structures that worked through and with Eurocentric structures and yet maintain their dedication to community and tribal sovereignty. Speaking back, according to Ellen Cushman (Cherokee Nation), is a method of cultural perseverance. This perseverance is "a place where Native cultures, for example, enact part of their sovereignty—a process that allows them to name who they are, what practices count, what structures govern, and what technologies allow for adaptation" (Cushman 2011, 12). Speaking back to dominant structures, then, is not just accepting assimilation; it serves as a survival practice and a rhetorical practice of enacted sovereignty. "Sovereignty," as Scott Lyons points out, "denotes the rights of a people to conduct its own affairs, in its own place, in its own way" (Lyons 2000, 450). The adaption of the seminary model was not an erasure of Cherokee-ness by the Cherokee Nation but rather a way to maintain the balance between, as Rose Gubele tells us, truth and appearance. Explaining that the "dominant culture of the time had a definite agenda" of assimilation, Gubele explains trickster tactics of survival (Gubele 2012, 51). "We gain strength from our history, our culture, our stories," Gubele writes, "However, we have to survive in this world as well, so we need to wear a mask. . . . If we remain Cherokee inside, then what we 'appear' to be doesn't matter. It is just a survival tactic" (Gubele 2012, 51). For the Cherokee Nation, education became a means to not only navigate pressures from white colonizers but also improve the nation and re-tool the forced structures handed to them from outside cultures. Mount Holyoke educational model offered a means to provide access to every member of the Cherokee Nation, regardless of gender, wealth, or status.

One of the challenges of researching the Cherokee National Seminaries is that, on the surface of it all, the founding of such schools could very well be read as an imposition of a white-serving institution. While the curriculum was based on Mount Holyoke's model—one that promoted education in the sciences, history, Latin, rhetoric, and composition, what was distinctly lacking was any sort of curriculum that discussed Cherokee culture, Cherokee language, or Cherokee traditions (Mihesuah 1998, 62). However, according to historian Althea Bass, "The school was not, as people unaware of the history of the Cherokees might suppose, a brief and superficial attempt to imitate a popular achievement of the white man; it was part of an elaborate and carefully studied plan of education evolved by the leading men [sic] of the tribe" (Bass 1937, 8–9). The Cherokee school system also hoped to improve the lives of the Cherokee beyond the basics of education. Through the school system, the students participated in literary, debate, and drama societies, and as they left the school system, they continued to participate in these societies, bringing the students and community together, where these societies thrived in larger towns (Parins 2013, 68–69). Cherokee students understood that the formation of these literary societies would help them not only form a community at home but also spread the intellects of their society abroad. Wam-Da, a Cherokee student at the male seminary wrote in the *Sequoyah Memorial* about the role of their literary societies: "The time is approaching when we as members of this society shall go abroad into the world to discharge the duties while will devolve upon us in future life, when we shall have completed the course which we are at present pursuing; both in school and in this society; and when we shall be scattered abroad in the world to successfully or unsuccessfully discharge the duties and responsibilities which at present rest upon our fathers. Now is the time to form our characters and minds in such a manner that we may be honored and also may be good examples for those who may come after us" (Wam-Da 1855). While Wam-Da was writing in the early days of the seminaries, the tradition of having literary societies continued up through the very end of the seminaries, always serving as a way to bring the community together. One specific example of these societies was the Pocahontas Club,[2] which was formed by Ida

---

2. The name Pocahontas certainly is not taken from Cherokee history, as Pocahontas is a well-known Powhatan, and it may conjure up scrutiny as sounding like a club for those to "play Indian" such as "Red Men" societies for whites. While I have yet to find founding documents for the Pocahontas Club in Cherokee archives, perhaps due to the very nature of why there are few archives from this time in Cherokee history, the context of the founding of the club and the writings I have read in the student newspapers from the time the club was founded suggests that this was not a club to "play

Mae Collins in 1899. The Pocahontas Club, which was a social club for the preservation of Cherokee history and the welfare of the Cherokee Nation, began as a club for only the seminary women; however, after some interest specifically from Will Rogers, they allowed the men to join as well (Fry 1988, 102). The Pocahontas Club, which has been an active Cherokee society since its founding and still today, acts as a means to continue gathering as a community to promote the well-being of the larger Cherokee Nation as well as sustaining Cherokee histories and maintaining Cherokee culture. This example showcases the ways that Cherokee continued to practice their culture in ways that adapted to the nineteenth and early twentieth centuries and help us understand the public ways that the Cherokee maintained that culture. While there are critiques of the seminaries for not holding courses on Cherokee culture, there is just as much evidence that the Cherokee culture and language was still circulated and practiced outside of the seminaries. Perhaps the Cherokee did not see it as necessary to "teach" Cherokee culture since they were living it each day, sharing stories at home, and teaching Cherokee ways through the house. We tend to still practice our cultures in these ways, often gathering in social groups or clubs to discuss Cherokee welfare, or we spend time talking with elders and listening to stories. We are taught by example and by listening, not through a Cherokee government curriculum.[3]

Indian," as it was founded specifically for Cherokee women to *be* Cherokee women and *practice* their culture as a way to maintain it for their community—the same role the Pocahontas Club maintains today. As in the past, all current members must be enrolled citizens in the Cherokee Nation. Given this, my best educated assumption is that the name Pocahontas for the women at the seminary would be equivalent to names such as Betsy Ross, Queen Elizabeth, or Martha Washington for Indigenous people—Pocahontas was and is a well-known woman, dignitary, and important historical figure. She is perhaps seen as the "first lady" of Indigenous written Eurocentric histories. What this means is that her name is recognizable to a *whiter* society, even during the 1800s. While romanticized through novels and eventually through Disney, for these Cherokee women, Pocahontas was a feminist icon that existed in both an Indigenous and white world. Coincidentally, her name would receive recognition from a white society while maintaining a truer identity for Indigenous women as someone whose name has prevailed through histories and in stories. My hope is that more research can be done on this long-serving society to the Cherokee people.

3. These community gatherings still occur today in the Cherokee Nation. At the time of writing this manuscript, many of these community gatherings have shifted to a wider, digital format because of the ongoing Covid-19 pandemic. As an at-large citizen, I now have access to many of these cultural gatherings and teachings through the Cherokee Nation's YouTube channel in addition to receiving many digital invitations to synchronous meetings so that we can all participate, no matter our locations. These practices of community knowledge-making are alive and well in Cherokee country, and my assumption is that they always have been.

My assumption here is that nineteenth-century Cherokee did the same. A formal education wasn't needed for Cherokee culture, as they were already living it. Joshua Nelson agrees, explaining that "education is not a means by which civilization supplants traditionalist culture but a means of defending its independent character and physically preserving Indian lives" (Nelson 2014, 177). He notes that Cherokee leaders, knowing that Cherokee was still used and taught at home, did not see the need to provide formal education in the Cherokee language (Nelson 2014, 104). While there wasn't a need to teach Cherokee as a language (as it was widely spoken), the Cherokee government did see the need for printed materials for its Cherokee-speaking citizens and developing school system. In addition to developing Cherokee teachers through the seminaries, the efforts of the tribal government went into securing a printing press in Park Hill (the same place as the seminaries) during the 1840s. The Cherokee Nation not only put a Cherokee newspaper in press but also developed a Cherokee primer, children's books, a "child's guide," an almanac, and other secular and religious texts, all of which were written in Cherokee and, to understand the scope of this endeavor, the Park Hill Press had published more than a million pages of text in 1845 alone for the Cherokee Nation and the neighboring Choctaw and Creek Nations (Cushman 2011, 137–38). James Parins also chronicles the evolution of using Cherokee as the language of instruction in Cherokee schools. He notes that after the disillusionment of the full-blood Cherokees whose spoke primarily Cherokee with the mission schools established prior to removal, the Cherokee faced several issues of maintaining full-blood enrollment without Cherokee language instruction in the schools, including the seminaries. The problems facing the nation were multiple: First, there were few Cherokee teachers available before the seminaries had graduates to teach. Second, there was a lack of textbook and teaching materials available in the Cherokee language due to the shortage of adequate printing presses in Indian Territory. The process of setting up an entire education system in Cherokee took much of the nineteenth century; however, by the 1870s, the Cherokee government deemed that they had the resources and teachers available to have schools using only the Cherokee language, especially in areas with predominantly Cherokee-speaking citizens (Parins 2013, 75–87), which resulted in teaching approaches that included teaching English as a second language.[4] As Nelson argues, "education emerges as the

---

4. I expand more on the use of Cherokee language in Cherokee schools as well as second-language instruction in the following chapter, as it plays a larger role in the language and writing curriculum in the Cherokee Nation schools and seminary training.

primary strategy by which politicians can uphold their protective duties to the people. For [Boudinot] and other Cherokees, securing access to education was a paramount responsibility of the political arm" (Nelson 2014, 177–78), and along the way, the Cherokee found ways to incorporate their culture and language by their own means.

However, even during the nineteenth century, the Cherokee did not cease to practice their culture, and often mentions of specific dances appear in seminary student narratives. In Maggie Culver Fry's collection of narratives, she includes a note about one of the seminary alumnae, Rosa Gazelle Lane. She mentions that Rosa suffered a broken hip late in life and was in the care of Doctor Orange Starr, one of the "boys" she had grown up with. Doctor Starr, along with several other Cherokee men, performed a Stop Dance at the Indian hospital, where Rosa was being taken care of. They brought her into the ring and she danced alongside the men (Fry 1988, 134). Even within Eurocentric education models and outside pressures from the federal government, including removal from their homeland, the Cherokee found ways to keep hold of their cultural practices, language, and livelihoods much in the same way that twenty-first-century Cherokee still do—by finding balance between two worlds in the tensions of contact.

PEDAGOGIES OF DUYUK'TA

Soon after removal, tribal leadership saw the need to reestablish an education system that would serve the Cherokee people in addition to educating the community. James Parins points out that the Cherokee saw the modern equivalent of what we would now call a "brain drain" from the newly formed Cherokee Nation as other institutions of higher education were opening near the borders of the Cherokee Nation (Parins 2013, 88). Many of the mixed-blood Cherokee families wanted access to the kinds of education they were sending their children to back East and many full-bloods wanted a Cherokee national system of education that specifically served Cherokee purposes. The tribal government concluded that in addition to an education system that served every age of each Cherokee student, they would need Cherokee teachers to teach in those schools. While the seminaries served as an institute of higher education for the Cherokee, one of the main purposes of the seminaries was to provide extensive teacher training so that these Cherokee teachers would be able to leave the seminaries and teach in the Cherokee school system and at the Cherokee Orphan Asylum (Parins 2013, 88; Reed 2016, 323). In 1841, Chief John Ross outlined a plan for the national school

Figure 5.4. Cherokee public school near Chusty, Indian Territory, 1902. Photo by Jenni Ross Cobb, Jenni Ross Cobb Collection, Courtesy of the Oklahoma Historical Society.

system, indicating that all Cherokee, from ages six to sixteen, would have access to a free public education, including orphans who would be housed with Cherokee families that lived near schools.[5] Although attendance was voluntary, families worked hard to send their children to school since students would be taught an extensive range of education including reading, writing, arithmetic, spelling, geography, and history. While the Cherokee Nation initially had to import teachers from back East, by the mid 1870s, the seminaries produced enough graduates to fill teaching vacancies with Cherokee Nation citizens (Parins 2013, 77). The Cherokee understood that their world was about to be thrown out of balance with colonization and assimilationist policies, and to counteract that, they sought out ways to make these changes work with the Cherokee so that they could survive and, through their survival, resist

---

5. Later, the Cherokee Nation would establish the Cherokee Orphan Asylum in 1872, which was dedicated to supporting and educating the Nation's orphans as well as transmitting Cherokee traditional values and practices. See Julie Reed's "Family and Nation: Cherokee Orphan Care, 1835–1907" in *American Indian Quarterly* for a detailed history of the Cherokee Orphan Asylum.

colonization and assimilation. Because of the need to train teachers, the seminaries offered teacher training courses in addition to a slate of courses that met and even rivaled courses at schools back East, with courses in ancient languages, grammar, rhetoric, composition, literary criticism, history, geometry, chemistry, natural and mental philosophy, physiology, botany, astronomy, and zoology, to name a few.[6] Each seminary also boasted large libraries that included pedagogical texts, such as *History and Progress of Education, from the Earliest Times to the Present: Intended as a Manual for Teachers and Students* by Philobiblius[7] (psued.). One of the many ways that the seminaries perpetuated a culture dedicated to pedagogical innovation and teaching methods was by encouraging teachers at the seminaries to spend their summers continuing their own education through teaching institutes, sponsored by the Cherokee Nation and held locally, as well as sending teachers to teaching resorts back East.

Whereas other historiographers in rhetoric and composition studies have turned to textbooks as the source of pedagogical documentation (Kitzhaber 1990; Berlin 1984; Brereton 1995), I had a difficult time following their research models due to the nature of the artifacts that were preserved in the archives I visited. If there was a theme in pedagogical materials I had access to, it was the preservation (and digitization) of course catalogs from both seminaries, which provided a place to start making connections across seminaries, especially since these catalogs described courses taught at the seminaries. While the dates of what catalogs are preserved are haphazard across the nineteenth century, I was able to compare the male seminary catalog from 1886–1887 to the female seminary catalog from the same years through a process of following the stories and teachings of Selu and Kana'ti. While both catalogs offer the same course listing for each grade taught during the same semesters, the male seminary catalog offers descriptions of the courses offered. While I am not sure of the reason behind this, except that each catalog had a different author, I feel confident in the shared pedagogical implications that are uncovered within the male seminary catalog due to the evidence of continued joint teacher training. There

---

6. I expand on the details of the seminaries curriculum in the following chapter.
7. "Philobiblius" is a pseudonym for coauthors Linus Pierpont Brockett and Henry Barnard. Brockett, born in 1820, was a graduate of Yale Medical College in 1843 and published several works spanning from histories to encyclopedias. Barnard, born in 1811, was also a Yale graduate and an educational reformer. He served as the editor of the *American Journal of Education* from 1855 to 1881. Writing under the pseudonym, Philobiblius, Brockett and Bernard perhaps selected the name as it means "booklover."

is later evidence as well that the seminaries shared courses (Parins 2013, 91), and when the seminaries joined together in the early 1900s as coed facilities, many of the female students shared stories of learning the military routines and taking military training courses that were traditionally offered at the male seminary (Fry 1988, 128).

While the seminaries were initially divided along gender, the teaching institutes that the seminary instructors attended were not—another indication that the seminaries shared a curriculum and pedagogical interests. In the archives at Northeastern State University, there is a document with the meetings from the *Teacher's Institute of the Cherokee Nation*. This document, dating from 1881 and 1882, serves as evidence that teachers from both seminaries were meeting regularly to discuss pedagogical concerns and strategies for curriculum building. Each year, the *Cherokee Advocate*, the newspaper published by the Cherokee Nation, would list the program of the institute, as well as the expectations and outcomes. According to the June 26, 1885, edition of *Cherokee Advocate*, teachers from all of the Cherokee Nation schools were required to attend the two-day event as well as present essays that added to the teachings and might be adopted by other instructors. If instructors did not attend, they would be docked pay. The mission of the Teacher's Institute is summed up within the newspaper article:

> We would say the Institute will be just what you make it. There is a growing demand for a better grade of school work in the country, and the demands of society scarcely ever wait upon the tardy foot-steps of the individual. Those who will not advance will of course be left behind in the long run. But the Institute is designed to help you. Will you be helped? The teacher should not only be able to meet the demands of the country, but he should be prepared to move in the advance. (Cherokee Advocate 1885)

In addition to specific classes listed, including classes on elocution and grammar, the meeting also provided space to discuss the best methods for teaching English to Cherokee speakers, whether or not a textbook should be used to teach morals, and if there should be a pedagogy class at both seminaries. The names that appear in the program were often instructors from both seminaries who were presenting such topics as "Instruction of Arithmetic Methods," "Instructions in Physical Training," "Methods in Object Lessons," and so on. The Teacher's Institute, the presentations, and the shared pedagogical knowledge-making would be easily recognizable by any modern-day teacher who has attended a national education conference. Perhaps the main difference would be that the 1880s institutes often included musical performances, poetry readings, oratories, and even dramatic plays. What is most telling is that these institutes are a combined effort between seminaries to maintain balance in educational models as pedagogical models were not separated along lines of gender, but collaborative and balanced in representation.

The Cherokee invested heavily in their teachers, and in addition to paying a high salary, they sent teachers to teaching resorts during the summer months. One such resort was the Monteagle Teacher's Resort in Monteagle, Tennessee. I found evidence of this resort in *The Daily American*, a Nashville-based newspaper, which included an article about the purpose and ongoings at the resort in the Sunday edition from July 12, 1885. The article explains, "The summer schools are open to teachers of every State. For the sum of $10[8] they are admitted to all the various branches taught. Mathematics, French, Spanish, Latin, Greek, Hebrew, higher English, drawing, music and elocution are taught by teachers whose abilities are above suspicion" (Daily American 1885, 7). According to the article, the teacher's school met for six weeks each summer, where teachers would take classes from "the most distinguished educators of the country, while the list of subjects embraced almost everything from psychology down to the making of mud pies—to speak disrespectfully of Prof. Frye's geography work" (Daily American 1885, 7). In addition to this certain Professor Frye, the article gives sketches of other professors and teachers who were a part of the resort from all different subject areas, often outlining the teacher's educational background, disposition, success at the resort, and brief character sketches about their teaching and methods.

While the article boasts about the facilities and grand success of the resort, the July 25, 1884, edition of the *Cherokee Advocate* includes a letter from one of the Cherokee Female Seminary instructors, Ada Archer, who detailed her stay at the Monteagle Teacher's Resort. Ada Archer, a member of a prominent Cherokee family, comments about her own experience as a Cherokee at the resort, writing, "Of course, the fact that *real live Indians* were on the ground created a little sensation at first, but we are to have a Cherokee street, and one of the temples is to have a Cherokee name," alluding to the area where they had to set up temporary structures to house all of the attendees (Archer 1884, 1). She describes her day as beginning with courses in various subjects followed up by special lessons. After a midday break for lunch, she explains that afternoons are devoted to courses on teaching methods and general instruction while evenings are filled with various lectures (1). Much like the article describing the resort, Ada Archer writes, "The instructors in

---

8. Accounting for inflation, $10 is roughly equivalent to $287 in 2022, which is not an inconsequential sum for an academic institution.

the various departments are among the best in the United States, all are wide awake, and zelous [*sic*] in the cause of education . . . I never had the pleasure of meeting so many intelligent people at once before; everyone is bright and pleasant while the genial sociability which characterizes the cultured class renders the society here, perfectly charming" (Archer 1884, 1). Indeed, while the resort sounds intellectually intense, the joy that such a place devoted to teaching existed comes through in each of her descriptions. She ends by assuring the Cherokee public that "your National teachers hope to go back to you physically, mentally, socially and spiritually renewed" (Archer 1884, 1) and that she hopes that the Cherokee Nation would continually send teachers each year so that the Cherokee people would be greatly represented and that "the results would be good for us individually, and as a people" (Archer 1884, 1). Her testimony adds further evidence to just how much the Cherokee Nation devoted to their educational system, how much they valued having Cherokee citizens serve as educators, and, more importantly, how instructors understood that this education was for more than just individuals but was for the benefit of the whole Cherokee community. Clearly, representation was also at stake, and much like we consider the importance of diversity and representation today in our educational institutions, the Cherokee were tackling such issues during the nineteenth century. They understood the need to teach Cherokee students with Cherokee teachers and that there were community bonds that formed within these relationships. By investing in the continual education of its teachers, the Cherokee Nation looked to pedagogy and teaching methods as ways to restore *duyuk'ta* that was upended by removal and broken treaties with the federal government.

According to Emmett Starr, historian of Cherokee history and families, the Cherokee Nation saw a lot of benefits in the seminary model, especially regarding the roles of the teachers and the community they formed with students. Of the seminary education proper, he explains, "This school possesses many advantages over similar institutions, from the fact that teachers and students are together. Teachers instruct and direct, not only in the text book studies but in general reading, in the use of reference books and library work—a thing impossible when students have not libraries and books of reference in their homes or boarding houses" (Starr 1921, 232). This expectation that teachers would be readily accessible demonstrates that the Cherokee Nation valued the mentorships and relationships that formed between teachers and students. The 1886–87 female seminary catalog outlines the roles and responsibilities of all of the faculty, and specifically states that "Harmony in action should be strictly observed by the members of the faculty and all employees, and all of the moral support possible should be given by each others" ("Catalogue of Cherokee National Female Seminary 1886–87" 1887, 11). Education didn't end at the ring of a bell but continued throughout the day to lights-out (and even after). In almost all of the narratives of Cherokee seminary students, alumni mention the bonds they formed with the teachers and the invaluable life lessons that they passed on to them, often prompting them to reach higher and expect more of themselves because they were capable of doing such.

Out of all of the seminary records available in archives, there is only one principal that has file folders dedicated specifically to her and her influence on the Cherokee Female Seminary. While it is difficult to trace a lot of the records of teachers and principals, Ann Florence Wilson's time at the seminary, from 1875 until 1901, is best documented. In fact, to leave her story out of the fabric of the seminary's purpose would be a disservice to scholarship and her impact on the Cherokee community. Wilson was originally from Arkansas, and according to the souvenir catalog, her family was close friends with many of the Cherokee families who traveled west before the Trail of Tears.[9] Wilson taught in the Cherokee public schools before she became the principal of the seminary (Cherokee National Female Seminary1906, 13). These close working relationships with the Cherokee made her an ideal candidate to serve the seminary for so long, as she had spent her life around and being with the Cherokee. Of Wilson, the Cherokee Female Seminary souvenir catalog explains, "This woman was destined to become one of the greatest educators in the country and it was upon her that devolved the duty of moulding [sic] the characters of hundreds—yes thousands—of Cherokee women. And to say how well she did her task you have only to look over the nation and find the mothers and daughters—living monuments to her fame. There is no name in the Cherokee Nation today that is held in more living and thankful remembrance than that of Miss A. Florence Wilson" (Cherokee National Female Seminary 1906). Her legacy is remembered in almost every narrative collected by the students that attended the seminary.

Students often comment on her keen awareness of any misgivings going on at the seminary, yet in each account of her handing out demerits or requiring seminary students to stand in the corners of the classrooms, their stories are peppered with loving comments about her kindness, leadership, and abilities to teach. Each summer and during the years

---

9. These families are often called "old settlers" in Cherokee history and genealogy.

the seminary was closed after the fire in 1877, Wilson would attend at the Normal School at Oswego, New York (Cherokee National Female Seminary 1906, 13), and had a penchant for mental arithmetic, which some of the alumnae claimed was more like a hobby than a duty to her while being one of the most difficult classes they took (Fry 1988, 62). She also oversaw the girls' physical education, instituting a somewhat mandatory daily walk through the pastures surrounding the seminary promptly at 4:15 p.m. in addition to the physical culture class that was also required (Fry 1988, 62). Her guidance went beyond just mental and physical instruction, and she was seen by the seminary students as much more of a mentor and mother. Maggie Waters Culver explains that often the girls at the seminary acted in ways that Miss Wilson didn't always approve of but ultimately tolerated, with a mild reproach reminding them of the ways women acted. Miss Wilson, a white woman, was the longest standing principal at the female seminary and was loved by her students and the tribe. Maggie relates some of the advice Miss Wilson would give the girls, such as, "The mark of refinement for every young lady is her ability to have self-assurance in the presence of young men," and she assures the reader that this was "undoubtedly the sentiment of Miss Wilson" (Fry 1988, 119). Yet while she was strict, several accounts also acknowledge her caring nature and kindness that ultimately guided her response to student conduct (and misconduct). Students often recalled how they would hear her tell other teachers how she did not like to reprimand students and often could see their side in such matters, or how she allowed students who failed final exams the ability to study and retake the exam. One student recalled how she had ordered two students to leave the seminary and immediately revoked her order when she remembered one of the girls boarded with her very young sister, as they were orphans (Fry 1988, 65). In addition to daily care, students recalled that Miss Wilson also spent a lot of time helping the Cherokee full-blood students, who spoke little English and often kept more to themselves, stating that Miss Wilson knew and understood Cherokee families and genealogies as well as Emmett Starr, one of the most prominent and official documentarians of Cherokee family histories (Fry 1988, 66). Her legacy is representative of the community bonds that the seminary forged and the relationships between students and instructors, who notably signed their names in students' autograph books with the title "friend" (Fry 1988, 59). While some of the teachers came in as outsiders and some were seminary graduates themselves, what is evident is that they provided a vital service of maintaining the Cherokee community beyond merely intellectual support but as intermediaries between the Cherokee and the whites.

Stories Emerging from Dusty Boxes   161

Figure 5.5. Students from the Cherokee National Seminaries eating watermelon, 1896. Photo by Jenni Ross Cobb, Jenni Ross Cobb Collection, Courtesy of the Oklahoma Historical Society.

In addition to the community bonds within each seminary, the seminaries often spent time together and created regular community events. As I've been reading narratives of Cherokee women from the female seminary, one of the most enduring and often repeated events remembered by these women was the ways in which they interacted with students from the male seminary. There is one story in particular that frequently comes up throughout the various primary documents I've read and in student narratives. From the collection of female seminary narratives, compiled by Maggie Culver Fry, here is Maggie Waters Culver's story, who attended the seminary sometime between 1871 and 1879:

> One moonlit night, Lucy and I were in bed when we heard the most beautiful singing, all male voices. To the accompaniment of a guitar or banjo, they were singing the old favorites and the newest popular songs.
>
> "O, O, O—Josephine, my Joe, / Don't tease your Baby so / if that's your O, O, O . . ."
>
> "Boys from the Male Seminary. They've come to serenade us girls," Lucy whispered. "Grab your wrapper or drape a dress around your shoulders so your nightgown won't show. They've come all the way here to entertain us, and every girl in the school is allowed to go to the windows and listen, just as long as we don't start talking to the boys. All the teachers will be listening, even Miss Wilson."

> The deep tones ebbed and swelled in full harmony as they ended on "Good Night Ladies."
> The uniformed males left as silently as they had come, but none of us could forget such an occasion and many a girl lay staring into the dark, blissfully re-living it all. (Fry 1988, 118–19)

This is just one of the often-told student rituals at the seminaries. The female seminary also hosted students from the male seminary during open houses, during which the students as the female seminary entertained the students from the male seminary (Fry 1988, 119). During these open houses, there would be a boy for each girl, roughly the same age. Maggie Water Culver's narrative tells readers that "they would sit at tables and draw pictures or sing or play games under the supervision of the teachers. From ten-year-olds to young ladies old enough to graduate, there were boys to be entertained" (Fry 1988, 119). These sorts of rituals mirrored the balance of Selu and Kana'ti in the ways that girls and boys interacted in social situations. Nelson contemplates that, for Cherokee women especially, having a community of like-minded people was "a source of much-needed spiritual and physical strength in desperate and dangerous times for the Cherokee people, during which their traditional religion was for a multitude of reasons providing less support to increasingly fewer people" (Nelson 2014, 108). He continues, "This erosion was not total, however, insofar as traditional principles and practices directly and indirectly continued to inform politics, attitudes toward community, gender roles, and Christianity itself" (Nelson 2014, 108). Serving as the evolution of the vestiges of a matrilineal clan kinship, the Cherokee boys and men would travel to meet with the women and girls in their seminary to interact and entertain each other. While supervised, they were still maintaining *duyuk'ta* and the teachings of Selu and Kana'ti in new contexts, operating in a white world that imposed separate spheres.

For some outside (white) teachers, they maintained order through that supervision, but the Cherokee students also had the ability to practice core tenets of their culture. One of the more logical reasons to keep the schools separate has more to do with the living arrangements and boarding practices at the seminaries. Students and teachers lived together at the seminaries, and teachers acted as educators and guardians of the students who boarded with them, as outlined in the establishment act. Because many of the teachers came from white society and eastern schools, the model to separate schools by gender followed, which is why it is necessary to understand the purpose of the seminaries from the understanding of the Cherokee and not from white society. Without doing so, Cherokee women and their histories are subjected to a double burden of being both Indigenous and female. For Jaimes*Guerrero, the "double burden" of racism and sexism as a product of prejudices against Indigenous populations is described as "patriarchal colonialism." She explains that "deconstructing [patriarchal colonialism] demands an understanding of the US American colonial history as a legacy that brought over Eurocentric notions of the inferiority of other non-white or non Western 'races,' and of women in general versus the presumed superiority of the Anglicized Euroamerican male" (Jaimes*Guerrero 2003, 65). This calls for "the historical agency of 'Native Womanism' . . . in order to preserve and restore the sacred kinship traditions among these bioregionally-based indigenous peoples and their respective cultures, to envision precolonialist and prepatriarchal times, which promotes a prospective vision of a more humane and gender-egalitarian future exemplary of 'being Indigenous'" (Jaimes*Guerrero 2003, 68). Jaimes*Guerrero's call addresses the issues of American Indian women who are still subject to stereotypes and colonization of identity and reminds us that precolonialist and gender-egalitarian visions of Indigenous people were never erased. Rather, like the ways the Cherokee seminaries adapted cultural practices of *duyuk'ta* in their own ways in a colonized society, tradition never was erased. Prior to seminaries, there is evidence that even at missionary schools, the Cherokee maintained ritualistic culture, such as playing stick ball (Perdue 1999, 181), as well as stories of seminary girls getting caught in their rooms cooking a traditional Cherokee favorite—wild onions and eggs—that they procured on an unsupervised trip out of the seminary (Fry 1988, 63). The students and the community they formed maintained Cherokee culture and practices in ways that adapted to their current circumstances.

When the Cherokee Female Seminary closed in 1909 due to the purchase of the building and grounds by the State of Oklahoma, the seminaries still served as a key culture keeper for Cherokee society. The students and teachers from the female seminary joined the male seminary at this point, so that the education of Cherokee could continue. Again reminiscent of Selu and Kana'ti, the young men at the seminary would go out during the winter and hunt rabbits to bring back to the young women at the seminary if they were courting, according to Charlotte Mayes Sanders, a seminary student after the seminaries joined tougher in 1909 and whose narrative was collected by Maggie Culvers Fry (Fry 1988, 161). She explains that at that time there were roughly one hundred young women and seventy-five young men attending the National Seminary (as it was now known), and the rigors of coursework and instructors remained the same, regardless of gender. According to Sanders, "Our coursework was regular and very hard for us. Along with our study and daily chores we had time for recreation, however, and we were a big happy family, teachers and students" (Fry 1988, 160). Her narrative once again emphasized the role of the seminary as a place for Cherokee to come together as a community and continue their cultural practices as they adapted to the upheavals of the early 1900s as the new state government of Oklahoma seized control of Cherokee education. The joint National Seminary had only one year on record as its end mirrored the tragedy of the first female seminary building. Sanders's narrative ends bittersweetly as she recounts the day that someone ran into the Sunday church service and yelled that the male seminary was on fire:

> The whole town and countryside from all directions seemed to be racing to the fire. Buggies, wagons, people everywhere on foot or on bicycles—any way to get there [to the seminary building]. Since the fire started in the cupola of the Seminary, it could be seen for miles. . . .
> Paden Banks, our cook, whom we all adored, had carried huge pans of peach cobbler from the burning kitchen to the tables under the trees. Some ate; some did not. We were all a frustrated group. Our school and all of our Easter clothing had gone up in smoke. Now, we would all be separated.
> Everyone lingered about the ruins and on campus until nearly dark. The whole city of Tahlequah opened up its homes to the students who could not go home that afternoon. . . .
> These are my recollections of that terrible day which affected the lives of so many in their struggle for education and which contributed to the decline of the Cherokee Nation as an administrative body. (Fry 1988, 162–63)

When reading Sanders's narrative, it's hard not to think of the odd set of coincidences of fires destroying the seminaries on different Easter Sundays nearly twenty years apart and think of how the Cherokee Nation through education had persevered against the policies and erasure done by the federal government. The beginning of Oklahoma as a state set into motion the end of what was a robust education system that served to preserve the Cherokee. Much like a funeral, Cherokee people gathered and shared in a sort of disheartening picnic to bid farewell to the institutions that sustained them out in the new territories that they eventually made their homelands. Yet, through this sadness and closure, we still get a glimpse of the ways that the Cherokee formed their community with and through the seminaries, and what began as an experiment in resistance and sovereignty ends with a foundational tenet of Cherokee pride, culture, and community even today.

"THIS WAS NOT WHAT WE WANTED, BUT PAPA SAID WE'D HAVE TO GO ALONG WITH IT."

While much of the scholarship on the Cherokee during the nineteenth century focuses on the tensions between full-blood and mixed-blood ideologies as binaries between tradition and assimilation, spending time with the stories and histories of students at the seminaries has helped me understand the complexities that binary reasoning removes. Education for the Cherokee wasn't a pathway to become white and the tribal leaders, teachers, and students never envisioned that existence for the seminaries. Rather, the Cherokee understood that a national education system that was controlled by the Cherokee meant that they maintained sovereignty during a time when every dealing with the federal government meant to take that away. During my research, I came across two stories that embodied the desires of the Cherokee government in their hopes to navigate the complexities of a changing society in a culturally rich and tradition-based way of life. The first comes from the narrative of Nannie Waters McGee. She begins by chronicling her early days at the seminary with details about music, plays, forbidden dances, and the love and influence of her teachers. She explains that later in her studies she became quite interested in Cherokee politics, especially as her father was a council member (something she is quite proud of). She details the ways in which the Dawes Commission was impacting the tribe, explaining that her father spent much of his time going around to various Cherokee households explaining the purpose and the reason that other Cherokee signed the Dawes' Roll and proceeded with the allotment process, saying, "That was not what we wanted, but Papa said we'd have to go along with it" (Fry 1988, 129). Her father explained that many Cherokee didn't understand why they had to sign up for the allotment, and these Cherokee would become lost if they were not on the Dawes roll and the Cherokee would lose their lands.[10] This moment for Nannie and her father represents the navigation the Cherokee had to make as their culture resided both in the space of contact with colonial powers and a space of transformation and adaptation. As seminary students who also found themselves in the nexus of those spaces, Nannie explains, "I believe we [Nannie and her father] were closer that afternoon than

---

10. Citizenship in the Cherokee Nation is still dependent on the Dawes Rolls. Rather than having a set blood quantum requirement, enrollment in the Cherokee Nation is based on whether or not you have a direct ancestor on the Dawes Rolls. Without an ancestor, you cannot enroll in the Cherokee Nation. In many ways, Cherokee who didn't sign the Dawes Rolls were "lost," as are their descendants in that they are still unable to claim citizenship.

we had been before. Papa was also one of those who believed in the old ways of his people and wanted no change. His beliefs and those of the Keetowahs[11] were the same, but adjustments had to be made" (Fry 1988, 132). Yet in all of these adjustments, the purpose of the Cherokee seminaries as well as the role of Cherokee culture was to help Cherokee people become helpful and useful citizens to their Nation.

Early in the seminaries' history, students understood and communicated the importance of Cherokee education as to go beyond just bettering oneself intellectually. In the *Cherokee Rose Buds*, the student newspaper of the female seminary, there is a story published called "A Dialogue Between Susan and Ellen" in the August 2nd edition from 1854 (just a few years after the founding of the seminary). In this dialogue, Susan convinces Ellen that she should attend the seminary; however, Susan is reluctant because she values her freedom to do what she chooses and when she chooses to do it. Knowing that Ellen would appreciate the structure of the seminary and its education, Susan explains, "Come to the Seminary, then, and be faithful in your studies, upright in your deportment, obedient to rule, and you will find no difficulty. And at the close of the four years, you will leave with honors to yourself and friends, prepared to exert a good influence, and to be useful to those around you" (Cherokee Rose Buds 1854, 5). These two stories, both told and written by seminary students spanning the earliest beginnings of the Cherokee National Seminaries to their sunset days illustrate that the mission and purpose of the seminaries rarely strayed from the ways the Cherokee leaders of the time envisioned it. The students knew that education was for the Cherokee people and that it was their role to help sustain their community and Cherokee practices rather than seek an education solely for the benefit of the individual. The Cherokee expected these experiences to span generations, passing on the need to tend to the welfare of the nation through its young graduates. As alumnae explain, "By whatever means, they all came eager, excited, *thrilled*, these girls of earlier days watching to catch a glimpse through the blackjack trees of the brick columns that meant the seminary, and later, their daughters watching for the red brick towers of the building that replaced the original" (Fry 1988, 58). The hope is that each generation of Cherokee would be able to experience the seminaries just as their mothers and fathers had been able to so that they could continue the communal kinship ties and help their nation in their own ways. It

---

11. The Keetowahs, were and still are, traditionalist Cherokees and are now considered a distinct federally recognized Cherokee tribe along with the Cherokee Nation and Eastern Band of Cherokee Indians.

was within this context that coursework was adapted and developed to serve the Cherokee people rather than assimilate them. Even today, it is in this context of Cherokee education that the citizens of the Cherokee Nation still find their pride and strength in the history of the seminaries through memorializing the remaining pillars, still visible through the blackjack trees in Park Hill, Oklahoma, and, just like the Cherokee people, their culture, and their practices, they are still here.

What marks Cherokee as being different in records? How do they story their experiences to a white audience that does not understand why the Cherokee have created an educational system for themselves and what they are able to accomplish? Yes, they can study Shakespeare just like any of their peer schools on the East Coast; however, it is different for them because of their Cherokee-ness, and it's not of their culture. We need to remember that this was soon after the federal supreme court ruled the Cherokee as wards of the nation, equating them to children who must be taught and assimilated. So, being able to read and study Shakespeare and do it well wasn't a mark of assimilation away from Cherokee but a claim that the Cherokee could take care of themselves in their own way and have the same outcomes as students in white schools.

The seminaries served as a haven for Cherokee thought, practices, and traditions that met the nineteenth century with the adaptability and living embodiments of storytelling. Awiakta tells us listening to these stories is all about the context: "If Selu's story is kept in its own riverbed, its own cultural context, the flow runs clear and to the point" (Awiakta 1994, 251). Hearing/reading Selu and understanding the knowledge in the story clarifies what the seminaries were to the Cherokee people. This knowledge is networked and spread throughout the community following a Cherokee *gagoga* rhetoric, (Teuton 2012), which is not placed within one individual who passes the knowledge down to others. Instead, it is knowledge that exists in a networked state with the role of the community as knowledge producers, just like the community of Cherokee at the seminaries. Teuton further explains, "Each reader brings his/her own viewpoint experience, and unique skills to the task of interpretation. The act of returning with new knowledge and fresh interpretations creates new terrain upon which the community may continue to grow. Knowledge is sought and valued in relation to the collective harmony and survival of the community as a whole" (Teuton 2008, 197). Selu's body tells us of this harmony and this community that is held in the balance of each other and of survival. Just as Awiakta asks, "How do we remember Selu in this?" she also tells us, "From our pockets, each of us retrieves a sturdy corn kernel. 'This thing they call the corn is I.' The kernel is deep red, like a drop of the Corn-Mother's blood. Or like a drop of our own, where genes bring the seeds of memory into the present, so we can have a future. 'We are the stories.' We have to remember that. We are the stories. We are creating them now" (Awiakta 1994, 215). So, we continue our stories, both traditional Cherokee stories and the narratives of Cherokee seminary students, double-woven together, as we both listen and tell of Selu, corn, and our blood. In this way, we continue the living knowledge that is created and maintained within the community following the traditions of the seminaries. This is the story that contextualizes our revisionist history—whereas others focus on a male-dominated space to contextualize pedagogy and disciplinary history, we can locate other stories that are balancing on the intersections of race and gender. This context not only gives us a different read of disciplinary history but also locates pedagogies of *duyuk'ta* in a place that speaks to cultural and societal boundaries and asks those pedagogies to respond directly to the context of the day. It may not have been in the ways they had initially wanted, but it was the ways that they needed to survive and resist.

6

"WHERE BRIGHT THOUGHTS LIKE RIVERS FLOW"
Composing with and for the Cherokee Nation

ANI-KUTANI: THE PRIESTHOOD WHO WRITES

There are older stories—from before the Cherokee had any contact with European settlers and before they were ever called "civilized" because of their writing by white society—of a powerful, priestly clan of Cherokee who used writing in powerful ways. What we know of this priestly clan is handed down in snippets and traces. I've read stories and heard them called the "Ani-kutani," "Nicotani," "fire priests," and the "Unanti." The Ani-kutani, according to the accounts by Chief John Ross and Doctor J. B. Evans in *Myths of the Cherokee and Sacred Formulas of the Cherokees*, were a "mystical, religious body, of whom the people stood in great awe, and seem to have been somewhat like the Brahmins of India" (Mooney 1982, 393). This family or clan was built on hereditary power, which went against the more egalitarian structure of Cherokee politics and social organization. Although they inspired awe through their knowledge and writing, they "did not hesitate to rend asunder the tender relations of husband and wife when a beautiful woman excited their passions" (Mooney 1982, 393). Feeling oppressed and inspired by a young man who was brave enough to go against the Ani-kutani, the people rose up against the Ani-kutani and massacred the clan, got rid of their writing practice, and, in doing do, solidified the Cherokee adherence to egalitarian social structures rather than hereditary ones.

Other stories tell of a distant clan of peoples, known as the Unanti, who may have been the Mound Builders living north of the Cherokee. The Cherokee traveled north and became "one" with this clan of Mound Builders. However, this priest clan began to kill the Cherokee who were among them through human sacrifice. In an act of rebellion, the Winged One, who had a serpent head and bird's body, called upon the bird warriors and gave them the ability to fly. They flew toward the priest clan and killed most of them. Teuton records this story and

https://doi.org/10.7330/9781646425228.c006

shares Hastings Shade's storytelling about this priestly clan. Shade tells us that "[the Unanti] were mean. And they were not . . . they were not of this world, the elders used to say—*tla elo unadehnv yigese.* . . . They was wanting domination. They wanted to dominate 'em. Slaves, I guess, if you wanted to call it that" (Teuton 2012, 59–60). However, because the Cherokee had intermarried with this priestly clan of Mound Builders, they brought some of their knowledge with them, including mound building, and those that were of mixed blood with this clan became Cherokee medicine people. According to Shade, "the blood that was mixed between the ones not of this earth and some of the Cherokees. That's how the blood mingled. And that's how we got our teachers, you know, our medicine people. The people that taught things, you know" (Teuton 2012, 60). While these stories retell histories of migration, pre-European contact, wars, and beliefs, the threads of this story come back through the story of the syllabary, connecting the genesis of it not from the awe of a European advancement but from the knowledge of writing that had been contained through the role of teachers, priestly clans, and elders.

Joshua Nelson mentions that the Ani-kutani stories are interpreted as allegorical by some Cherokee thinkers to serve as an admonishment of governmental abuse and the loss of responsibility and accountability to their people, and these stories of the Ani-kutani serve as a critical reception of a hierarchical ruling structure. Nelson argues that there is more nuance in the story of revolt and massacre of a priestly clan in that it also suggests that the people had the power to change society and eschew authoritative religious practices in order to solidify the equity of knowledge, practices, and even stories as belonging to the people (Nelson 2014, 62). What interests me in this story is the element of writing and the power it contains to withhold knowledge from the people. The priestly clan used an ancient writing system to keep away sacred formulas out of the knowledge of the people, and then abused this power. To release this knowledge from one source, the people revolted and continued to spread knowledge through orality, thus making these formulas. Yet, according to Nelson, the introduction of Sequoyah's syllabary played a part in the eventual dissolution of Cherokee medicine men, who were perhaps a remnant of the Ani-kutani. Rather than training and passing knowledge from one medicine man to another, the syllabary gave Cherokee the ability to write down these sacred formulas and caused a diffusion of knowledge among the people to the point where medicine men were not as necessary as they once had been (Nelson 2014, 63). I see two parallel lessons on the power of writing for the

Cherokee. Writing, if used by only a few, captured knowledge and withheld it from the people. Stories released that knowledge out. Yet, when needed, writing also could serve as a way to share and give equitable access to that knowledge. What this relied on, however, was a dedication to widespread literacy so that writing could both preserve and diffuse knowledge. Sequoyah, who may have been familiar with the stories of the Ani-kutani, identified the moment of exigence for a (re)turn to literacy for the Cherokee people.

Just like Sequoyah and other Cherokees who encountered these stories, our encounter with them also comes with a reflection on the axiology of stories here in ᏄᏕᎵᎬ (*wudeligv*), the west, asking ourselves, "What is considered valuable in research? How does my work contribute to the field?" This is the rib that I struggled with as I moved my research forward, perhaps a struggle shared by Sequoyah as others looked at his work on the syllabary and talking leaves as nothing more than nonsensical whims of a silversmith or perhaps even more cutting, a desire to assimilate as white settlers continued their advancement into Cherokee lands. Like the value Sequoyah saw in developing a written language for the Cherokee, I knew that my work on Indigenous rhetorics had value and contributed greatly to areas of the field that were underrepresented; yet would it have impact outside of these circles? What value would the larger field see in this? For that, I turn to Shawn Wilson's definition of axiology that is grounded in Indigenous research paradigms and framed through an ethical and moral lens. He contends, "If reality is fluid and the objective of research is to chance and improve this reality, then other ethical principles must be implied. Axiology is thus asking, 'What is it ethical to do in order to gain this knowledge and what will this knowledge be used for?'" (Wilson 2008, 34). Framing axiology through these Indigenous guiding questions, I then asked myself, How am I giving back to the community when I gain this knowledge, and how will this knowledge sustain the community that gifted me access to this knowledge through their stories and guidance? These stories told in ᏄᏕᎵᎬ (*wudeligv*), the west, by ancestors gift us the wisdom to understand what should be valued, but also by what means they should be valued.

***

To understand why the Cherokee valued language, education, and writing as their greatest weapons against colonization, we need to step back and follow the path that brought the Cherokee to this point in the nineteenth century. Being an eastern nation, the Cherokee had been in contact with English settlers since the seventeenth century. While early interactions dealt mostly with trade, the Cherokee were quickly wrapped up in European affairs, siding with the British as they fought the French in North America as early as 1710. What often gets written down in history as a relationship between the Cherokee and the British was in reality an unbalanced relationship that asked the Cherokee to cede land, took advantage of the Cherokee's decentralized government and spread-out towns, named a town leader as "Emperor" of the Cherokee who pledged loyalty to King George, and named him the Cherokee protector. Along with this relationship, white settlers introduced smallpox, which devastated the Cherokee populations. Increasing numbers of white settlers during the seventeenth and eighteenth centuries further drove the Cherokee people into military and trade treaties, increased factionalization among the Cherokee, and resulted in the loss of land throughout the East. As the eighteenth century came to a close and the colonists took up arms against the British, the conflicts between Cherokee and white settlers increased during a time known as the Chickamauga Wars. This armed conflict between the Cherokee and white setters resulted in the loss of Cherokee territory, eventual peace treaties, and the reorganization of tribal leaders and warriors into the Cherokee Nation. As the Cherokee moved into the nineteenth century, the demands that they relinquish the last of their lands in the East plagued the tribal nation once again. This time, the pressure came from the newly established federal states that used the might of the courts rather than relying only on military might to deny sovereignty to the Cherokee Nation through the *Cherokee Nation v. Georgia* supreme court decision handed down in 1831. The United States saw the Cherokee as no more than wards of the nation, giving them the rhetorical upper hand to deny the Cherokee of their sovereignty and the civil power to enact policies that broke any existing treaties the Cherokee held. The United States sought to factionalize the Cherokee even more while the Cherokee looked for ways to regain sovereignty, and this factionalization of the Cherokee shaped the history of the Cherokee peoples throughout the entirety of the nineteenth century (Nelson 2014, 156) as they faced removal to the West.

Yet during this time, the Cherokee resisted factionalization and the policies of the United States aimed at destroying the nation through what can also be seen as an explosion and strengthening in Cherokee identity through the establishment of an education system. This education system was created by tribal leaders to serve the Cherokee people, provide upward mobility as well as strategies to navigate a colonized experience, and to promote Cherokee literacy through writing with a newly created syllabary. Early in the nineteenth century, from roughly 1810 to 1820, Sequoyah developed the Cherokee syllabary—a writing system based on visual representations for each syllable in the Cherokee language. As testament to the cultural importance of the Cherokee writing system, the tribal council adopted the syllabary in 1821 and the use of the syllabary spread throughout the nation. In only a few years, the majority of Cherokee could read and write in their own language. Ellen Cushman, a Cherokee rhetoric scholar, attributes the quick adoption of the Cherokee syllabary in everyday life to the cultural affirmation and identity the writing system provided the Cherokee people and the tribal council during the nineteenth century to the present. She explains, "As one tool important to the tribe, this writing system has allowed Cherokee to protect, enact, and codify Cherokee knowledge and perspectives. It has enabled the Cherokees to weave foreign ideas about governments and religions into the fabric of everyday language and life: the massive social change in the tribe was made in—if too rarely on—Cherokee terms" (Cushman 2011, 9–10). Through continued efforts by its people, the Cherokee Nation celebrated language and writing by embracing Sequoyah's Cherokee syllabary and the creation of the first tribally run newspaper press in the country, which the Cherokee Nation saw as a means to promote a sense of cultural identity during an era of upheaval. "With uncommon acumen, the [Cherokee] government foresaw not only the cohesive, nationalistic force a newspaper would inspire, compensating for the proliferating fragmentation of other social and religious structures," Joshua B. Nelson, Cherokee citizen and Indigenous scholar in film and media studies, explains, "but also its persuasive potential in offering sympathetic audiences alternative accounts of the depredations they faced in resisting the expansion of American empire" (Nelson 2014, 159). Because the Cherokee now had a written language, the Cherokee government could promote the spread of literacy through the newspaper and also do the double work of creating and controlling a Cherokee identity separate from an assimilation cultural identity thrust upon them.

    Sequoyah understood the impact of colonial encounters and loss early on, as he grew up in the Overhill towns of what would later become eastern Tennessee. Because the Cherokee of the Overhill towns had sided with the British during the Revolutionary War, the new colonists, led by Andrew Jackson, took lands away from the Cherokee in this area. Despite criticism from other Cherokee, Sequoyah saw a system of writing as a way for the Cherokee to garner respect from outsiders and become a source of self-respect for the Cherokee as well as a technology that had benefits beyond national pride (Cushman 2011, 35). As they were forced into a dependent state by the new federal government, the need to both preserve and diffuse traditional knowledge was immediate, as there was a distinct threat to Cherokee knowledge-making. Writing wasn't meant to replace orality for the Cherokee and was never meant to serve in opposition to orality. It was a necessary means of survival and preservation of Cherokee spirituality and tradition.

The Cherokee written syllabary is still doing the work of keeping the Cherokee language alive, and the importance of this continual work started by Sequoyah situates writing as a material mode of survivance—not just of the language but of the ways Cherokee understand the world and their culture ("Tom Belt: Cherokee Language Teacher" 2011). For the Cherokee, the work of writing is more than just a vessel of content or external storage; writing is a material technology that is a source of self-determination, an act of resistance, and a preserver of culture. To understand the relationship between Cherokee education, literacy, language, writing, and orality, we need to frame our understanding of Cherokee writing in the same way that Sequoyah and subsequent Cherokee thinkers and proponents of Cherokee education did: writing was and is material survivance of orality, not the division of writing and orality. However, the stories of Sequoyah have been muddled by existing textbook and colonized messages of how the Cherokee came to writing—not as a means of material survivance but as a way to "civilize themselves" to exist in the white settlers' manifested space. According to these whitewashed stories, Cherokee had had our famous relative who invented that writing—Sequoyah, one of the most famous Cherokee (second only to Will Rogers), in his red and white turban and blue striped jacket, gracefully smoking a pipe while showing the world a writing of strange, rarely seen symbols on a long piece of parchment. He could be found in those museum displays across the state, on postcards ready to buy and be sent anywhere, and he was even a glorified bronze statue proudly gifted by the new state of Oklahoma in 1917 to the federal government. He was, and still is, the Cherokee to know about. Even more, he was in school textbooks. The story told in our classrooms across Oklahoma is that Sequoyah, having encountered civilized white people, was so impressed with the writing he saw that he decided to also invent a writing system. He worked and eventually came up with the Cherokee syllabary—a system of writing that gave each syllable a symbol. To convince others that his writing system was useful, he sent his daughter into the council to read Cherokee. At first, they said, the Cherokee elders and chief were mystified by this "magic." They didn't believe it, so Sequoyah worked to convince each of them to tell only him something, and he would write it down. He then brought this writing to his daughter, and she was able to tell the council exactly what they had said, even though she wasn't in the room with them. After convincing the council, the Cherokee Nation quickly adapted the syllabary, and within a few years, almost every Cherokee could read and write. And just like that (according to the textbooks), the Cherokee were now worthy of being called a "civilized tribe."

As much as I loved the story of Sequoyah and his "talking leaves" and saw him as a childhood hero, that story is only a muddied reflection of the stories I heard later in life. Hastings Shade tells a story of Sequoyah that upsets the histories within faded Oklahoma history textbooks and page after digital page of what is passed around online. While many are told that Sequoyah created the syllabary on his own, he tells us that "back in the time Sequoyah was born. 1760s or 70s. There were seven elders that come from the Rocky Mountains that had some type of written form of language. And after Sequoyah got old enough to want to do the syllabary, they kind of presented it to him and kind of gave him an idea what to do" (Teuton 2012, 100). He continues, "*Goligwogi anugayvlige unilustv.* And that's what that means: seven elders came. And they wrote not on paper but on cedar or mulberry" (Teuton 2012, 100). Shade explains that these elders had learned to travel from the Winged One, who had given travelers the ability to shapeshift; perhaps these elders were once Unanti or remaining medicine men from the Ani-kutani. These elders gave Sequoyah the knowledge of a writing system that had long been unused until it was time to bring it back. (101) While these stories perhaps offer a retelling of Cherokee history before the Cherokee used writing to record it, the stories also disrupt the power of written language from being a record of knowledge and tool of the oppressor, kept to one clan or to a literate, civilized people. Museums may claim that writing is what civilized the Cherokee, but the Cherokee knew the power that writing held. For them, writing became a means for the Cherokee people to survive yet another encounter with people who seek to oppress them, to resist being only a "civilized tribe" in museums.[1]

In a Eurocentric worldview, Ong associates writing with "wonderful worlds" (Ong 2009, 8) and characterizes it as "enhancing" (Ong 2009, 9).

---

1. The five tribes, Cherokee, Choctaw, Chickasaw, Seminole, and Muscogee (Creek), all who endured removal to Indian Territory (Oklahoma) during the 1800s, were referred to as the Five Civilized Tribes by the popular press and various federal and local institutions. Even when I was in high school in the 1990s, these five tribal nations were still being called the Five Civilized Tribes in Oklahoma history classes. Specifically, here, I am referring to the Five Civilized Tribes Museum in Muskogee, Oklahoma, which still operates under this name today. In chapter 7, I interrogate this naming practice.

However, he also readily points out the power of writing over orality by stating, "Though words are grounded in oral speech, writing *tyrannically* locks them into a visual field forever" (Ong 2009, 12). While Ong and perhaps early Cherokee thinkers familiar with stories of the Ani-kutani might share this apprehension, their worldviews differ on the rhetorical meaning-making of orality. For Ong, orality is seen as a connection to the past and as a simple dialect with only a few thousand words (Ong 2009, 8). In this way, Ong continues to frame orality as othered against writing, even setting up an inevitable dichotomy between orality and literacy, all while acknowledging that "written texts all have to be related somehow directly or indirectly, to the world of sound, the natural habitat of language, to yield their meanings. . . . Writing can never dispense with orality" (Ong 2009, 8). There is a sense in which writing will never rid itself entirely of orality, and we begin to see the connections and relations between these two opposing structures. Even though he acknowledges the relationship between writing and orality, writing still remains privileged over orality in Ong's theory. He explains, "Without writing, human consciousness cannot achieve its fuller potentials, cannot produce other beautiful and powerful creations. In this sense, orality needs to produce and is destined to produce writing. Literacy, as will be seen, is absolutely necessary for the development not only of science but also history, philosophy, explicative understanding of literature and of any art, and indeed for the explanation of language (including oral speech) itself" (Ong 2009, 14–15). This positioning of writing, even as it has a dependence on orality, holds a colonial privilege over speaking. But what does this do for oral-based cultures, especially when orality is the balancing link that holds communities together? Ong's position and the ways it has influenced rhetorical theory continues to subjugate Indigenous knowledges, Indigenous experiences, and Indigenous rhetorics. However, this is not to be confused with the notion that oral-based cultures are more attuned to primacy of orality or as a nostalgic look at orality and that written cultures are somehow alienated from this "first" and "natural" method of communication and the word. Instead, I want to show how neither is privileged above the other but once again work in a networked and balanced relationship.

The differences between orality and literacy as a part of graphic representation of those discourses is that oral discourses are "living forms of cultural knowledge" kept within the community while graphic discourses "record tradition for posterity" (Teuton 2010, 32). Together, these are held in relation by a third impulse that Teuton describes as a balance that doesn't remain static but is seen as always in flux. This arises from the consciousness of the community and responds to both the oral and graphic as a need of survival (Teuton 2010, 34). However, rather than viewing all of these as dichotomies, Teuton explains, "the oral and graphic are not opposites, but interpenetrating media that, brought into concert by the critical impulse, allow for a flow of ideas that may account for tradition as well as innovation, individuality as well as community, memory as well as record" (Teuton 2010, 34–35). In this way, the critical impulse acts as a way to decolonize the graphic and oral impulses as it breaks down the potential for hierarchy created by viewing writing as a linear progression from the oral. Another way the critical impulse decolonizes writing is by recognizing systems and ecologies of communication of which the oral, graphic, and critical impulse are all a part. Another shift is that communication, and even agency, does not place responsibility on the individual as an agent. Rather, this creates a community-centered approach as a method of communal survival when identity has been stripped from that community. In this way, American Indian rhetorics, as Teuton explores, focuses more on the community and a sense of we-ness that is more attuned to the nature of rhetorical ecologies. We can view this as distinct from a Eurocentric worldview that historicizes the importance of the individual—an I-ness—that takes away from the nature of rhetorical Indigenous ecologies.

HOW CHEROKEE ORALITY CALLS MATERIAL RELATIONS INTO EXISTENCE

In order to approach a Cherokee-centric composition study in the Cherokee National Seminaries, I have framed my understanding of Cherokee writing through the ways that Cherokee have created a relationship *with* writing during the early nineteenth century as a material survivance of orality. The story that unfolds during this time is the rapid transition of a society that operated primarily through orality into a society that sought to preserve their Cherokee-ness and orality through writing. While student writing is difficult to recover, I have expanded out my definition of archives related to Cherokee composition to include the rhetorical uses of writing from documents collected during the early nineteenth century, such as Mooney's work, which collected Cherokee histories, stories, and sacred formulas through a missionary's lens as well as early social documents from the nineteenth century that were written in Cherokee and collected and analyzed by Cherokee folklorists John and Ann Kilpatrick. Archives are typically viewed as collected portals into the past and as material contextual clues in the content of what was happening through a windowed view. Journals, recipe books, letters, scrapbooks, and more are artifacts that become written preservers of the everyday, whose content serves as an important role to understand what was often not documented formally and provides places to locate the histories that are unvoiced and overlooked. Yet, much like stories, archives can tell us the what of the everyday as well as explain the how of thinking, reasoning, and understanding the world. It is in the how that I approach the written documents of the Cherokee so that I can better understand how writing functioned epistemologically for them as they transitioned through a primarily oral-based society and culture into a world so ingrained in writing and print that orality was seen as a shaky, pixelated and unreliable knowledge. However, when stories are plotted out in print, they can become disassociated with the storyteller. They are bound in books, categorized as objects, placed on shelves, and subjected to the agency of the reader through the means of a publishing press that is often controlled by the oppressor (Weaver 1997, 22). So, while print can record and document these stories, print can also colonize these stories in the same way that Indigenous peoples were (and still are) recorded and documented through the Bureau of Indian Affairs. I argue that the "supremacy" of print in nineteenth-century archival research is under the same colonization that Weaver posits. The thingness and permanency of print is colonized; however, we need to investigate the ways that the orality of stories and storytellers is preserved and actively breaks the restraints of print in Cherokee writing.

While there was some cultural apprehension, Sequoyah developed the Cherokee writing system ten years prior to the removal policies of Jackson. This writing system is based on syllables rather than individual letters that graphically signify each full sound as it is pronounced in Cherokee with the materiality of writing representing the orality of the language. In describing the process of altering the Cherokee script for the printing press, Ellen Cushman explores the importance of the Cherokee-ness of this written language. She writes, "At both the visual and linguistic levels for Cherokee audiences, then, Sequoyan in print would have retained its aura as a writing system because it traces visually to the original longhand and linguistically to tradition" (Cushman 2010, 637). What this means is that the aura, in the Benjamin sense, of the spoken language would have been encapsulated in this written word. Language, for the Cherokee, has always been theirs whether spoken or written. The transition from speaking to writing is recorded during this time through a collection of social documents from 1862 forward in the book *The Shadow of Sequoyah*, compiled and translated by

Jack Frederick and Anna Gritts Kilpatrick, who together wrote several books about the Cherokee language as well as Cherokee tales. In their preface, the Kilpatricks remind us of not only the importance of the Cherokee linguistic tradition but also the weight of its disappearance: "One reads over and over, for example, that with astonishing rapidity Sequoyah's people became literate after his contribution was made available to them. Seldom in print is one reminded of the sad truth that Sequoyah's syllabary and the whooping crane stand in approximately the same relationship to oblivion" (Teuton 2012, 100). These texts that they have preserved, then, are invaluable in terms of rhetorical scholarship as well as the importance of archival artifacts from the seminaries that are written in Cherokee. Not only do they allow us to analyze the beginnings of a written culture situated in an oral-based one, but studying texts like these help us understand the cultural rhetorical practices within Cherokee writing. Even more so, as compositionist, we can take a moment to pause at the importance of writing to the Cherokee based on the rapid, and perhaps unprecedented, adaption of writing to the creation of school systems and institutions of higher learning in the Cherokee Nation. The history on paper is dense, but the timeline from the 1820s to the 1840s is a blink in the annals of historiography.

Also engaged in nineteenth-century history, the Kilpatricks' work often focused on archives of written letters and other ephemera from Cherokee during the same time period that the seminaries were open. Looking through a dusty copy of *The Shadow of Sequoyah* that includes a collection of social documents of the Cherokee from 1862 to 1964 that were compiled by the Kilpatricks, I noticed that the majority of these letters had a striking written pattern. Most letters, and especially the older ones, relied heavily upon the word "now" at the start of each new section even if it didn't fit contextually. A brief glance down the page brought my attention to this footnote: "While gha? has a variety of meanings, it is most commonly used in writing to preface a new thought. There are other words in Cherokee for 'now' used in the adverbial sense" (Kilpatrick and Kilpatrick1965a, 5). I took this footnote for what it was and moved on. It wasn't until I was looking through another collection by the Kilpatricks that I took notice of the use of this "now." In their book *Walk in Your Soul*, which is a collection of love incantations of the Oklahoma Cherokee, the use of "now" is profuse. In this text, the Kilpatricks explain the use of "now" in much more depth: "The 'Gha?!' with which the majority of Oklahoma Cherokee conjurations and incantations begin is an interjection that could be translated in a number of ways—'attention!' or 'hear this!' or 'well!' for example—but 'now!'

appears to us to be the most appropriate rendering. It is not ritualism; it is generously employed in workaday writing and conversation for the purpose of prefacing a new thought" (Kilpatrick and Kilpatrick 1965b, 18–19). Cushman's work on the Cherokee syllabary identifies this syllable as an interjection that could also mean "listen to this!" or "attention!" and if used at the end of a word, it can mean that the speaker expects the listener to respond positively with a "yes" (Cushman 2011, 54). This syllable "*gha*," or in Cherokee, Ꭰ, while still often translated into English as "now" is essentially an untranslatable utterance in that there is no English equivalent to what it actually means, but rather carries a signification that produces a meaning.

What does this all signify? And how are the orality of spoken Cherokee and the materiality of Cherokee writing brought into balance? This is where rhetorical sovereignty can be seen at work as it becomes a way to enact orality within rhetorical ecologies of both the oral and the written. Scott Lyons explains, "Sovereignty is a guiding story in our pursuit of self-determination, the general strategy by which we aim to best recover our losses from the ravages of colonization: our lands, our languages, our cultures, our self-respect" (Lyons 2000, 449). Lyons contextualizes the importance of sovereignty to American Indians as a means of survival and a mode of self-determination. Through this analysis, we can surmise that when Sequoyah was creating the Cherokee syllabary, he saw a need for a specific symbol, Ꭰ, for the purpose of introducing new thoughts. In other words, Ꭰ was important enough syntactically that it deserved its own symbol and memorialized a trace of orality in written form. We can see how it is used in the following excerpt of a letter written by a young Confederate soldier named Tse:gh(i)sini on July 20, 1862, to his near relatives:

> I:no:li, allow me to write you at this time, Sunday evening. I am getting along well.
>
> Now! A few days ago I send you a letter giving you permission to get the hat. I forget to tell you to let me know quickly if you were able to do what I asked you to do. . . .
>
> Now! I also want to know how those quite a few sick at home are getting along. We believe that someone has gone to search for someone. You tell me that, too.
>
> Now! For us to visit you is a hopeless situation, even though we do want to visit you. . . .
>
> Now! Now I have just stopped writing. I hope that you are well v:ghini:li I:no:lie, and all of your family. . . .
>
> Now! I greet you this evening from far away. Now! I, Tse:gh(i)sini, just scribbled this. I am well. You also, I suppose. How are all the women at home getting along? Very well?
>
> Now! I greet you this evening. (Kilpatrick and Kilpatrick 1965a, 7–9)

This letter, much like many of the other letters in this collection, is not only a glimpse into everyday language between Cherokees during the time of the Cherokee National Seminaries, but it also captures the use of Ꭴ in written Cherokee. However, what is interesting about this letter is its awareness of the written form of this communication. This letter is written only forty years after the Cherokee adopted Sequoyah's syllabary. Not only does it show the reach of Cherokee writing during this time, but also its style is much akin to speaking. Both of these put this text in close proximity to speaking. This style of written communication continues through this collection up until the last letter written in 1962, although it is used with less frequency. This symbol then becomes a residual of the oral in writing—it is the writing of orality coded in the syllabary. This coding sustains a place where the Cherokee enact orality as a means of maintaining their oral traditions within a technology that is conflated with a distancing of the oral and written binary. However, as we see here, enacting orality leads to rhetorical sovereignty. In order to explore this further, we need to look at how this utterance is used—that is, how it functions rhetorically as well as technologically.

Since the utterance Ꭴ doesn't easily translate and doesn't seem to have an absolutely defined meaning, we can look at how the word is used. As the Kilpatricks noted, the word is used to introduce new thoughts. We can see in the above letter that it acts in the same way the beginning of a new paragraph would act. However, it seems to be more than just a punctuation marker. In order to explore this utterance more, the Kilpatricks have also compiled a collection of love incantations of the Cherokee. According to the Kilpatricks, these love incantations are part of the magical texts of the Cherokee that were used mostly by medicine men and women and also by the common layperson. These were written down anywhere that there was free space. While they are often referred to as sacred formulas, the Kilpatricks explain that this term does not describe these magic texts. They explain, "The Cherokee designation for one of their texts, i:gawe:sdi, is a far more meaningful term; for most Cherokee magical rituals consist of something that one says (or merely things) or sings, called the i:gawe:sdi ('to say one'), and some recommended physical procedures, called the Igv:n(e)dhi ('to do, one'), although some have no igv:n(e)dhi at all" (Kilpatrick and Kilpatrick 1965b, 5). The magical texts have the same structure throughout—each one starting with Ꭴ followed by the name of a spirit plus their ritualistic color, the location of the spirit, and a statement of the spirit's omnipotence (Kilpatrick and Kilpatrick 1965b, 6). The following is an example of a typical magic text:

Now! Listen!
Red Raven!
Very quickly you have come to hear. You Place of Peace is Above.
You fail in nothing. (Kilpatrick and Kilpatrick 1965b, 133)

These magical texts act as a sort of invocation, reminiscent of the Roman Catholic Mass, but only serves as a vehicle to what is actually being performed through thought. The Kilpatricks explain, "In any magical ritual all generative power resides in the thought, and the *i:gawe:sdi*, which focuses and directs that thought, alone is inviolate. The *igv:n(e)dhi*, which merely augments the authority of thought, or serves more effectively to apply or disseminate it, may be expanded, curtailed, altered, or dispensed with entirely in conformity with personal preference, special circumstances, or the broad general principles that govern Cherokee medico-religious practice" (Kilpatrick and Kilpatrick 1965b, 5). In other words, not only are these incantations merely vehicles for thought, the words themselves don't hold specific signification. There is not a correct phrase or sentence that one needs to speak even if the formula remains the same.

Given these varied examples of the utterance Ꭴ, we assume that this word is used in written everyday texts as well as ritualistic texts. It can be written or spoken. While it has no real translatable meaning, it is commonly translated across the board as "now!" So, what is this word doing? Since Ꭴ is both oral and written, it works as the signal for bringing meanings into a relational existence at that point in time. It carries the essence of language into the material, spoken world. In this way, early Cherokee writing becomes a case study for Teuton's theory of the oral, graphic, and critical impulse of communication (Teuton 2010). It can also help us establish a theory of rhetorical sovereignty as it creates a method of cultural survival through orality. By acting as both oral and written, this symbol helps us see how orality, as being both rhetorical and technological, is enacted. In this sense the Cherokee have created a space of rhetorical sovereignty, as these oral techniques of writing are not seen as being something primitive or natural but as always already technological. When this becomes the style or way of being for a people such as the Cherokee, they are able to enact rhetorical sovereignty as a move toward self-determination. In addition, we can now situate the breakdown of the oral and written binary as something ecological and in balance/*duyuk'ta*, much like Cherokee gender, since they are both existing together and not tied to a linear progression from one to the other or in Eurocentric hierarchical power relationships.

COMPOSING PUBLICLY WITH THE CHEROKEE THROUGH PERSEVERANCE AND DEVELOPING NATIONALISM

The Cherokee of the nineteenth century knew the importance of writing as a weapon against assimilation and erasure, and because of their history with white settlers and the United States, they knew they needed a tool that could sustain their culture in the future when the United States would once again seek to completely erase the Cherokee. In 1828, the Cherokee tribal council formally established the country's first tribally owned and operated newspaper, the *Cherokee Phoenix*. Much like the mystical bird the newspaper is named after, the newspaper to this day remains a testament to the importance of Cherokee writing to the Cherokee people, as the editors made a point to publish stories in both Cherokee and English in each edition of the newspaper. Phillip Round, in *Removable Type: Histories of the Book in Indian Country, 1663–1880*, briefly contextualizes these early years of the Cherokee people's turn to literacy through the council's development of the *Cherokee Phoenix*. The council picked Elias Boudinot as the newspaper's first editor, who "saw the relationship between print and government as a matter of giving voice to Cherokee experience within the dominant public sphere." (Round 2010, 133). According to Round, "In his own way, Boudinot was proposing a counterpublic discursive space from which to enunciate an emerging Cherokee nationhood" (Round 2010, 133). This was done on two levels: first, the content written in English was specifically aimed at a "distant white audience" to not only illicit general sympathy to the Cherokee cause but also perform a sort of civility that countered white beliefs that Natives were still savage, uneducated, and poor. Often, he would print tribal laws, Cherokee government documents, speeches, as well as culture, literature, and local stories. (Round 2010, 136) The content written in Cherokee was clearly aimed at the Cherokee people and included letters, news stories, local happenings, and other typical newspaper content. However, because of the removal policies and hardships the Cherokee faced during this time, the *Cherokee Phoenix* had a short run before the press was seized by the state of Georgia in 1835, three years before the Cherokee Nation was forcibly removed to what is now northeastern Oklahoma. (Round 2010, 139) By this point in tribal history, the Cherokee press had already had a lasting impact on the Cherokee people. Round mentions that the Cherokee census in 1835 reported that only 18 percent of tribal members could read English, but 43 percent could read Cherokee (Round 2010, 139). The newspaper clearly played a role in the spread of Cherokee literacy and the need to promote Cherokee goings-on in Cherokee was vitally important to the survival of the tribe. With the removal and upheaval of the tribe into Indian Territory (present-day Oklahoma), the Cherokee would not have a tribally run newspaper until the creation of the *Cherokee Advocate*, another dual-language newspaper, in 1844. The *Cherokee Advocate* had a much longer run than the original *Cherokee Phoenix*, lasting until the Cherokee press published the last edition on March 4, 1906, when the United States government dissolved the Cherokee Nation, effectively shutting down the Cherokee people's ability to have a tribally run and sovereign press. These early newspapers served as both a space for Cherokee to share their writing with one another and for the Cherokee to write publicly for a white audience. The dual languages in the newspapers served a purpose rhetorically to both promote and retain Cherokee culture and identity.[2] Chris Teuton explains, "Sharing knowledge is a part of Cherokee traditional culture, but that does not mean that all Cherokee knowledge is open to all Cherokee people, much less the general public. Sacred knowledge—of spiritual matters, family matters, and knowledge of medicine, among other kinds—are only shared with those who need to know these things" (Teuton 2012, 4). The newspapers allowed the Cherokee to maintain a public and Cherokee identity. This rhetorical move sustains actual Cherokee cultural practices and values that survive through oral stories and protects it from colonial settler narratives. In this way, the Cherokee have fully taken advantage of what they once saw as an oppressive power of written language held by the Ani-kutani. The immortal power of written words constantly creates and sustains Cherokee sovereignty through language and literacy as long as those written words remain in circulation.

Even when the Cherokee acted on the offensive by taking advantage of a nationwide literacy program, a bleak future was always on the immediate doorstep for the Cherokee as more settlers moved into Indian Territory through federally run land runs in which settlers literally raced onto free plots of land that the government had taken away from Indigenous nations. With the influx of white settlers, the push for a statehood grew stronger, and in 1907, the United States determined that Indian Territory should be admitted as the state of Oklahoma.[3]

---

2. I expand on this point more in chapter 7.
3. Originally, the people of Indian Territory wanted to be admitted as two states: Oklahoma, which would be inhabited by white settlers, and Sequoyah, which would be inhabited by Indigenous sovereign nations. This movement failed at the national level as President Roosevelt admitted a joint state of Oklahoma. As part of the statehood ceremonies, the new state held a symbolic wedding between Oklahoma and Indian Territory, in which a prominent businessman from Oklahoma City represented the groom—Oklahoma, and a young woman represented Indian Territory.

At this point, the Cherokee Nation entered what some have called the "Cherokee dark ages" (Teuton 2012; Nelson 2014). During this time, the state of Oklahoma took possession of the Cherokee National Seminaries, turning the Cherokee Female Seminary into a teaching school, also commonly known as a "normal school," later becoming Northeastern State University. The United States also passed the Indian Allotment Act, known as the Dawes Act, that shifted communal ownership of land to individuals to further break down Cherokee society and practices, and by 1924, American Indians were declared to be United States citizens, ending any claims to tribal sovereignty and tribal citizenship. As United States citizens, the Cherokee were drafted into the United States foreign wars and suffered considerable loss of lives and tribal members. With each life loss, the number of Cherokee within traditional communities shrank. The United States government formally declared that it would not recognize any tribal governments until the 1970s when the American Indian Movement along with the Civil Rights Act put an end to termination policies and reestablished tribal governments, bringing a close to the Cherokee dark ages (Teuton 2012, 85–89). Despite this, Cherokee culture survived (and even thrived) through a continued dedication to the Cherokee language, which is the life force of what it means to be Cherokee. "Everything we do traditionally, it starts with the language," Hastings Shade explains, "Our stomp grounds. Our fire. It only understands the Cherokee language. Once the Cherokee language is gone, we're going to lose our fire" (Teuton 2012, 89). To be Cherokee is to see, understand, and relate to the world through the Cherokee language, and because that language can be documented, read, and immortalized through writing, Cherokee culture is still here, still existing. While the decline of spoken Cherokee continues at an alarming rate, written Cherokee still preserves Cherokee culture and orality. While some may

---

Complete with the pomp and circumstance of the wedding march, Ms. Indian Territory was greeted by the groom, Oklahoma, who had this to say of the matrimony: "Out of sympathy for the young bachelor, I now propose to Indian Territory, who I am sure is matrimonially inclined, that the proposal be accepted, and that the union be consummated here and now. It should be understood, however, that nothing should be said about the age of the bride. It is a case when youth and age are to be blended together in harmonious union, and that under the constitution and laws, no divorce can ever be granted. This is not exactly a case of love at first sight. A lady by the name of Sequoyah interfered with the courtship and at one time tried to break up the match. But having failed to do so, and tired of the loneliness of single blessedness, she gracefully surrendered to the inevitable, and has ever since been in favor of the marriage." A Baptist reverend then performed the marriage ceremony (from the transcript of Oklahoma statehood proceedings reproduced in *The Oklahoman*, Friday, November 16, 2007).

claim that the Cherokee only adopted writing as a means to assimilate into white culture, Joshua Nelson argues that "this argument holds only if we accept the implicit assumption that 'the ways of their conquerors' (never mind the implicit assumptions of this naming)—for example, practicing religion, education, diplomacy, and so on—were exclusive provinces of whites, that precontact societies did not worship, teach their children, negotiate with other tribes. There may have been marked differences in the ways Cherokees and whites understood and enacted such practices but they were not so alien as to be categorically distinct" (Nelson 2014, 64). The teaching of composition at the seminaries needs to be framed through this mindset as well. Composition for the Cherokee was not another means of assimilation just as it was not a progression from an oral to a literate society or a primitive to a civilized society. Rather, composition shifted Cherokee orality and literacy into a relationship with one another through a means of survivance that is a balance between the materiality of writing and the living nature of storytelling.

LISTENING TO THE ARCHIVES: RECOVERY WORK

In order to situate the seminaries within the disciplinary boundaries of rhetoric and composition, we can compare pedagogical space created by the cultural locations of the seminaries to the rise of current-traditionalist composition methods. Current-traditionalism evolved from the Harvard model of composition instruction from the early nineteenth century and a surge of textbook publications after the Civil War. Today, the notion of current-traditionalist pedagogies can easily fall into the space of the catchall term used to describe any outdated model of teaching composition. However, I am specifically referring to the pedagogical practices rising out of the shift in composition pedagogies during the mid-nineteenth century seen in textbooks by Harvard professors Adams Sherman Hill and Barrett Wendell, as well as Amherst professor John Franklin Genung and the contemporaries following their early works (Berlin 1984, 58). Berlin categorizes current-traditionalist rhetoric as "the triumph of the scientific and technical world view" that championed the "most mechanical features of Campbell, Blair, and Whately, and then the sole concern of the writing teacher" (Berlin 1984, 62). This focus on mechanics is deeply rooted in the roles of universities after the Civil War; instead of an educational space for the aristocratic elites, universities provided upward social mobility for the rising middle class, and the ability to write—and write effectively—was one of the skills needed to succeed (Berlin 1984, 60). Following the Harvard Reports, which were developed to track and assess writing curriculum during the late nineteenth century, the most noticeable and traceable aspects of writing were grammar, mechanics, and even penmanship. According to Berlin, the Harvard Reports "thus gave support to the view that has thus haunted writing classes ever since: learning to write is learning matters of superficial correctness" (Berlin 1984, 61). Current-traditionalist practices are not arbitrarily bound in our histories; just as the seminaries are situated in Cherokee practices and needs for educational practices, current-traditional practices are situated within socioeconomic pressures and university models during the nineteenth century. Without the necessary recovery work that many historians and scholars have attended to in our discipline, including Brereton, Berlin, Crowley, Gold, Enoch, and others, these boundaries remain obfuscated in our disciplinary narratives.

While the school followed traditional women's seminary educational models with roots at Mount Holyoke, the Cherokee Nation both modeled their courses from other female seminaries and aligned the curriculums at both the female and male seminary so that they offered the exact same courses, provisions, and instruction.

By situating the Cherokee seminaries within Cherokee teachings of gender balance as well as the importance of education to the nation as a means of cultural acceptance, I look at traces of pedagogical practices that speak to socially and culturally conscious and egalitarian educational models. For the Cherokee nation, models for their own education system needed to respond to the social pressures of acculturation and accepted gender roles as well as the need to develop a model of teaching writing that considered the needs of Cherokee-speaking students as second-language speakers and writers. Continuing through the evidence within the archives, we need to contextualize the Cherokee Female and Male Seminaries' course offerings and descriptions within the concerns and contexts specific to the education of Cherokee women and men. At first glance, there doesn't seem to be much room to counter the prevailing emphasis on grammar, penmanship, spelling, and forms that speaks to a current-traditionalist model of composition study, especially since each of these courses (grammar, composition, penmanship, orthography) are not only mentioned in the catalogs but verified as being integral to the curriculum for some time. However, one of the mentioned debates at the Teacher's Institute, held by seminary instructors in the summer of 1882, was the question of how to best educate Cherokee speakers ("'Teacher's Institute of the Cherokee Nation: July 5, 1882' Meeting Notes" 1882). Unlike Harvard, the Cherokee seminaries used grammar classes not as a way to emphasize form over content and authorship, but as a means to help non-English speakers take command of the English language because of the pressures of assimilation and oppression Cherokee-speaking peoples faced. This context can also be juxtaposed with the description of composition classes in the male seminary catalog, which clearly outlines:

> It is recognized that the English language is a living language and that a correct use of it can be learned only by practice in speaking and composition. Technical grammar is taught, but the student is not burdened with forms. Rhetoric teaches the most effective way of expressing thought. The composition in connection with this course aims to make the student familiar with figurative language, and to give him skill in the proper use of it. Special attention will be given to the study of content of words and to the choice and use of words. ("Catalogue of Cherokee National Male Seminary 1886–87" 1887, 8)

While grammar is acknowledged as part of the English courses at the seminary, grammar and forms are not the sole focus of composition, and rhetoric seems to still be the preferred means of teaching composition, emphasizing the meaning-making of language rather than the superficialities of grammar instruction that Berlin discusses with current-traditionalism.

To further back the claims that the seminaries were not adhering to the Harvard model and current-traditionalist methods following that model, we can look to a list of the library books housed in the male seminary. We already know that both schools had equal access to materials through the establishment act, and it stands to reason that both schools were following similar teaching methods because of the annual teacher's institute. The Cherokee Male Seminary catalog from 1888–1889 lists the contents of the library. This list is mostly focused on fiction, philosophy, religion, history, science, and reference books; unfortunately, there is little mention of textbooks that might have been used. Yet, under the "Miscellaneous" heading, Richard Green Parker's *Aids to English Composition* text is listed. Carr, Carr, and Schultz describe Parker as "overlooked" as a serious pedagogue since he has been categorized as producing several textbooks during the nineteenth century as a sort of textbook mill (Carr, Carr, and Schultz 2005, 171). Parker's approach to composition was focused on invention strategies and the student/author as an integral part of the compositing process (Carr, Carr, and Schultz 2005, 172). Carr, Carr, and Schultz call his approach "maverick" and "groundbreaking" for the time, especially with the rise of current-traditionalist works (Carr, Carr, and Schultz 2005, 168–69). While Carr, Carr, and Schultz are working with his earlier texts, the edition of *Aids to English*

Composition in the male seminary library is prefaced by Parker, arguing, "It would be presumptuous for any author to attempt to give rules, or to lay down laws, to which all the departments of English composition should be subjected. Genius cannot be fettered, and an original and thinking mind, replete with its own exuberance, will often burst out in spontaneous gushings, and open to itself new channels, through which the treasures of thought will flow in rich and rapid currents" (Parker 1875, iii). This preface speaks not to the mindset of current-traditional practices and emphasis on mechanics but harkens to the student-centered teaching practices implemented by Mary Lyon during the early years of the nineteenth century at Mount Holyoke and illustrated in the structure of her composition courses (Mastrangelo 2012, 70). The influence of Mount Holyoke's early curriculum on the Cherokee seminaries is clear in these shared pedagogical moments and artifacts.

However, as Mount Holyoke's curriculum began following the Harvard model later (Mastrangelo 2012, 70–71), the Cherokee seminaries started establishing their own pedagogical pathways to meet the needs of Cherokee students who were to potentially become Cherokee teachers in the nation's school system. While the female seminary catalog only mentions these courses, we can cross-reference evidence of composition methods focused on student-centered models in the newspaper produced by the Cherokee Female Seminary, *A Wreath of Cherokee Rose Buds*. There are relatively few copies of this newspaper in existence in their original form, and the copies in the archives at Northeastern date from 1854 to 1857. However, these newspapers serve as writing samples from students attending the female seminary. These writings strike a familiar chord with the pedagogical practices of Parker that have students describe objects, moments, feelings, connections to other subjects, and so on (Carr, Carr, and Schultz 2005, 174). We can see this in the various topics, such as "sin," "beauty," "A Visit to the Fortune Teller," as well as other compositions written by female students. One of the earliest available student publications from the female seminary's newspaper, *Cherokee Rose Buds*, includes a poem written by Corrine, one of the students at the seminary, which gave the students and the newspaper their names. Titled, "Our Wreath of Rose Buds," this poem describes the role of the seminary as a garden for Cherokee women to grow intellectually. After naming the women at the seminary "rose buds" and asking the reader to ponder where these buds grow, Corrine writes, "No, our simple wreath is twined/From the garden of the mind;/Where bright thoughts like rivers flow[4]/And ideas

---

4. The title of this chapter is taken from this stanza of poetry written by Corrine as a homage to the ways the seminary women viewed themselves and also as an example

like roses grow" (Corrine 1854). From the earliest days of the seminary, students were aware (and writing about) the ways in which they formed knowledge. It wasn't through rules and mechanics but through freewriting and thought. These means would produce intellect and expand the mind, echoing Parker's sentiments on the matter as well. While Corrine's poem perhaps romanticizes the wonderfulness of these teaching methods (keeping in mind that this poem was written for a wider audience), not all of the students saw composition as a means to tend the garden of the mind. One piece in particular stands out, titled "A Week at the Female Seminary." Published in 1857, this anonymous text describes Wednesday as "composition day." She explains, "One third of it is gone, before the wide ranging, unwilling thoughts can be collected in a space sufficiently small to compose a dozen lines that will harmonize with the subject selected. The most appropriate name for this dark day would be, I think, the Bable [sic] of Sentiments" (Wreath of the Cherokee Rose Buds 1857). What she describes is a method, albeit in her words, a "dark" method, of invention—a rhetorical practice displaced with the rise of Scottish common sense realism. In these two examples, we get a glimpse of the outcomes of such composition methods, but also an image of the rigors of writing in such ways. More importantly, students seem aware of the means of writing instruction, echoing the teaching methods found in Parker's textbook as well as the course descriptions.

During Ann Wilson's tenure as principal at the female seminary, the catalogs and courses reflected the influence of the Oswego Normal School of New York she attended and included courses titled Object Lessons. Object lesson pedagogy is grounded in sense perception, observation, and a focus on thingness. Object teaching in writing stems from the early nineteenth century education leaders looking to the Swiss education reformer, Johann Heinrich Pestalozzi, who lived from 1746 to 1827. While Pestalozzian pedagogy is often observed in early elementary education, Lucille Shultz documents the influence of Pestalozzian object teaching on nineteenth-century college composition, which emphasized that writing was best learned through the experience of writing and not by rote memorization of grammatical rules, through the connections between John Frost's 1839 textbook *Easy Exercises in Composition* and its predecessor in Pestalozzian teaching, Elizabeth Mayo's 1830 textbook *Lessons on Common Things* (Schultz 1999, 66–67). Frost borrows object lesson teaching and applies its principles more directly to writing so that students can learn writing from writing. The common means of teaching

---

of how students contextualized their own learning and writing practices.

from sense and experience works as follows: The teacher would bring in a piece of glass, while students sit around. According to Mayo's teaching lesson, "Glass has been selected as the first substance to be presented to the children, because the qualities which characterize it are quite obvious" (Mayo qtd. in Schultz 1999, 70). As they pass the glass around so that the students can examine and hold the object, the teacher begins to ask students what they see and to spell it out so she can write it on the slate board and so that the students will now know the subject of their writing. Then, the teacher will ask the students what they observe, noting that perhaps they will observe it is bright (Schultz 1999, 70). While our contemporary courses might see this as a form of early technical writing, nineteenth-century teachers used object lessons as a method of inquiry and invention in writing. After this lesson is demonstrated, Frost's text gives examples of the kinds of writing that the teacher should expect from these exercises from Mayo to illustrate the ways that experiencing the glass will encourage students to abstractly extrapolate on the meaning of glass as an object. The entry on glass reads as follows: "Nothing illustrates the utility of glass more finely than the green-house. By this happy contrivance we are enabled to enjoy, in the depths of winter, the flowers of spring, and the fruits of summer and autumn, and to bring perfection in our northern climates the productions of the tropical regions" (Schultz 1999, 71). Shultz notes that the Oswego Normal School that Wilson attended during her tenure at the female seminary was one of the most visible schools that supported Pestalozzian teaching methods. Shultz notes that in general, these schools "promoted a benevolent classroom environment and a pedagogy that moved from the simple and concrete to the complex and abstract" (Schultz 1999, 75), and it is this teaching method that Wilson brought with her to the Cherokee seminaries. At this point in time, the seminaries moved away from the strict influence of Mount Holyoke and began to join a national trend of following the education reforms of Pestalozzian and Herbartian (from German teaching philosophies) progressive education methods, which were made popular through the Oswego Normal School so much that it became known as the Oswego movement. Because this movement was based in experiential learning, it dramatically impacted women's education in ways that shifted it away from preparing women for society and toward preparing women for life and more academic and educational pursuits (Mastrangelo 2012, 5). We can see that influence in the seminaries through the composition course description from the male seminary's course catalog in 1886: "The pupils are first exercised in writing simple sentences, descriptive of objects placed before them. They are taught the use of different kinds of sentences, and how to punctuate. Later drills consist in the outlining the reading lesson; in constructing sentences containing new words, and in learning synonyms for such words as awful, nasty, nice, etc. Strict attention is given to the grammatical statement of thought, both in written and oral work" ("Catalogue of Cherokee National Male Seminary 1886–87" 1887, 6). While there is some degree in which students are learning grammar, perhaps because the teachers were working with students whose first language was Cherokee, and not English, we can still see the influence of Pestalozzian pedagogy adapted to a Cherokee environment.

Even though archival evidence is sparse, we can still construct histories of composition practices and teachings through the connections between course listings, library listings, and textbooks that challenge our dominant narratives of current-traditionalism in the nineteenth century. When we view this adapted pedagogy through the lens of Cherokee teachings, language, and stories, I argue that this choice in pedagogies wasn't happenstance or based on the whims of who they hired as principal. As I explained earlier, Cherokee thought and practices are the confluence of the material and the abstract in the ways they understand material relationships within their worldview,[5] which is perhaps most easily illustrated in the Cherokee language. Cherokee is a verb-driven language; however, the case endings are not dependent on gender. Rather, they are dependent on the number, location, and even physical characteristics of the nouns they are acting upon. Cherokee has roughly forty of these "classificatory verbs" in which the stem of the verb includes a morpheme that indicates the physical properties of the noun object. There are five such morphemes in Cherokee that indicate whether the object is living, flexible, long, liquid, or compact. The connections I see between Cherokee language speakers and an introduced composition method are revealed more when we focus on the influence of materiality of language and orality on Cherokee writing instruction. To teach a people composition effectively and to keep a student-centered perspective, teachers at the seminary may have seen that it was beneficial, even necessary, to ground that teaching in a way that fit the Cherokee worldview. In this case, current-traditionalism would not have had the same traction at the seminaries in the ways that Pestalozzian teaching and composition instruction would have thrived. Much like at Mount Holyoke, current-traditional practices ultimately did not constitute the entirety of composition practices at both the male and female seminaries. Mastrangelo

---

5. See chapter 3.

explains, "As the overall drive in composition instruction for correctness at the expense of content continued, other influences also began to work at dismantling such a hierarchy between student and teacher, correct and incorrect as had been formed by Harvard" (Mastrangelo 1999, 57). The Cherokee Nation was struggling with acculturation that demanded a "correctness" to speaking, especially when educating second-language learners, but the writing practices of these students followed a student-centered approach that aligned with Cherokee teachings and worldviews in pedagogical teachings during the nineteenth century. The intersections between Cherokee culture and progressive educational methods provided a model of education that adapts and to cultural tensions and demands of socially driven pedagogies. Current-traditionalism, as it was taught at Harvard, does not open up a space and location for this culturally situated education and writing, and instead, the Cherokee seminaries follow what Mastrangelo calls a "Deweyian Progressivism" that can be characterized in part by viewing education as an equalizing force as illustrated in the early and later educational models of Mount Holyoke (Mastrangelo 2012, 6–7). This dismantling not only changes our historical perceptions of composition histories and the relationships between faculty and students, but it also dismantles the normative structures of origin stories and helps us situate composition history within cultural and gendered locations.

RELANDSCAPING: LOOKING BACK TO LOOKING FORWARD

Even as we construct metaphoric locations of the discipline, we are acting as geographer and landscaper, imposing our own frameworks that can ultimately create boundaries and borders that divide our landscapes and locations along accepted and othered. Ultimately, locations are contested. However, these contested locations can be unbound and relandscaped in ways that can be empowering and act as a recovery of narratives that are buried under the uncontested canons of histories. Because a storytelling methodology celebrates and creates a space for participatory knowledge-making praxis, the ecologies of these artifacts are realized through all our material relationships that seek to indigenize the connections in those relationships. The result is revisionist history, but it's also a returning present reality—the reality that these archives have always already been Indigenous even in a colonized state, the reality that our research methodology needs to navigate colonial structures still present, and the reality that we, as scholars, must seek reflective practices that are vigilant against our own cultural ecologies.

Ultimately, what this case shows is that not only are our locations situated, but we—as scholars, historians, pedagogues—are also situated in our own cultural embodiments. While there is much work to be done in the archives, the teaching practices of the Cherokee Female and Male Seminaries help us understand how our writing and writing histories are always responding to cultural locations, and that our histories are still needed. More importantly, research writ large has a need for storytelling methodology as an Indigenous knowledge-making praxis. By listening to the stories tucked away in dusty locations within archives, our histories of composition instruction grow into lived practices and locations of culturally situated research and storytelling.

In the waning years of the Cherokee National Seminaries as Oklahoma statehood became a reality, the female seminary put together a souvenir catalog in 1906. This catalog, one of the most digitized and widely available documents from the female seminary, contains a brief history of the seminary, the impact of Sequoyah's syllabary on the Cherokee Nation, the stories of notable leaders from the schools, lists of graduates, daily schedules and course lists, pictures of buildings and students, and poetry from students memorializing the school. All of these textual remnants of the seminary are bound together and printed on glossy paper by the Indian Print Shop in Chiloco, Oklahoma. This print shop, which also printed the monthly school journal, "A Magazine Printed by Indians," was a part of the Chiloco Indian Agricultural School that was established through the same executive order signed by President James Garfield that established other Indian boarding schools, such as Carlisle Indian Industrial School and Haskell Indian Nations University as part of a federal effort to assimilate American Indian children through residential boarding school. I'm not unaware of the somewhat sad fact that one of the lasting documents from one of the first tribally run institutions of education was handed off to be printed through a federally run residential boarding school at the beginning of an era of assimilation and erasure for American Indians. I stop a moment to think of the passing of these documents between the two schools and the story this widely shared document is telling us through what it symbolically signifies and ironically captures during the last few years of the Cherokee National Seminaries before they were forcefully bought by the state of Oklahoma. I also chuckle just a bit to myself as I realize that, even though this document is one of the most influential artifacts on my research, I've never seen the original copy—just online pdfs or old printed copies that are held in several archives across the United States. These are just some of the ways that this document has shared many stories with me as I've gone back through, time and again, reading passages, comparing course lists and class schedules, and stumbled across names and references in other documents. Even as I sit here to edit this chapter, I am reminded how artifacts, like this souvenir catalog, tell us different stories at different times and how these artifacts keep stories back for other times.

One of the first stories I encountered during my research was an anonymous poem, written by a "nineteen-five senior," that has been found long life in the opening pages of the souvenir catalog. It's always been this last stanza that I kept coming to, and it serves as one of the ribs of my research questions and framework during the time I've spent with the archives:

And the maidens now departing
From this dear old Alma Mater,
From this dear old second Mother
Who has cared for them so gently
Through the sweet years of their girlhood
Leave the wish and prayer behind them
That, as future years roll onward
Blotting out our race of people,
She may stand here always ready,
Glad to welcome Indian children
And to keep alive tradition—
Of this proudest Indian Nation.[6]

During a time when federal policy was aimed at "blotting out our race of people," what does it mean for the Cherokee "to keep alive tradition"? Reading through this verse again, I think of how top-down the act of blotting is, a slow and methodical wiping out as treaties were broken, rulings were made, people were separated and removed from their homes, documented on rolls, blood quantum given, land allotted, and over time, place names became anglicized and tribal governments were disbanded. Yet, what remains alive are those traditions, however they may adapt to survive and resist. So, what looks like it has been erased still stands ready. While I haven't been able to find out who wrote this poem, I imagine them thinking back on the pillars from the original seminary building that still stand there in Park Hill. It makes sense to me that this place is home of the Cherokee Heritage Center, where the genealogical records of Cherokee families are held. There the three pillars stand in the heart of it all, a constant reminder of the struggles, resilience, and pride of the Cherokee people—their dedication to education as a founding institution of their sovereignty.

---

6. Poem from *An Illustrated Souvenir Catalog of the Cherokee National Female Seminary, Tahlequah, Indian Territory, 1850 to 1860* (Cherokee National Female Seminary 1906).

7

"TO KEEP ALIVE TRADITION"
Survivance and Writing at the Cherokee National Seminaries

> *"Does not the heart of every Cherokee parent swell with emotions of pure delight, as he or she passes through the intervening Prairie and beholds on either side, one of the stately edifices which have been erected by the wisdom of our Nation and dedicated to the intellectual and moral culture of her youth? Or in other words, fond parents, are not your very hearts filled to overflowing with pleasure, when you see us—your sons and daughters—drinking of this fount of knowledge, ye yourselves have planted in our midst?" (TBW 1855)*

After searching through legal documents, old course catalogs, and newspaper clippings in the various archival boxes and vertical file folders filled with the materials of the Cherokee National Seminaries' past, my research turned to the ephemera of student life that still remained. During that hot summer's research trip, the fires that destroyed the Cherokee National Seminaries at various times during the nineteenth century felt as close as they possibly could. Little evidence of student work, if anything, was left of what had been described in institutional documents as a robust student academic life. However, as I walked across the hall from the archives to the special collections at Northeastern State, I found old copies of microfiche with student newspapers tucked away in obtusely labeled file folders. As I read through these worn-out copies of copies, I felt a nearness to the seminaries that engaging writing can bring. Peppered throughout the worn and faded papers were poetry and prose by student authors whose names were in Cherokee and in English. Making yet another copy of a copy, I left that day with only two editions of these newspapers and feeling as though I had been sitting in Park Hill, Indian Territory, in the 1850s, talking with students about their daily trials as seminarians out in the prairie. Wishing there were more copies, I kept wondering what may have happened to the other copies and whose grandmother may have stashed away a copy as

https://doi.org/10.7330/9781646425228.c007

a treasured family heirloom kept in a box in a forgotten closet—that is, until one day when trying to find some of the families of the students mentioned through genealogical research. A quick search online led me to various archives throughout the United States and turned up additional copies of different editions, digitized from the originals and accessible to anyone able to download a pdf. I had that same feeling of hearing whispers that lead you in a thousand directions, only to stumble across what you are looking for absentmindedly, as I began to piece together the publication histories of these newspapers and the role these student writers played in establishing a Cherokee National identity by preserving Cherokee culture through and with writing.

THE CHEROKEE ROSEBUDS AND THE SEQUOYAH MEMORIAL: A BRIEF HISTORY

In 1854, the Cherokee Female Seminary began publishing their student newspaper twice a year. The *Cherokee Rose Buds*, named for what the women seminarians called themselves. Following the same publishing practices of the *Cherokee Phoenix*, the first newspaper of the Cherokee Nation and the first tribally run newspaper in the United States, the *Cherokee Rose Buds* published stories in both Cherokee and English in each edition, which is one of the most striking aspects of this small student newspaper. A year after the first *Cherokee Rose Buds* was published, the Cherokee Male Seminary followed and published their own newspaper, the *Sequoyah Memorial*, named for both the great Cherokee Sequoyah and a similarly named literary society at the male seminary. Like the *Cherokee Rose Buds*, the *Sequoyah Memorial* was student-produced; however, it focused more on political stories and civic matters and did not seem to publish very many articles in the Cherokee syllabary. Yet, one of the connecting features of these newspapers was the inclusion of student compositions written for a public audience rather than kept to the classroom. These student compositions were nestled among more traditional news content from current political events and announcements of various meetings, deaths, and marriages in the Cherokee Nation and at the seminaries.

While it can be easy to overlook these newspapers as there are so few copies that we know of remaining in existence, the insight that they provide into Cherokee intellectual thought remains extremely important historically, as there are very few written documents that still exist that illustrate the rhetorical awareness that these students saw as a necessary response to federal policies of eradication. To fully understand the survivance work that these newspapers accomplish, we must read and understand these newspapers as a portion of a constellation of work that resists dominant erasure through more Eurocentric research methods. By constellating Cherokee perspectives of nineteenth-century history, Cherokee rhetorical practices in their writing and, most importantly, Cherokee traditions that are sustained through their stories, the theoretical work of storytelling, and especially Cherokee stories of balance can recover relationships within ephemera that has largely been severed from its original context. From colonizing histories of erasure and assimilation, the *Cherokee Rose Buds* and *Sequoyah Memorial* instead represent the rise of Cherokee nationalism, preservation of culture through written language and printing, and the rhetorical strategies of student writing at the Cherokee Female Seminary that was caught in the crossroads of conflicting gender roles, cultural expectations, and outside assimilation policies. These worn-out and faded student newspapers are a part of a much larger and complex history and are the material remnants of Cherokee tradition; to understand the work that they do to serve Cherokee culture, we need to step back and understand the larger constellation.

LEARNING AND WRITING WITHIN THE CONTEXT OF THE BRAVE, THE MIGHTY WARRIOR

Caught up in a time of quickly shifting power struggles within their own nation and the ever-increasing pressure from the United States to eradicate the ways of life the Cherokee had known and to take their land away, the people of the Cherokee Nation looked for strategies to survive as a people, as a culture, and as a nation. The old ways of diplomacy through treaties and military conflict had been stripped away by years of negotiating power dynamics with the influx of white settlers and eventually succumbed to a newly formed United States that turned their might inward to remove and erase Indigenous peoples by taking their lands, children, and language. The once powerful Cherokee Nation now had to find answers to the ever-pressing question of mere survival. During the nineteenth century, when the Native way of life was threatened and physical conflict and war was no longer a viable option of survival, the Cherokee turned toward language and literacy as a means to continue to follow the very heart of what it meant to be Cherokee. "Natives are created in words, their sacred names are derived in nature, and their presence is forever related in stories," Gerald Vizenor explains (Vizenor 2003, vii), and Cherokee stories serve as pathways toward balanced relationships within that word world.

Guided by stories, the Cherokee traveled along the path through survival, and stories like the one about the brave and boastful warrior provide the context of Cherokee survival strategies. The story goes that there once was a brave and mighty warrior who was full of pride and arrogance and told everyone of his great deeds, of battles he had won, and foes he had overcome. Even though everyone knew he was a great warrior, he took every opportunity to tell them again, and the village soon became annoyed of hearing how great he was. Each time he made a new weapon, he boasted about how his war club was the greatest, how his bow was the strongest, and how his arrows were the sharpest. Again, he told everyone of his greatness even though the old man told him how this boasting would cause him to fail in the end. Soon, the tribe went to war with another tribe, and although the brave and mighty warrior brought the best weapons and tools, he was knocked unconscious from behind and taken captive. The enemy saw all of his fine weapons and tools the brave warrior had used against him. They gathered his weapons and tools, tied the warrior up, and shot him with his own arrows[1] (Duncan and Arch 1998; 90–92). On the surface, this story makes an easy case that boasting can lead to a person's demise; yet, in a playful slip of meaning, reading the story of the brave and mighty warrior in context of the upheavals of the nineteenth century reveals a path of survival when one group takes up the mantle of an enemy and uses it for themself and on their own terms. "Native traditions arise as a creative practice," Vizenor argues, "and are sustained by a crucial sense of presence and survivance in stories" (Vizenor 2003, vii). In other words, this story and other stories do the work of not only sustaining Cherokee tradition but also bringing the Cherokee into presence by surviving and resisting forces that try to blot them out of resistance. As long as they tell stories and live through these stories, the Cherokee survive. Vizenor likens this mode of survivance to N. Scott Momaday's arrow maker, who crafts word arrows as weapons of language and literature against erasure (Vizenor 2003, vii), and like the brave warrior in the Cherokee story, these arrows, which are often naively categorized as tools of the oppressor meant to assimilate Native culture, are turned on and used against the dominant society. In this story, the boastful warrior is not unlike the prideful United States that declared Manifest Destiny a right, given by God, and the Cherokee were very aware of the ways the United States used nationalism, court orders, and federal policies as weapons against the Cherokee Nation. And like the brave warrior's enemy, the Cherokee

---

1. Story adapted from Davey Arch's storytelling, recorded in Barbara Duncan and Arch's *Living Stories of the Cherokee* (1998).

looked toward these institutions as models for strategies they may adapt as a means of survival. For nineteenth-century Cherokee, education, literacy, and writing were the sharpened arrows that, when deployed on Cherokee terms, could take down even the bravest warriors.

CHEROKEE WRITING, NATIONALISM, AND NEWSPAPERS

While the Cherokee were devoted to promoting their own issues in their own terms and language during the tumultuous nineteenth century, the press wasn't without its own hardships. Even though the *Advocate* had a successful run, the press was interrupted in 1853 to 1870 due to lack of funds. However, during this interim, the Cherokee seminaries stepped in with their own student-led (compared to tribal government-led) publications. The *Cherokee Rose Buds* and the *Sequoyah Memorial* took up the role of promoting Cherokee interests and was made available outside of the seminaries and sold to a general readership. Like its predecessors, the *Cherokee Rose Buds* (later called *A Wreath of Cherokee Rose Buds*) and the *Sequoyah Memorial* included stories in both Cherokee and English, and like its predecessors, it filled the dual role of reaching out to a wider and whiter audience through English and created space for specifically the Cherokee people through stories that were only published in Cherokee. While the female seminary's newspaper included essays that focused on Cherokee life, the male seminary's newspaper included more specific details about the curriculum of the male seminary in addition to several essays on the importance of education. Both newspapers routinely published the poetry of seminary students. The creation and direction of each of the newspapers seemed to be led by students at the seminaries, and every edition I have recovered lists the names of students who served as editors.

While there are no documents that have survived that explain why the newspapers were created, several short articles across the newspapers give us insight into what the students saw as the purpose of their newspapers. The *Cherokee Rose Buds* was created first, and in the August 1, 1855, edition, editors Elizabeth Duncan and Lucinda M. Ross write of an exchange program with other women's colleges across the United States. Although they are thankful for the robust exchange program and the numerous papers they have received each week, they worry that the *Cherokee Rose Buds* may lack in quantity and quality because it is only published twice a year and, up until recently, very few of them spoke or wrote in English (Duncan and Ross 1855). While it is unclear if the *Sequoyah Memorial* was part of a nationwide exchange program, the male students

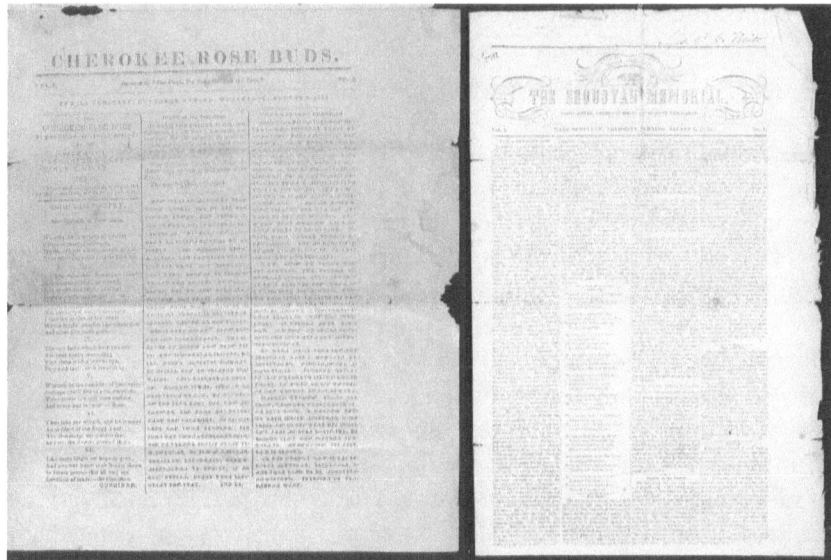

Figure 7.1. An 1854 copy of the Cherokee Rose Buds from the Cherokee Female Seminary and an 1853 copy of the Sequoyah Memorial from the Cherokee Male Seminary. Both are some of the earliest editions published at both seminaries. Images courtesy of the Beinecke Rare Book and Manuscript Library, Yale University.

were encouraged by the female students to start their own student publication. In the year following the first edition of the *Cherokee Rose Buds*, the editors of the *Sequoyah Memorial*, D. L. Vann, Joel B. Mayes, and C. H. Campbell, humorously explain in the first edition that "The Rosebud is *very* anxious that our paper should be forthcoming! They are *so fraid* [*sic*] we will fail!" (Sequoyah Memorial 1855). The *Sequoyah Memorial* also explains the public role of their newspapers as their "object is to improve the morals and intellects of mankind. . . . By reading newspapers a person can become acquainted with the character of different nations of the world, and know whether the public acts of those nations will elevate or degrade them" (Sequoyah Memorial 1857a, 3). With both newspapers published with the public reader in mind, both editions of the newspapers carefully crafted stories that brought the reader into intimate conversations with the students of the seminaries, often employing humor throughout. The *Cherokee Rose Buds* often employed a sort of self-deprecating humor through subtle takes on expected gender roles in addition to adding witty little stories and jokes in the white spaces between articles. The *Sequoyah Memorial* also included jokes throughout the paper and inserted wry commentary into the articles themselves. In the same article that states the public nature of newspapers was intended to raise the morals of the reader, the author goes on a tangent about various ads in newspapers, even ads seeking wives. The author remarks, "If a man has not enough of manly ambition and respect to mankind to keep him from advertising for a wife, I don't think he ought to have one" (Sequoyah Memorial 1857a, 3). The humoristic style throughout the newspapers is perhaps best illustrated by the *Sequoyah Memorial*'s very first edition. Under the header, the editors write: "It is common for most pin-hook editors to puff a little about their paper, but we'll only say buy a copy—or as many copies as you please, and judge for yourselves. However, we do not think you will lose much by such an operation, for 'tis very cheap, only ten cents per copy" (Sequoyah Memorial 1855). The writing style and rhetorical aspects of each newspaper illustrate a counternarrative to current-traditionalist practices that are emblematic of nineteenth-century student writing. The newspapers even call out the critics of form and writing, claiming that the best poets and writers have had their feelings "berated by their severe attackers," and that "if these terrible fault-finders were only here on 'composition' day and note the deep lines of countenance of those who are trying to grasp [unreadable] thought" (Leila 1855). The aim of writing, according to the students writing in the newspapers, is to share "bright thoughts that have taken to themselves wings" (Leila 1855). This is evident throughout the newspaper stories published as they focused less on mechanics and form, and instead, engaged more in rhetorical wordplay, nontraditional essay structures, humor, and more importantly, practices politically motivated writing as a means to establish a Cherokee national identity.

THE CHEROKEE ROSE BUDS: THE SELF-DETERMINATION OF CHEROKEE WOMEN WRITING CHEROKEE

The *Cherokee Rose Buds* took up the mantle of establishing a culturally identifying force through the continued dedication to publishing in the Cherokee language. The *Cherokee Rose Buds* included several stories on each page written in Cherokee, while the *Sequoyah Memorial* only has a few stories in Cherokee in a later edition. Much of the written Cherokee has not yet been translated into the English, although what little has been translated creates a dual audience within the newspaper. According to the *Cherokee Rose Buds*, by 1857, some of the seminary students had only been speaking English for four to five years (Wreath of the Cherokee Rose Buds 1855), meaning that the majority of the Nation still operated everyday life in the Cherokee language. English, however, was not seen as a superior language by any means and there is no evidence, written or spoken, that the Cherokee sought to replace their own language with English (Nelson 2014, 173). In addition to practicing Cherokee culture by printing in Cherokee, the *Cherokee Rose Buds* also illustrated the rhetorical ways that Cherokee used this balancing act to their advantage in the same way that the *Cherokee Phoenix* did. According to Rose Gubele, Cherokee scholar and professor of Native American rhetorics, the *Cherokee Phoenix* operated through trickster tactics as it switched between Cherokee and English and employed rhetorics of accommodations and resistance (Gubele 2015, 108). The use of Cherokee and English in the *Cherokee Rose Buds* mirrors the rhetorical strategies of its predecessor, and in knowing that their writings would be read by two audiences for different purposes, the student newspaper continued the work of developing a Cherokee identity for and by the Cherokee (Gubele 2015, 112). According to the Cherokee Language Council, some of the stories in the newspaper are written only in Cherokee, signaling that they are for a specifically Cherokee audience while other stories have been written in Cherokee and English.

In one of the early editions of the newspaper from 1854, Na-Li[2], who self-identifies as a full-blooded Cherokee with dark skin, writes, "An Address to the Females of the Cherokee Nation" in English as well as in Cherokee. In both versions of the address, she explains that education is available to all Cherokee, regardless of status. She builds on her own experience as evidence, explaining that her parents, now deceased, never attended school. In the English version, Na-Li explains that although her parents were "common class," they "loved their children as well as the rich" (Na-Li 1854). In the Cherokee version, translated by Anna Huckaby, she writes that they were told that the rich used to be the only people to send their children to school, "These people were wrong. My parents were Indians. Not rich, not poor, just everyday Cherokee. But they loved their children in a way that these other people can't feel" (Huckaby n.d.). While both addresses argue that Cherokee education is important and that it is available to all Cherokee, the differences

---

2. In several of the student narratives in Maggie Culver Fry's collection, the students at the Cherokee Female Seminary often mention how they would receive a nickname in their early days of attending the seminary, usually given by an older student. These nicknames tended to come from an experience, a character trait, or something else. In the student newspapers, it seems like some students used a Cherokee name, like Na-Li or Qua-Tsy, to sign their writings while others used a given nickname, like Icy or Fanny. Because they did not use their anglicized names, they were in a way reclaiming agency, away from white culture, and instead used their peer-given names. Unfortunately, now we have no clear way to connect their authorial names with their anglicized names that are used in government documents (typically collected by the federal government).

between the Cherokee and English versions clearly establish that these addresses were for different audiences. The version in English gives a detailed account of how Na-Li's prior education with the missionaries prepared her for the seminary, and that she feels that "it is no disgrace to be full Cherokee. My dark complexion does not prevent me from acquiring knowledge and being useful hereafter" (Na-Li 1854, 3). The English version concludes with a description of what students learn at the seminary and as long as these women attend a public school prior to enrolling at the seminary, they should be able to succeed or at least keep trying to succeed. The Cherokee version makes no mention of her complexion or status as a Cherokee, and it does not mention missionaries or all of the classes that the women will take when they enroll. Instead, it ends on a much more confident note, stating that even though Na-Li had the benefit of a prior teacher, she is "certain that anyone could make it into this school if they set their mind to it" (Huckaby n.d.). This story is not the only time we see students writing in both English and Cherokee for different audiences. In a later edition, a student named "Icy" writes an overly Christian parable titled "The Two Companions" that tells a story of how a woman was helped along a journey by Faith and Hope (Icy 1855, 5). In the Cherokee version titled "Two Should Walk Together," however, the characters have been drastically changed to a male protagonist and an older woman who helps him on the path. The Cherokee version tells a story that, while Christianity is a worthwhile pursuit, it is almost impossible to attain. The Cherokee man sets out alone on a difficult path that is hard to follow, but when he meets up with his elderly companion, she explains that it takes two to walk in harmony along the path (Alves 2009, 89–93). While the English parable, written for a white audience, lauds Christian ideals, the Cherokee version, written for a Cherokee audience, explains the importance of relationships and harmony/balance in finding the right path—a path of *duyuk'ta*. While there are more stories to translate into English, what we learn from these two examples is telling. The Cherokee used their dedication to education to show how they were "civilized" to whites and that being Indian did not stop them from attaining that. However, the act of being educated, for the Cherokee, helped give them the strategies to double-voice their use of education and preserve the core values of Cherokee culture and nationalism through their continued use of Cherokee.

Since Cherokee was unreadable to a white audience and appeared only as something "strange" and "exotic," the Cherokee were able to protect these stories and resist the influence of Eurocentric ways of thinking while they navigated their own identities through perhaps the most difficult times in Cherokee history. The shared discursive space of Cherokee and English in the newspapers produced by the Cherokee Female Seminary is an act of rhetorical sovereignty in a moment of survivance, an active and dynamic negotiation of survival and resistance (Powell 2002; Stromberg 2006). Using both Cherokee and English becomes an act of rhetorical sovereignty (Lyons 2000), which is "the inherent right and ability of a *peoples* to determine their own communicative needs and desires in this pursuit, to decide for themselves the goals, modes, styles, and languages of public discourse" (Lyons 2000, 449; emphasis in original). These newspapers and student writings are public yet maintain sovereignty by what they do not give to that distant white audience. These few copies of the *Cherokee Rose Buds* still act as living ephemera maintaining Cherokee sovereignty through stories written by Cherokee and producing meaning in a Cherokee way as the ultimate act of self-determination.

THE *CHEROKEE ROSE BUDS*: CHEROKEE WOMEN RHETORICS OF SURVIVING TRUE WOMANHOOD

While Cherokee women wrote in Cherokee as a means to preserve their culture, Cherokee women at the seminary were also caught within the "cult of true womanhood" that characterized femininity and established gender roles in the nineteenth century, ultimately imposing subjugation to a patriarchal system. Cherokee women were faced with seeking out balance between surviving and resisting imposed gender roles with their own cultural gender roles. Nelson builds on the work of Barbara Welter to situate the tensions of gender expectations for Cherokee women in the nineteenth century. The attributes of true womanhood, according to Welter, could be categorized as piety, purity, submissiveness, and domesticity. These teachings were spread throughout Cherokee culture prior to removal through the influence of missionaries on what they saw as the elite and ruling families in the Cherokee Nation (Nelson 2014, 92). Within the *Cherokee Rose Buds* newspaper, the portrayal of true womanhood permeates throughout the content, and the even the newspaper dedication "The Good, the Beautiful, and the True" echoes these gendered nineteenth-century sentiments; however, under the surface of those ideals in the newspaper, Cherokee students carefully balanced a performed assimilation to the ideals of true womanhood by resituating these ideals as part of the already known strength and power in the roles that Cherokee women had long held in their society.

Instead of stories of submissive women, Qua-Tsy, a student enrolled at the seminary in 1855, wrote a piece titled "Female Influence." She begins by claiming, "How often have we hear it re-iterated [*sic*] that the destiny of the world depends on woman—that woman is the appointed agent of morality—the inspirer of those feelings and suppositions which forms the social nature of man." (Qua-Tsy 1855). Following this proclamation, Qua-Tsy makes a connection to the fate of the Cherokee people, stating, "The elevation of our race does depend on the manner in which woman executes this commission. Nor does the destiny of man as an individual alone depend on female influence, but that of nations, kingdoms, and empires" (Qua-Tsy 1855). In this short opening, Qua-Tsy makes it clear that the role and influence of women isn't relegated to the home or individual man but rather that women's influence extends outside of that domestic sphere and into areas of society traditionally occupied by Cherokee women but denied to them by Eurocentric gender roles. She continues with numerous mentions of women who would be recognized by anyone familiar with Greek and Roman history—Aspasia of Athens who "instructed Socrates and Pericles, so much that they had to acknowledge their indebtedness to her," "world-renowned" Helen of Troy, and Cleopatra, whose "influence over some of the leading men of Rome was almost boundless" (Qua-Tsy 1855). Breaking from ancient history, Qua-Tsy also describes Madame de Stael, a French revolutionist who was exiled by Napoleon for writing *Delphine*, by exclaiming that "the proudest monarch of France would tremble before a single female [de Stael] sooner than he would at the approach of armed foes" (Qua-Tsy 1855). In her description of contemporary influential women, Qua-Tsy upends the traditional domestic sphere of women by exclaiming that men like George Washington had influential character only because they had even more influential mothers. After establishing that women have always been influential and powerful, Qua-Tsy makes a connection back to the role of women in the Cherokee Nation during her time. She asks, "If this influence has been so universal in past ages, is it not equally powerful in our day. . . . The elevation of the Cherokee People also depends upon females; and, perhaps, particularly upon those who are just springing into active life" (Qua-Tsy 1855). To her, then, the education of women is absolutely necessary, not to make them subservient creatures to men and restricted to domestic duties, but to uphold the Cherokee Nation so that "when we are called to other stations and our field of effort widens, our influence may have an elevating and enabling effect upon all with whom we come in contact" (Qua-Tsy 1855). While we can never be certain how Cherokee women defined gender roles during the nineteenth century, Qua-Tsy's story helps us contextualize how Cherokee women understood the role of education in relation to their gender roles. Education, for the Cherokee, wasn't a means to assimilate but a tool of self-determination for the continuance of the Cherokee Nation. Cherokee women could write of ideals like piety and beauty in the *Cherokee Rose Buds*, but these ideals, when constellated with Qua-Tsy's story on female influence and the importance of Selu as Corn Mother, are characters of powerful women who can influence the Nation. Their writing doesn't mean that Cherokee women viewed traditional practices in conflict with or subservient to the imposed Eurocentric culture of "true womanhood" prevalent during this time. Instead, as Perdue argues, Cherokee culture was not dying, but rather, Cherokee notions of gender especially were well established and even surviving the imposition of true womanhood. That is, "Selu had met Eve, but she had not surrendered" (Perdue 1999, 184). This encounter between Selu and Eve is evident in student writings, and ultimately, these students' writings are stories of survivance and perseverance. To survive the onslaught of assimilation and removal policies during the nineteenth century meant to perform to the cult of true womanhood; to resist the erasure of Cherokee culture during this complex time meant to continue Cherokee practices, especially writing and speaking Cherokee, even if Cherokee culture was kept (perhaps purposefully) out of colonial eyes.

"CIVILIZED" WRITING IN THE *SEQUOYAH MEMORIAL* AND THE *CHEROKEE ROSE BUDS*

Previous work done on the seminaries' newspapers echoed a clear theme regarding the writing: The newspapers extol the virtues of being civilized and demean a past, "savage" way of life; therefore, these educated Cherokees were fully assimilated and essentially "white." (Mihesuah 1998; Alves 2009). Indeed, it's hard not to read statements such as "It has not been two centuries since our part of the human race were living the savage life in a state of ignorance and barbarism, unacquainted with any of the improved arts and sciences of the present age, and cared and done but little for the improvement and cultivation of their minds" (W. 1856) and immediately cringe each time the words "savage," "ignorance," and "barbarism" jump out from the page. Were the Cherokee already so defeated and erased that they did the work of the United States by labeling themselves as savages? If read through a settler colonial lens, then it does appear so. Or do we shift the context of these words back into the stories and traditions of the Cherokee people writing these words? Do we stay caught in the binary of savage and civilized, or can we recognize that this binary was forged as a tool of colonization? Ultimately, when we look at these words like the arrows of the brave warrior that caused his demise, we shift our questions. Instead, we can lead with the question, Who gets to call themselves civilized? Does the colonizer get to label the Cherokee as civilized to erase the Cherokee culture? Or do the Cherokee appropriate these rhetorical word arrows as a means to define what Cherokee civilization means to the Cherokee? Much of what is written in the student newspapers echo the trickster rhetorics employed by Elias Boudinot, the first editor of the *Cherokee Phoenix*, and while he had passed away almost twenty years prior to the publications of the student newspapers, the student writers seem to be influenced heavily by his writing style. Boudinot, who, along with Chief John Ross, was a staunch supporter of Cherokee education, is often labeled through historical narratives as a Cherokee who sold out his tribe to white acculturation and assimilation. However, Gubele explains that Boudinot was a much more complicated figure in Cherokee history and emblematic of a discursive trickster figure who navigated this identity through accommodationist rhetorics and protest rhetorics (Gubele 2015, 108). "Language play is the signature of trickster discourse, but the play has a serious purpose that carries transformative power," Gubele explains (Gubele 2015, 107). Often seen as a figure that supported accommodating white culture, Boudinot often used the newspaper as a subversive space that disguised the language of accommodation and used it to call out the savagery of white settlers (Gubele 2015, 107–9). Like Boudinot, the Cherokee students at the seminary used Native stereotypes as a means to assert their own cultural identity as "human" rather than an exoticized other and disappearing race. The trickster discourse acts as a slippery rhetorical device that navigated the political aims of the Cherokee Nation (sovereignty) with the cultural identity of the Cherokee. "There is a dialectic between political desire and Indian identity, the one influencing the other in a relationship that is rarely if ever mutually exclusive," Lyons argues, "However, I do not want to suggest that any of these identities is inherently positive or negative" (Lyons 2010, 66). Trickster discourse serves as a means to navigate settler colonialism when other navigation tools, like treaties and alliances, are denied. This process is not a binary choice between becoming white or living an Indigenous existence and identity; it's an active relationship between shifting and evolving identities to reach political goals and maintain cultural survivance. It's not a severing of traditional ways by assimilation; it's a performance of identities for political means, and it is played out in the battleground of faded newspaper pages (Gubele 2015, 111).

The newspapers use of "civilized" rhetorics and "civilized" Natives continues to repeat throughout post-removal history, and even today, you don't have to look very hard to find the Native Americans of Oklahoma be called and still refer to themselves as the "civilized tribes." Like every child going through the Oklahoma education system and learning Oklahoma history, I learned about the Five Civilized Tribes of Oklahoma, memorizing their tribal names: Cherokee, Choctaw, Chickasaw, Seminole, and Creek, and all of the ways they were removed from their lands back East into eastern Oklahoma. As school kids, we seemed to be under the impression that each of these tribes were civilized in that they were considered more white than the other tribes who were often cast as the Plains Indian in buckskin and tipis in any movie that had a need for an exoticized other in the Wild West. We learned that these civilized tribes had rolls with the names of politicians, and if we could find our family names on those rolls, maybe we could call ourselves Native. We learned that these tribes also had allotments of land, colloquially called "Indian land" instead of the name the land had been given by her original inhabitants to be passed down through generations, and maybe our family still held on to our "Indian land." But these were the claims in textbooks and reinforced in museums sponsored by oilmen, and our Cherokee stories were much older. For every museum display celebrating our civilizing, we also had glimpses of what mattered to our communities and what threads of tradition were still woven in with colonized tapestry. Museums may claim that writing is what civilized the Cherokee, but the Cherokee knew the power that writing held. For them, writing became a means for the Cherokee people to survive yet another encounter with people who seek to oppress them, to resist being only a civilized tribe in museums.

WRITING TRICKSTER RHETORICS OF CIVILIZATION

Reading about civilized Cherokee was not a new mode of discourse to soften Indigenous histories for twentieth-century school children and museum goers; in fact, the use of the word "civilization" has been employed by and for the Cherokee since the early nineteenth century. Throughout the *Cherokee Rose Buds* and the *Sequoyah Memorial*, a rhetoric of civilization is woven throughout various stories. Yet, it is often misunderstood and defined through settler colonial terms in the same way that Boudinot often gets cast as an assimilationist. As Joshua Nelson points out, the goal of prominent Cherokee leaders like Chief John Ross and Elias Boudinot was not to pursue cultural assimilation and the various aspects of society like education, worship, and trade, which weren't imposed by colonization; rather, the Cherokee had already implemented these pursuits in some way even in their traditional society, just as they had done with writing, giving writing a distinctly Cherokee narrative. "They did this work for the Cherokees," Nelson explains, "for other Indian peoples, and for nonnatives, and they lent to it a distinctly Cherokee perspective" (Nelson 2014, 182–83). According to Lyons, the Cherokee of Boudinot's time were living through a systematic ethnic cleansing carried out by Andrew Jackson's federal government. Boudinot spoke as a Cherokee who searched for any means necessary to survive. During this time, Boudinot made perhaps his most well-known and most criticized speech, "An Address to the Whites," in 1826 that dared to make the argument that the Indian was a human being, no different from whites. Even though Boudinot described the Cherokee at times as "ignorant heathens" and "savages," Lyons explains, "Boudinot's rhetorical charge, quite literally a matter of life and death, was to convince the whites that Indian identity was no more than the product of one's environment, that underneath our circumstances humans were essentially the same as God's children and made of the 'same materials.' As an early Indian identity theorist, one who at the time happened to be staring down the Trail of Tears, Boudinot was by urgent necessity both a universalist and a constructivist" (Lyons 2010, 37). With Boudinot's writing as their rhetorical model, the Cherokee seminary students also utilized a rhetoric of civilization in their publications. More importantly, they knew it was meant for a public audience that more than likely included non-Natives who would understand the meaning of civilization as assimilation, whereas the Cherokee reading would understand that civilization meant progressive practices for and by the Cherokee. Being able to play with the slippage of rhetorical and cultural understanding of civilization also meant that the Cherokee could make a case for their sovereignty through publications.

For the seminarian students, their declaration of Cherokee sovereignty came through in their writing, and through their writing, they rhetorically utilize a slippage of referents, specifically embracing rhetorics of "civilization" by using it to promote a specifically Cherokee civilization rather than applauding the attempts of civilizing and assimilating of white settlers on their nation. Scott Lyons argues that the act of writing for Indigenous peoples uses the slippery connections between words and ideas that have been historicized as "white" as acts of Native sovereignty. "None of these meanings or materials is any purer than any other, although some are clearly older. All are constructions; all can be legitimizing, resistance, or subject identities depending on their particular contexts and uses," Lyons explains. He continues, "Making an x-mark means more than just embracing new or foreign ideas as your own; it means consciously connecting those ideas to certain values, interests, and political objectives, and making the best call you can under conditions not of your making" (Lyons 2010, 70). Therefore, when these Cherokee students use writing, and especially in the public forum of newspapers that, as a medium, encourage circulation, their rhetorics and messages are not assimilated or acculturated but are a complicated and nuanced Cherokee perspective and expression of sovereignty.

In the later of the two copies of the *Sequoyah Memorial* that I could locate, the very first editorial that appears on the 1856 edition supports Nelson's claim by arguing that the Cherokee had not succumbed to "white" ways; rather, the whites had adopted the progressive practices of Cherokee civilization and enlightenment—practices established for the Cherokee and grounded in Cherokee ways. In an impassioned editorial, a student who signs the piece as "W." opens by exclaiming the Cherokee were the "bravest of the brave, the noblest of the noble, first in all the virtues of savage life, the most successful in the chase, the most dreaded in war, implacable in their enmity, and everlasting in their friendship" (W. 1856, 2). He calls out the introduction of "true religion" the downfall of their "savage nobility," and yet the Cherokee Nation responded by transforming their society, adjusting the ways they employed power in the past.

Throughout the editorial, W. frames the Cherokee society as a *civic* society, introducing the Cherokee concept of civilization as one of civic-mindedness, not one that emulates whiteness. He writes of the unparalleled patriotism Cherokees had for their nation that brought about transformation, but it was not without bloodshed and a "hasty endeavor to push the nation to as high a standard of excellence as they had attained" (W. 1856). The bloody and war-torn history that W. describes gives a uniquely written Cherokee perspective of the events of the seventeenth and eighteenth centuries when the Cherokee were at war with other tribes, allied with the British, and factionalized because of the decentralized government system the Cherokee had in place of which the British took advantage. This "transformation" he mentions more than likely was the result of the Chickamauga Wars that brought together a tribal council that centralized and strengthened the Cherokee government. "We have had orators, before whose native eloquence, malignant prejudice would not trust itself," W. writes, "Statesmen whose diplomatic acuteness, bitter foes will not question. Poet and Editors, who have respectable reputations abroad" (W. 1856). W. reminds readers that these are not the advancements of whites but that these are Cherokee accolades for a Cherokee society. W. makes the case for the already established sovereign Cherokee Nation that is, again, wholly Cherokee: "We are truly a Republic, have a code of laws *exclusively our own*. We have wise legislators, learned judges, eloquent lawyers, and zealous executive and ministerial officers. Our laws cannot be violated without impunity" (W. 1856, emphasis mine). W.'s move to purposefully present a civic society of Cherokee follows what Lyons labels as *legitimizing identity*, which is an identity introduced and approved by dominant institutions, which in this case is the federal government. By making claims that the Cherokee Nation is as civilized as the United States by having a similar mindedness toward a civic and political society, W. also rhetorically places the federal government in a position to recognize the Cherokee so that the United States will "authorize Indians to be Indians" (Lyons 2010, 61), which at this time, may have seemed like the only path of survival. When read through the framework of Cherokee stories and rhetorical patterns that are seen across mediums, W.'s performance of assimilation was for a public audience as a means to establish a legitimizing discourse so that the Cherokee would be recognized as Cherokee rather than being completely erased.

In addition to rhetorically positioning the Cherokee within a legitimizing identity, the student newspapers also navigate the other "legitimate" identity that the United States imposed upon the Cherokee—stereotypes of a Noble Savage. "Yes, your typical tribally enrolled, phenotypically correct Indian automatically shares something meaningful with Disney's Pocahontas: a political function," Lyons argues. "As two sources of Indian meaning, both federal recognition and stereotypes produce the kinds of Indians that the dominant society ultimately approves of, because both in turn legitimize the dominant institutions in our society" (Lyons 2010, 61). When that identity becomes a peoples very narrow path to still exist, the performances of those assimilated identities become a tool of survival and one that can be used against the dominant society by the mere fact that recognizing the Cherokee meant they wouldn't disappear. Several of the students' writings rhetorically take advantage of this predicament by drawing upon the stereotypes of the disappearing Native. The Cherokee people saw their current way of life, including their cultural practices, society, and political functions, as being overwhelmingly threatened, and as a means to promote their causes, they wrote stories of idealized pasts in almost a lovingly eulogistic form. In a story titled "The American Indian," an anonymous student writes that after the "happy race of people" welcomed white settlers into America, treated them well, and offered them shelter (Sequoyah Memorial 1857b), the white settlers grew and went to war with the race of people who had treated them as brothers, and pushed American Indians out of their lands in the east to the foothills of the Rocky Mountains. "[The American Indians] look back with grief upon the grass of their forefathers. About three centuries ago their war-hoop and death songs could be heard from the Atlantic Ocean to the Mississippi and from Florida and the Gulf of Mexico to the Hudson Bay," he writes. "The smoke of their wigwams could be seen curling from every village. This is all past. They have been thrust into the mighty wilderness of the Rocky Mountains there to perish" (Sequoyah Memorial 1857b). We see a similar use of death and passing in W.'s "A Glance at the Past and Present Condition of the Cherokees." After establishing that the Cherokee Nation existed as a political nation and civically grounded one, W. continues that the Cherokee Nation is not a free and independent nation and is facing a crisis. "We who once acknowledged no superior, are now compelled to assume the humble attitude of a ward, with our younger, overgrown, powerful sister for a guardian, doomed but the voice of prediction, to utter annihilation," claims W., echoing the recent outcome of the *Cherokee Nation v. Georgia* ruling (W. 1856). Yet in both of these stories, the writers do not accept that perishing and being eradicated are the only options left. W. claims that since the "United States government turns a deaf ear to them all" (W. 1856), he has no confidence in battles even considering such is foolish. The anonymous writer's take is much more optimistic: "Yet still as in ages past, in the far west, the Indian hunter goes forth in the morning and returns at night laden with the spoils of the chase. When he retires to his camp, his happy children gather around him to share the sweet repose," he writes. "The warrior concealing his noble frame in the gigantic branches of the forest tree, still sends forth the whistling arrow to the heart of his bitter enemy. With the raging fury of a lion, he still wields his bow and arrow in deadly contest" (Sequoyah Memorial 1857b). Instead of giving up a national identity, both anonymous student writers answer this crisis by establishing new identities for the Cherokee to take. The Cherokee do not need to give up their traditions, but their power and weapons have shifted from battles to surviving still as an educated and civic society. Doing so would save Cherokee nationality.

When these writings are constellated within Cherokee stories and rhetorical practices, they are recast as a negotiating balance between what it meant to be Cherokee during this time and to write for a public audience that included non-Cherokees. As Mark Rifkin explains,

"Native peoples occupy a double bind within dominant settler reckonings of time. Either they are consigned to the past, or they are inserted into a present defined on non-native terms. From this perspective, Native people(s) do not so much exist within the flow of time as erupt from it as an anomaly, one usually understood as emanating from a bygone era" (Rifkin 2017, vii). Because of this, the Cherokee had to find the best available means possible to rhetorically assert their identities as Cherokee. This rhetorical strategy of building on what the dominant society had decided was the "correct" identity for a group of people it wants to erase is seen in multiple stories in both newspapers. Like the *Sequoyah Memorial*, the *Cherokee Rose Buds* employs the same rhetoric of civilization and loss of an idealized past. However, the young women's writing often focused more on the day-to-day Cherokee life, rather than grand narratives of history seen more in the *Sequoyah Memorial*. The *Cherokee Rose Buds* often included stories that focused on the day-to-day changes in Cherokee life from an unspecified past life to a contemporary, post-Removal life. While these articles seem to provide evidence that Cherokee women were ashamed of a primitive past and proponents of a contemporary existence in which they were more "white" and civilized, especially when read within the subtext of settler colonialism, with knowledge of Cherokee rhetorical strategies, like those present in the *Sequoyah Memorial*, or knowledge of Indigenous worldviews and stories, we see the important rhetorical sovereignty and pushing back against white assumptions that these students carefully navigate.

Similar to the male seminary students, the sentiments that female students Na-Li and Fanny detail are of a progressive version of Cherokee life for contemporary Cherokees. Together, they pen these sentiments in a joint story in the August 1, 1855, edition titled "Two Scenes in Cherokee Land." In the first scene, Na-Li describes a Cherokee family of the past, whose home lacked current characteristics typically found in homes—books, vases, landscaping—and describes the overall condition of the place as "wild and desolate" (Na-Li and Fanny 1855). Na-Li continues to describe the everyday activities for this Cherokee family, how the "swarthy-looking boys" have prepared their bow and arrows for a hunt and how two girls stand in a corner preparing a mortar and pestle to beat the "*conihany*"[3] in their "calico skirts and red jackets fash-

---

3. The closest approximation I can make of this word is that it refers to a traditional Cherokee food now called *kanuchi*, which is a delicacy produced by standing and beating hickory nuts in a tree stump with a long pestle. While this is an assumption, the context of traditional preparation and the fact that Cherokee pronunciation has

ioned with silver brooches, their feet covered with moccasins" (Na-Li and Fanny 1855). After describing the scene of a typical day, Na-Li notes that the only reprieve from this "passive, un-interesting" life is when the boys return after a three-week absence and the family would gather with other Cherokee for religious festivals, such as the Green Corn Dance. (Na-Li and Fanny 1855). This lonely scene from Na-Li situates the Cherokee in a past life, simple and uninteresting, but still fulfilling. She describes the balance in the roles women and men took in Cherokee families and communities that anyone familiar with the story of Selu and Kana'ti would clearly recognize. While this scene seems to relegate Cherokee culture to the past, the following scene of a contemporary Cherokee family complicates this simple narrative. In parallel form, Fanny describes the home of a Cherokee family as filled with books, vases, cut flowers, rows of cottages, and other signs that "civilization and nature are here united in our Cherokee land" (Na-Li and Fanny 1855). In describing current Cherokee life, Fanny refers back to Na-Li's scene and the "olden days," and asks what has happened to the Cherokee family now that they have been changed by missionaries. "Have they gone to a *ball-play* or to gossip at a *green-corn-dance* [sic] as in days gone by?" Fanny continues, "No; for the general observances of these customs has passed" (Na-Li and Fanny 1855; emphasis in original). These scenes, when read together, show a knowledge of traditional Cherokee culture and at the same time acknowledge that the missionaries impacted this Cherokee way of life. However, Fanny and Na-Li do not make the argument that the past way of life is inferior to this new way, and instead they take up the rhetoric of civilization as they make the turn to highlight the role the Cherokee education has had on their current society. Nelson explains that "encouraging education as a means of developing a specifically Cherokee civilization appears throughout the rhetoric of this period" (Nelson 2014, 173) and we see this clearly in Fanny's comparison. She writes, "Other festivals or 'gatherings' have taken their place, where the *mind* is exercised instead of the *body*" (Na-Li and Fanny 1855; emphasis in original). For her, the missionaries might have changed the Cherokee from their "old ways," but the new ways sustain the community in the same ways as Na-Li's description of the roles established by Selu and Kana'ti. Making her point more clearly, Fanny continues, "The Indian lad, in place of his bow and arrow, is now taught to use the pen and wield the power of eloquence. The girl, instead of engaging in the dance, keeping time with the rattling noise of the *terrapin-shells*, bound

---

several various dialects makes me feel fairly certain that the girls described are making *kanuchi.*

to her ancles [*sic*], keeps time with the *chalk*, as her fingers fly nimbly over the *blackboard*, solving some problem in Algebra or Geometry" (Na-Li and Fanny 1855; emphasis in original). Education, as an institution, is called "civilized," but this "civilized" definition has multiple meanings and employs a trickster discourse. For whites reading the newspaper, the Cherokee are seen as adapting to white culture, but for the Cherokee, education is not seen as better than traditional culture in the same sense. Rather, these acts of Cherokee "civilization" are performing the same function in Cherokee society as traditional culture, supporting Nelson's claim that they are done in a Cherokee way for the Cherokee people to uplift Cherokee society as a Nation.

We know from oral stories as well as documentation that the Cherokee were an agrarian society with a robust political structure based on a clan system that set up the governmental structure for each of the Cherokee towns. The pastoral images that the Cherokee students describe, however, are not entirely accurate representations of Cherokee life and in fact seem to mirror the colonial settlers' images of the Noble Savage. Were the Cherokee so far removed from their culture that they believed the settlers' stories of who they were in the past? The details about the specifics of Cherokee culture, including references to the stomp grounds, stickball, Green Corn Ceremony, and subtle repetitions of the role of the hunter, Kana'ti, and the Corn Mother, Selu, make it almost impossible to think that the Cherokee had forgotten who they were. Instead, what the students have done is create a mirrored existence through their writing of what the dominant society believes of the Cherokee. In all of these stories in the newspapers, the Cherokee students remark on how they are no longer this "noble savage" of white narrative dominance. By doing so, they shift their past and their culture onto a metaphorical past and culture that can be "erased" by claims of civilization. This rhetorical move and employing of trickster discourse sustains actual Cherokee traditions and values that survive through oral stories and protects it from colonial settler narratives. In this way, the Cherokee have fully taken advantage of what they once saw as an oppressive power of written language held by the Ani-kutani. The immortal power of written words constantly creates and sustains Cherokee sovereignty through language and literacy as long as those written words remain in circulation. These student newspapers are a celebration of that perseverance through language and survivance through stories, and although tucked away in archival boxes, once read and shared, these newspapers do their work to keep the fire.

THE IMPORTANCE OF CONSTELLATING EPHEMERA IN RESISTING ASSIMILATION

The *Cherokee Rose Buds* and *Sequoyah Memorial* ceased publication after a short run in 1857, and the very few physical copies of the newspapers that still exist are kept in archives and digital collections throughout the United States. While their runs were short, the stories in these newspapers are rich with details of Cherokee student life, poetic musings of young women and men about the beauty of the meadows on a warm summer's day, the joy and mirth surrounding an Osage wedding ceremony, and even the follies of plagiarizing another student's composition work. These surviving pieces of ephemera are almost all that is physically left of the robust tribally run education system. And yet, just as the great pillars[4] of the original Cherokee Female Seminary building survived fires and stand as almost an act of defiance against President Andrew Jackson's mission to remove and erase Indigenous nations during this tumultuous time following the Cherokees' forced removal, these newspapers illustrate the careful negotiation of Cherokee identity and rhetorical practices that sought a middle path between legitimizing the Cherokee Nation and resisting colonial institutions that sought out ethnic cleansing as a means to erase the Cherokee peoples.

The carefully crafted and nuanced student writings in the *Cherokee Rose Buds* and the *Sequoyah Memorial* are testaments to the Cherokees' dedication to use education as a means to uplift a nation, promote a national identity, and perform assimilation for a white audience. These young women and men understood what it meant to be Cherokee and the complex roles they played in establishing that identity. When encountering literary narratives that complicate notions of Native identity, especially during the nineteenth century, Joshua Nelson explains that scholars are quick to label Cherokee writing as "problematic" and explain away Cherokee writings as products of assimilation. He argues that "these critics adopt a historical pattern of dismissal that reduces Indian identity to a dichotomy in which Indians are either 'traditional' or 'assimilated,' the latter being code for 'not really Indian'" (Nelson 2014, xii–xiii). In the context of Cherokee education, this false dichotomy that is grounded in colonial thinking sets up the assumption that any steps that the Cherokee took to educate themselves gets coded as "becoming" white and that the seminaries are a site of assimilation

---

4. These pillars are still standing in their original location in Park Hill, Oklahoma, and are preserved as part of the Cherokee Heritage Museum. The pillars have come to represent Cherokee pride and nationalism as they remind the Cherokee of their dedication to education.

practices, not unlike federally run Indian boarding schools, which were also being established during this time. To theorize away Native identity through the continued problematic practice of labeling Native works and practices in a false dichotomy continues the work of colonialism that only provides one unattainable path toward authenticity—a path that can only be followed if we ignore the very recent histories and policies of colonialism. The *Sequoyah Memorial,* the *Cherokee Rose Buds,* and the students writing are denied an authentic Cherokee identity when we separate oral cultural practices of stories and language from literate practices of writing and education. What is happening through this narrow view is that scholarship about Cherokees in the nineteenth century continues the colonial work of denying the self-determination and survivance of the Cherokee people during this time and effectively shifts the right to education and literacy as belonging only to white people, or those whose Native identity gets whitewashed by labels of assimilation.

WE ARE STILL HERE, AND WE ARE STILL WRITING

When I visited the National Museum of the American Indian in Washington, D.C., in 2012, I remember wandering through the various exhibits that were curated by different tribes in their own ways. I turned the corner of a big room and saw "We Are Still Here" in large letters, making this declaration for all to see. The words are a part of the Cherokee Nation's exhibit that highlights Cherokee culture. The exhibit is centered on the importance of the Cherokee syllabary as the pride of the Cherokee people and the influence of Sequoyah. Celebrated together with some Cherokee history and artifacts, early government documents in Cherokee and English, and sound clips of spoken Cherokee are also some Cherokee stories. I remember laughing quietly to myself as I read the story of Spearfinger—the women who roamed the woods and used her spear-like finger to stab out the hearts of those who got lost—and imagined all of the people unfamiliar with Cherokee culture being just a bit scared of the power of our stories and especially our monsters. Even though everything was in a museum, the words "We Are Still Here" kept shouting out as a reminder that the United States did not erase the Cherokee and that the Cherokee did not assimilate into white culture to disappear. Instead, we are still here, using our language and living our culture and traditions through our means. And we have always been proud of the ways that we do that through writing and education.

When we widen the view of research to constellate the student writings from the *Cherokee Rose Buds* and the *Sequoyah Memorial* out of a static view of objects, we understand that these pieces of ephemera are culturally situated living stories practicing *duyuk'ta*. We understand that these Cherokee women and men were always in the middle of assimilation and tradition, but they had developed rhetorical strategies to help them navigate these tensions by balancing survival and resistance in a newspaper shared between two cultures. The performance of assimilation during this time does not mean that Cherokee women and men ceased all traditional practices. Cherokee tradition and culture is maintained and lives through the continued use of the Cherokee language and labels of civilization do not mean the loss of Cherokee identity. Cherokee students writing in the nineteenth century were aware of this, even when facing annihilation from the United States government and policies aimed at ridding the Cherokee of their culture. Through Sequoyah, the Cherokee reclaimed the power of writing from the Ani-kutani, but this time they used the power of writing on Cherokee terms. Because of writing and the ease of a syllabary for that writing, the Cherokee language is immortalized as long as those words are written and accessible. The student's writing trips, hops, and slips around literal meaning, word play, and performance for a distinctly public audience that existed outside of their culture. Writing, for these students, gave them a platform to establish that they were more than a helpless nation of wards to the state; they were bright, intelligent, enlightened Cherokee who stood by their Cherokee ways. In these few faded papers written so long ago, the legacy of Cherokee education continues to live on, keeping tradition alive.

PART 5

ᎤᎦᎾᎹ: ᏔᏧᏬᏔᎬᎵᎵ ᏕᎤᏂᏕᏆ

uganawu igatihaigvnedi dunadadudalv
South: Maintain Relations

As we move to ᎤᎦᎾᎹ (uganawu), the south, we pause to reflect on the ways and ceremony our ancestors have brought us along. They have asked that we spend this moment reflecting on how we continue to maintain our relations and constellate what we have learned through ceremony. While we have come full circle, counterclockwise around the medicine wheel, the work we have done is always active, breaking the linear progressions of research. The south invites us back into the north, holding our ceremony in balance between the poles of seeking knowledge and maintaining the relations made in the knowledge through story. What we have gained along the way in ceremony continues to prepare us for the living knowledge of stories and teaches us ways to give back in responsible reciprocity.

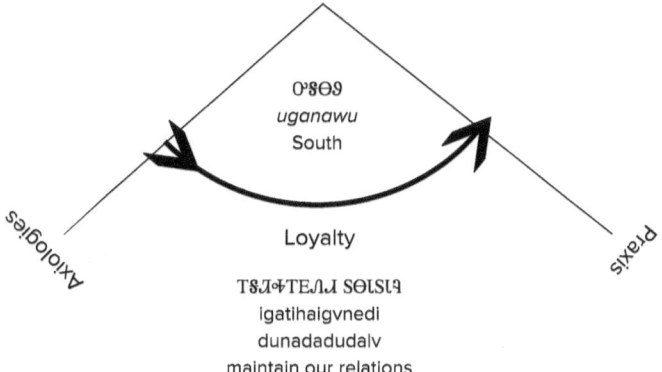

Figure 8.0. South: Maintain Relations.

GADUGI
Working Together (An Epilogue of Sorts)

We are a revitalized tribe. After every major upheaval, we have been able to gather together as a people and rebuild a community and a government. Individually and collectively, Cherokee people possess an extraordinary ability to face down adversity and continue moving forward. We are able to do that because of our culture, though certainly diminished, has sustained us since time immemorial. (Mankiller and Wallis 1993, xix)

MAINTAINING A STORIED WAY

Now that we have turned our eyes and our work to the south, ᎤᎦᎾᏬ (*uganawu*), our work is now to take up the ancestors' call and strive to maintain our relations, ᎢᎦᏘᎭᎢᎬᏁᏗ ᏚᎾᏓᏚᏓᎸ (*igatihaigvnedi dunadadudalv*). In other words, it's a place where we look back to look forward, acting as a bridge between our work and the actions we take now that we have gone on that journey. By constellating Indigenous histories with contemporary experiences of Indigenous peoples, we have journeyed together in ceremony through this text by walking with Cherokee ancestors on the path between survival and resistance. However, this journey was never meant to be a linear path whose knowledge is gained and banked. While we have come full circle, we still have work to do to carry this knowledge of *duyuk'ta* together in ceremony. Even though this book is coming to an end, the shared practice of storytelling continues to sustain us as a community of knowledge-makers across time, space, and even realties. I had a dream while writing this book, and as I opened up Google Docs to write, it spilled into those digital pages that eventually conceived this print. I was back in school, sometime around eighth grade but with all of the knowledges and reasonings of my almost forty-year-old life. We were assigned worksheets to do, and I had been breezing through them, keeping up and even surpassing my fellow classmates. Coming back to me was that rush of academic competitiveness and the confidence of a would-be valedictorian. I've got this and I've got my peers' respect (or ire coded in playful jabs of nerd-laced teases). My dream's day had become of routine until the teacher passed out another set of worksheets. Full of confidence, I picked up the pencil only to realize that the pictures made no sense to me, the order was out of place, I was missing what everyone else seemed to have. Everyone around me breezed through, and I struggled and shrunk into the imposter my mind created. The classroom became empty as everyone laughed, passed in worksheets, and went to lunch. I turned around and behind me was someone I hadn't noticed before. A strong, Indigenous woman, surrounded by books, adorned in colorful beads, and a billowing ribbon skirt. I asked her for help to understand the perplexing worksheet, and she just smiled and said, "Don't do it that way. You don't have to turn it in like anyone else. Follow my way. I take my time and think of it all at once. You don't need to finish it right now." I was swept away with relief, knowing that the rush I felt prior wasn't worth the competitive shadows lurking, and I didn't need to read these academic mountains in the way of others. I had my own path, cleared by the mentoring of Indigenous knowledges and wisdom of others. From here, the teacher's authority left my dreams, the peers I once kept disappeared. And I woke up. Ready to write with the company I kept in my dreams.

Whether I knew it at the time or not, that dream was a breakthrough moment for me in my research and writing process. Until then, my research felt very much like a solitary journey, and even a pretty selfish one at that. I had completed what I could of my archival research at the Cherokee National Seminaries, scoured what I could find online, and immersed myself into Cherokee culture and stories by seeking out those voices of Cherokee scholars[1] past and present. I had written my dissertation, fought with the formatting and template as I made sure to include the Cherokee syllabary in the appropriate type, and successfully defended and deposited that tome that helped give me the honor of adding PhD to my name. Even though I had a dissertation chair and committee that joyfully supported my work, a caring partner who went on research trips with me, and even strangers who acknowledged the value of my work with publication acceptances, my voice felt quiet and hesitant in the places that I felt that voices like mine were rarely heard. But I wasn't alone in those archives. In every artifact I analyzed and every narrative I read, I was (and still am) surrounded by the stories of my

---

1. I use the term "scholar" here both deliberatively and deceptively. For me, a scholar is anyone, living or having walked on, who teaches through story, practices, and conversation. Scholars can be our human companions as well as the plants, animals, rocks, and places we have been in community with. What "scholar" does not mean here is anyone who is only connected through institutionalized academia.

ancestors, who have been teaching me all along. Even though a good portion of this book was written in the middle of a global pandemic and in lockdown, I was never alone. Ancestors don't always listen to mandates of "social distancing." These stories from my ancestors sustained me, distant relatives reached out to me and sent me family artifacts, I met scholars whose work intersected with mine, and I shared with my partner and colleagues the lessons I was learning. Even the Cherokee stories and Cherokee language lessons my five-year-old son and I shared informed my writing and research and sustained my knowledge-making.

All along the way, my ancestors were there sharing their stories still in a way that felt like it was healing the generational traumas of being an Indian in the archive (Powell 2008). Generational and historical trauma is a sticky sort of material thing that takes the deep healing medicines of stories to even confront. As part of a study on how historical processes are embodied, Walters et al. define historical trauma as "an event or set of events perpetrated on a group of people (including their environment) who share a specific group identity (e.g., nationality, tribal affiliation, ethnicity, religious affiliation) with genocidal or ethnocidal intent (i.e., annihilation or disruption to traditional lifeways, culture, and identity)" and then situate the histories of American Indian and Alaska Natives as sustaining five hundred years of trauma and resistance (181). Research on gene expression investigates the ways that trauma has affected and still does affect the overall health and well-being of generations of these peoples through chronic illnesses, like diabetes, and mental health issues (Walters et al. 2011, 185). The knowledge of historical trauma is a "concept of embodiment . . . consistent with AIAN [American Indian and Alaska Native] spatial and relational worldviews, the ancestors and the future generations" and in these worldviews "environment, mind, body, and emotional health are inextricably linked to human behavior, practices, wholeness, and hence, wellness" (Walters et al. 2011, 184). The stories and experiences are not only expressed and experienced through physical markers in genes and in health but also network the lived experiences of trauma of generations before. These stories of trauma are continually experienced through future generations in very real and felt ways that affect the current health and well-being of a group of oppressed peoples. No matter the separation of time and space, this trauma is what we continually share with our ancestors.

While this text is limited by the linear order of physically bound pages, our community work continues together with the knowledge made both within the archives of the Cherokee National Seminaries and the process of researching, writing, and reading about the seminaries.

The healing and reconciliation of the past colonial traumas doesn't happen when we are embedded in the Eurocentric mindset of worldviews that situate archival work and Enlightenment-informed research methods and methodologies. Just as Shawn Wilson explains, "If we think of reconciliation as acting to restore healthy relations, then it is consistent with what we have been describing as the activity of Indigenist research" (Wilson and Hughes 2019, 17). When I stopped and really listened to all my relations in the archives, I recognized the need for balance, for *duyuk'ta*, in research as well as in the ways I write about that research. The work of scholars such as Malea Powell and Qwo-Li Driskill, both of whose stories are tucked alongside mine in this book, tell us of this balance as an embodied rhetorical act—an act that continues along a path of both knowledge and survivance. We all work together in an alliance of both listening and telling, and finding strength within our community, our bodies, and our practices. Our bodies and practices—Indigenous and academic—are our communal stories. And these stories are our knowledge. And yet, it's important to continually remind ourselves of the ways in which we learn and understand that knowledge, and so I return to Chris Teuton's lesson from the Cherokee elders of the Turtle Island Liars' Club: "'*Nijadolihvi jadetlosgwasdi. Tla yidetlosgwasdi.*' 'If you want to learn you're goin' to learn. If you don't want to learn you won't learn.' And if you learn, it's going to be yours. And if you don't learn it, that knowledge belongs to someone else" (Teuton 2012, 141). Without framing our research in ceremony and seeking balance, that knowledge perhaps belongs to someone else and we just won't hear or experience it. *Duyuk'ta* in research prepares us to see and hear the bodies and stories of our ancestors, who have always been there even if we may not have been listening in the right way to learn from them.

DOING THINGS TOGETHER AND SHARING KNOWLEDGE WITH ANCESTORS

Ending this book feels like an arbitrary moment—one in which I decided that I presented all that I could about the Cherokee National Seminaries, their pedagogies, and their writings. However, the truth that I face is that I am still learning from these archives and listening to the stories that they are telling. In a way, this moment captures the tensions between a storytelling model of knowledge-making praxis and the finality in written texts. Books eventually end, yet stories continue living. Cherokee National Treasure Noel Grayson, a culture keeper, bow maker, and hunter, remarks that knowledge is meant for sharing by explaining, "When I see someone take an interest in [knowledge], all you gotta do is keep that spark going, right? And it's gonna build up later;" however, Grayson continues, "It's your responsibility, you know to keep seeking that knowledge, to ask questions, and to be open to learning" (OsiyoTV 2020). Using the process of bow making, he explains that this is what the Cherokee call *gadugi*, that is, working together. Just as the rings of the wood of a bow need to work and bend together, so do we with the knowledge that we gain and share. Reflecting here in the south, not only is my research guided by Cherokee ceremony, my writing that I share also mirrors this pathway, breaking the constructs and constraints of Eurocentric genres of research. My research is a story that places my readers—ancestors as well as living humans and other-than-humans—into balance with the knowledge I am sharing, writing my research following the path of *duyuk'ta*, which is never a solitary ceremony but one that invokes and sustains community. This was the biggest takeaway I had, and which I hope I have shared in this book: In our *sgadug*, we spend our time *gadugi* as a way to maintain our *duyuk'ta*—not just with those who are present with us but with those who are our ancestors sharing their stories though living oral archives and material artifacts. Together, we are all working together to maintain knowledge. This is the core of what the Cherokee practice in stories and in writings, and this work has never ceased despite the times when the federal government stripped the Cherokee of their sovereignty. As Kirby Brown suggests, the "communistic ethic of kinship, place, and the grounded labor required" of the Cherokee not only renewed, restored, and sustained Cherokee communities, "it worked to uphold Cherokee Nationalism." He explains, "As the survival of Cherokee communities and the contemporary presence of the Cherokee Nation suggest, while the Cherokee national government might well have gone into a period of dormancy following allotment and Oklahoma statehood during the early twentieth century, Cherokee nationhood persisted as Cherokee continued to stoke the fire by cultivating and renewing relationships in a variety of ways" (Brown 2018, 214). Along with a national newspaper in both Cherokee and English, the Cherokees' focus on writing and education during the nineteenth century illustrates the ways that Cherokee often adapt Eurocentric structures not as a means to promote assimilation but as a way to practice *gadugi*—working together to keep the community together by the means best suited for the Cherokee ways of sharing knowledge.

These patterns of adapting technologies continue with the Cherokee even into the twenty-first century. In addition to the traditional written press and the continuation of the *Cherokee Phoenix* (the national newspaper), The Cherokee Nation has invested its resources in television production with the series *OsiyoTV*. This news program reaches Cherokee at home in Oklahoma and Cherokee like me, who are "at large" and live outside of the Cherokee Nation. *OsiyoTV* is a mix of Cherokee news stories, contemporary profiles of Cherokee such as Noel Grayson, traditional Cherokee stories and history, and language lessons broadcast on television, and it is available at any time streaming for free on YouTube. As Kirby Brown points out, the Cherokee Nation exists in its people and citizens, and those citizens are everywhere. Programs like *OsiyoTV* help Cherokee carry nationhood with them wherever they are (Brown 2019). I know that I have spent hours with my young son streaming *OsiyoTV* in our Ohio home, fourteen hours away from those prairies and blackjack trees in the Cherokee nation, learning about Cherokee culture as we practice learning Cherokee together. It doesn't take much to imagine a Cherokee family, removed from their traditional homelands in the southeast, opening up a copy of the *Cherokee Advocate* during the 1800s and learning Cherokee together while reading stories and news in Cherokee. It's in these moments that I know that, like my ancestors, we are all keeping our culture and sharing our knowledge to help sustain our communities and kinships. And it's our responsibility to continue to learn and share that knowledge.

In the middle of my research process, I had the opportunity as part of a linguistics seminar on Native American languages to travel to Cherokee, North Carolina, to meet with Eastern Cherokee members and elders. While the focus of the trip centered on a visit at the language immersion elementary school, the New Kituwah Academy, most of our conversations with tribal leaders and elders happened away from the school, on trails to Clingman's Dome through the Great Smoky Mountains National Park and a visit to Kituwah, one of the original seven mother towns of the Cherokee people. On a warm, pleasant day in the middle of May, Tom Belt, the Cherokee language coordinator at Western Carolina University, brought us out to Kituwah and began to tell us the history of how the Eastern Band of Cherokee (EBCI) was able to reacquire the land recently after it had been privately owned by a non-Cherokee family. He told stories of the founding of the town and the religious center for the Cherokee and walked us out to the mound where the council house once stood. Not worn away by years of farming and cultivation, the mound still stood as a historical artifact of survivance and simultaneously as a contemporary place of pilgrimage. He told us stories of the ancestors who lived here while pointing out how careful archaeologists had to be when excavating the foundations of buildings as the bones of the ancestors kept coming to the surface, as if to remind every visitor that Cherokee have always been here and will remain.

These stories spoke to me deeply on a personal level even though I had been raised in Oklahoma as a member of the Cherokee Nation. Tom Belt told us that Kituwah will always be home to every Cherokee. He pointed to the mountains, the valleys, the trees, the flowers, and the mound as the place of sacred fire, where we first came to be. And he told stories. Stories not meant for these pages, but stories that brought me and those with me into line with the local knowledges, teachings, and the place called Kituwah. While we participated in *gadugi* in the mountains of Kituwah, we encountered stories and joined in with all our relations and participants in that somber, moving, affective, sacred, and ever joyful moment. And yet, the stories told that day cannot be retold and be expected to produce the same knowledge. They are emplaced in that time, that location, and together with every blade of grass, every bone of my ancestors, every word, and every breath of those who were there; the stories create and sustain a community through knowledge that was shared and passed along. Hold up, you might say, didn't I just spend a paragraph or two explaining how it was the responsibility of all of us to share knowledge? Why the caginess all of a sudden? Just like the student newspapers and the national press of the Cherokee kept some of the stories only for Cherokee through their use of the Cherokee syllabary, stories also have their time and place when they can and should be told and shared. Yet, there is still knowledge being made together and shared if we attend to the rhetorical nature of storytelling. In stories, the act of telling the story creates agency within the knowledge that is shared and outside of the need for human centricity. That knowledge lives on, and when it is ready to be shared, the time and place will align. Part of our knowledge-making and sharing is knowing that, if the knowledge is meant to be ours, it will be, and if it is not, then it won't be. While this is but one encounter and one story, sacred stories such as this one have a way of producing encounters that are kairotic in nature, fleeting if not carefully attended to, and impactful if we acknowledge our roles as listener and participant in that moment. A moment by definition does not last but leaves behind traces of knowledge-making in its wake. These moments, networked through the storytelling, bring us (as researcher, student, scholar, etc.) into a knowledge-making system. While we must be ready to listen purposefully to stories, we also need to acknowledge that knowledge is meant to be shared and transmitted through stories so that the living work of storytelling and knowledge-making that connects us deeply to our ancestors can continue.

STORIED CONNECTIONS OF THEN AND NOW: KEEPING NINETEENTH-CENTURY STORIES IN TODAY'S WRITING PEDAGOGY AND ACADEMIC EXPERIENCE

> The past and present we know, but what of the future? We ask no higher reward than it be worthy of the name it bears and that its identity be not lost in the coming years, but may the thread that is broken now be woven in a brighter and fresher web. May its volume of usefulness be increased and enriched as it flows down into the remote future and may every Cherokee woman hand down to her posterity the fact that this institution was the creation of their forefathers and the pride of their hearts. The sun has set forever on the Cherokee National Female Seminary. —Mrs. R. L. Fite, a seminary alumna (1906)

As we near the end of our research ceremony, we have the ethical imperative to ask ourselves: So, what do we do with the stories of nineteenth-century Cherokee at the seminaries and how do we continue to maintain relations with the ancestors who have shared their stories with us? Thomas King tells that once you hear a story, it's yours; however, you can't say you've never heard it and just move on; it's up to you to do something with it. (King 2005) While the ceremony of *duyuk'ta* closes, the directions are never linear, and the cyclical nature of ceremony is that we end by actively maintaining those relations through the continuation of story and ceremony as to honor the living nature of knowledge-making. I'm reminded of a story told by Andrea Riley Mukavetz as she worked alongside intergenerational women. She tells it this way:

> To practice relational accountability, I had to shift perspectives and listen to these women as not only research participants, but as intellects who understood disciplinary conversations on ethical research methodologies and representations of American Indians in formal education. When I asked for their input, I listened to it. And I took it because they were right.
>
> From these relationships, the women became collaborators and colleagues. It is my responsibility to treat their stories the way I respect and honor our relationships. I do not write for them or on their behalf. The women can speak for themselves and choose what communities to speak to. Instead, my relationship to the women and to their stories becomes central. I carry the stories of the women with me while I speak to scholarly cultural communities about my concerns. (Riley Mukavetz 2014, 114)

From her story, I take with me the understanding that the ancestors in the archives are even more than just participants in my research; they are my intergenerational colleagues and collaborators. So, as I ask myself what are nineteenth-century Cherokee teaching us about our presents and our futures, our direct connections to this story and the foundation

Gadugi: Working Together (An Epilogue of Sorts) 231

Figure 8.1. Cherokee seminary women taking a break sitting in front of the new female seminary building in Tahlequah, Indian Territory, 1892. Photo courtesy of the Cherokee National Archives.

of it is how we think of Eurocentric systems, such as higher education, as sites of resistances and hope for Indigenous and decolonial work. Malea Powell argues for these presents and futures by calling us to reimagine our academic spaces as places for the stories and bodies of people who have traditionally been pushed out of the centers of power: "My final story, then, is a call for a reimagining of this disciplinary space that is conscious of, and conscionable in relation to, the ideological position of the Academy within this continent—a reimagining that listens carefully to those bloody, invisible bodies—and not just to the bodies of American Indians, but also to the bodies of the African slaves and the Asian laborers, as well as to the bodies of their contemporary relations who continue to resist the advances of imperialism today" (Powell 1999, 11). Just as the Cherokee seminary students existed in the tensions of academic and Indigenous spaces, their stories and teachings weave together a place of resistance. However, in these academic tensions, there is always a susceptibility and a vulnerability present that may cause a scholar/researcher/ pedagogue to privilege one story over another, or in the case of the

Cherokee students, there is a present tension that speaks over the survivance of these students to code it as a cultural giving in to assimilation. Yet, by taking time to reflect and listen to the knowledge-making and stories of these Cherokee students during the nineteenth century, I've learned that the history they have shared is practiced ceremony. Their teachings tell us that our ceremony calls us to remember the intergenerational and interrelational work between decolonizing and indigenizing the discipline that happens when we position ourselves to listen to the stories. These moves seek out a balance between sustaining spaces of nondominant voices and joining conversations with/in dominant voices. Because of this, I assert that understanding the characteristics of stories helps us as academics to know when and how a story/theory should be told.

I learned from the students that my writing balanced between modes of accepted academic assimilation and the rhetorical sovereignty of following Cherokee cultural practices. The text reads linear, yet it involved tearing apart a dissertation and reweaving the reeds around the ribs of Cherokee cultural practices. Even more, these knowledges given through ceremony are embodied and practiced through the "decolonial skillshare," (Driskill 2015) as Driskill explains, of the many baskets I have woven; each one still focused on the center of Grandmother Water Spider as she holds the ribs together; each reed passed around, embodying the practice of the medicine wheel, heading up the walls and back down to secure everything in place. My baskets have certainly taken on many shapes, full of holes and gaps, and yet, each one helps me remember to always practice in ceremony. While I often joke that my first basket (see figure 8.2) was my dissertation (since I wove it during the time I was writing), I see the beginnings of my learnings. Now that I have sat with these teachings, my baskets became more focused, smaller, and tighter. I look at these baskets sitting on the shelves in my office alongside the number of academic books I have amassed over the years, and I see no difference between them and the knowledges in those books. I also see no difference in them from my own writing practices. These baskets are part of all my relations, bringing together my writing, my culture, and my knowledges. Without the students and the seminaries I've learned from, the interconnectedness of these would remain a story, waiting to be told and waiting to be listened to.

ALLYING WITH STORIES AS ACCOMPLICES IN THE ARCHIVES

Rather than coding our stories as an addendum to educational histories or a practice only necessary in circles of cultural rhetorics, we can

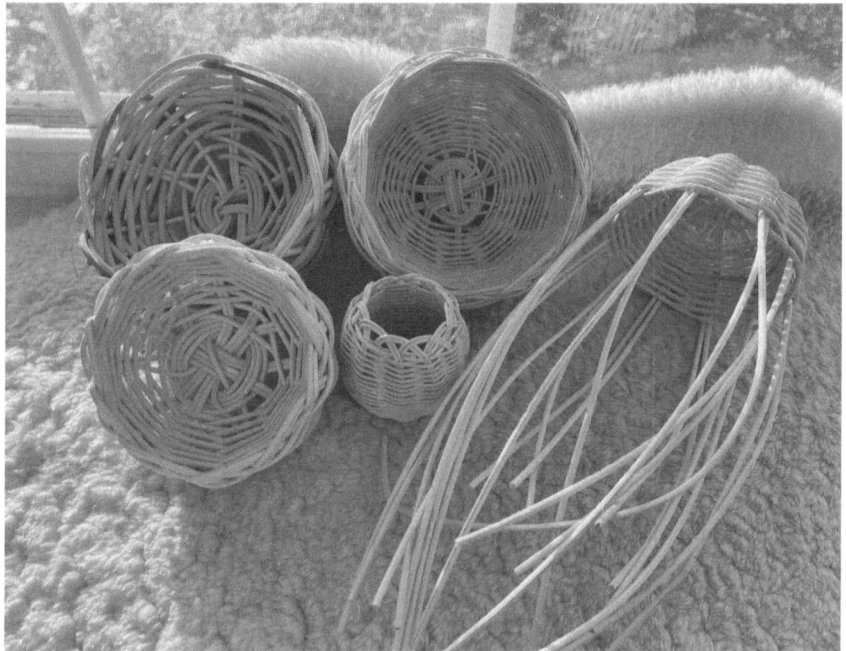

Figure 8.2. Cherokee double-walled baskets I wove throughout my research process on the Cherokee National Seminaries. Photo by Emily Legg.

acknowledge our stories as part of "all our relations" in our histories of the discipline. Gordon Henry Jr., Anishinabe poet and novelist, explains, "Theory like story may bring us closer to the impossibilities of reconciling our still extant needs, desires (even undisclosed pressure?) to legitimize our theories through our experiences and vice versa" (Henry, Pascual Soler, and Martínez-Falquina 2012, 19). Even as we seem to be writing about, with, for, or against theory, we cite or narrate our affiliations, and our cultural experiences, as though we know well enough, now, how to subsume one in the other, or both in neither, to keep writing our way in this strange complex of discourse we have entered into this engagement with cultures our own or otherwise. Our stories written and shared from experience grow from the same material pedagogies of object lessons that were implemented in the Cherokee schools and seminaries. Through each sense, we form experience, and from each experience, we form stories and do the work that Henry is calling for. This embodiment of material stories weaves together these experiences so that we can build a deeper, broader, and more comprehensive knowledge of our own methodologies. By doing so, we can continue to always navigate and indigenize these stories/theories regardless of the content or focus of our research and writing, knowing that stories do not just belong to Indigenous spaces. Stories gives us the rhetorical and epistemological means to materially weave together theories and frameworks of knowing, especially in archival research.

The weaving of story as theory, experience, and scholarly work is one of the foundational currents in reflective research and recovery work, especially in the areas of cultural and Indigenous rhetorics. "Native rhetoricians examine how American Indians make and disseminate knowledge within various intellectual sites: historiography, community-based research, embodied and material rhetorics, digital rhetorics, and composition theory to name a few," Andrea Riley Mukavetz explains, "Native rhetorics positions its scholarship and teaching within decolonial theories and social movements because of its commitment to privileging indigenous ways of knowing, acknowledging one's complicity in colonial rhetorics, and developing options for creating and sharing knowledge that does not use colonial rhetorical practices" (Riley Mukavetz 2014, 109). Although the research may look different, the rhetorical strategies of nineteenth-century Cherokee have always been an academic strategy of survivance. While the practice of unseeing, as Powell reminds us (Powell 2008), remains deeply rooted in historical narratives and scholarly practices, Indigenous scholars such as Angela Haas and Kimberli Lee perform recovery work and tell counternarratives—a re-seeing—through Indigenous and decolonial methods. In "Wampum as Hypertext," Haas explains that wampum, which are small beads made from shells and traditionally sewn into a band that served as a diplomatic treaty for several Eastern Woodlands tribes, "re-vision the intellectual history of technology, hypertext, and multimedia studies" (Haas 2007, 78). While wampum is multimedia and a material archive of Indigenous stories, decolonizing counternarratives extend beyond the material artifacts that we experience with our senses. Lee examines contemporary Native singer-songwriters to extend our understanding of contemporary storytelling and help students learn to listen as an act of decolonization (Lee 2015). To actively undo the practice of unseeing, both Haas and Lee locate decolonial ways to re-see Indigenous practices through sensory experience and story. In this tradition of re-seeing, stories of both the Cherokee female and male seminaries give us a location to understand the ways that our senses and experience are tied to Indigenous pedagogical knowledge-making. Those of us who have spent time in the disciplinary space of cultural rhetorics are embodied in these knowledge-making experiences; however, as Riley Mukavetz argues, "You do not have to be native, work with native people, or tell stories the way I tell stories to find these practices useful and meaningful. All research practices, methods, and theories are culturally located and specific. What relationality and there-ness, as intercultural research practices, can offer researchers is a way in to making cross-cultural (research) relationships visible" (Riley Mukavetz 2014, 121–22). So often in my research, I've encountered the phrase, "Well, that's interesting, but that's your thing." Or, "Oh, I'm not doing anything on Indigenous rhetorics, so I didn't cite any Indigenous people—I don't want to appropriate that work." And yet, when I read current scholarship, especially related to storytelling, object-oriented ontologies, "new" materialisms, I am struck by the similarities to my own research on Indigenous ontologies with the newest publications making the materialist turn as well as theories that marvel at the role of stories, and yet, the bibliographies read as a modern erasure of Indigenous voices.

One time in particular stands out. I was attending an interdisciplinary conference where one of the big buzz phrases was "digital humanities." After a talk about big data, tweeting, and digital humanities, the Q&A came down to a heated argument about how male-centric and white the digital humanities are. What happened during this heated Q&A was the following: Some of the participants were pointing out that the digital humanities institutes on their campuses weren't actually exclusionary (even with the caveat that it was true that most members were male and white). Several other participants shared stories claimed that these digital humanities groups had walked over to the cultural centers on their campuses and had asked those other people there if they needed them to do anything or to help. They claimed that these groups just weren't interested or didn't want to be involved. These cultural centers didn't "do" digital humanities, according to the brief conversations they had. At this point, two men sitting in front of me were having a side conversation about their philosophy department and their lack of diversity—not as a problem, you see, but as a symptom of "those" groups that didn't want to be involved. They casually pointed out that there were clearly no people of color at this conference, so what does it matter anyway and why was this conversation happening. "Those" people weren't *there*. In that moment, the stories of my grandmothers emerged in my thoughts. They reminded me that we came in with a notion that nineteenth-century Cherokee should be "Indian" and that dressing and adapting social institutions for Cherokee purposes made them lose their Indianness. The pervasive undercurrent that Indigenous people didn't belong or weren't a part of academic circles was happening to me in the twenty-first century. There are certain points where I have felt a need to "disclose" the fact that I am Cherokee and identify as an Indigenous scholar. That conference was one of those times. Seeing a chance to join in the conversation with the generative naiveté and collegial bravado of a newly minted PhD candidate, I mentioned that I was Cherokee and that I found that there is a need to talk about the pervasive whiteness of the digital humanities and that I actually was very interested in the intersections of race and digitality that was happening in the current lively discussion. They just looked at me—not perplexed or taken aback, but just looking and assessing. I got a "huh" as they packed up their bags and left the room as if I had never been seen in the first place.

I've reflected on this moment many times, and I'm left wondering if it was ignorance, awareness, or fear that caused them to not engage. Or was it the boldness of crossing disciplinary boundaries where walls are often historically in place that require us to adhere to what we've kept inside them that caused the two men to walk away? At that heart of each of these reflections was this: What is this fear of research areas attributed to? Is it a fear of the Edward Curtis Indian warrior, standing alone, face to the sun, and unapproachable in their stoicism? "That's your thing," they say. Or is it the pedestal placement of the Indian princess, their hair in braids and body in buckskin, a gentle relic of the past wrapped in Cherokee Trading Post gift shop culture along every American West highway? "I don't want to accidentally appropriate!" they say. They remind us that we can call out cultural appropriations of Native mascots because that's easy to wrangle and easier to be a "woke" Indigenous supporter in that fight (because who can't see the racial caricature of Chief Wahoo unless you actively avert your honoring eyes). We can half-heartedly listen and adapt land acknowledgments without working to actively participate because that feels safe on our universities' web pages. Yet, I ask again, is it too much of a foreign and exotic sight that my academic regalia looks more like the *National Geographic* photos of pow wows and ribbon skirts than the pomp and circumstance of eight-sided tams? The erasure of Indigenous ontologies and epistemologies *are* harder to wrestle with and acknowledge because *we* aren't those "Indians" that are consumed, but we are those NDNs[2] who remind you that we are still here, again and again, in our research, in our department meetings, and in our classrooms. We ask again, now that you've heard this story, what will you do with it? Because you can't say you haven't heard a word we've told you.

---

2. NDN is not an acronym but a reclaiming of the word "Indian" by North American Indians. It is pronounced just like "Indian" but each letter represents a syllable.

Even if you don't hear or see, we do have a word as well as a response to these kinds of experiences I have just shared: microaggressions. Microaggressions, such as claiming that race or cultural studies has no place in certain research, have the same effect that a small pebble dropped into a large body of water might have. The pebble, while seen by some as inconsequential, produces a ripple that grows exponentially. Now imagine a handful of pebbles dropped one after another. The ripples grow, interrupted by each other, and fan out to distort the entire body of water. Yet a pebble on its own can be seen as merely an annoyance that gets caught up in your shoe that comes with the often-heard advice that you just need to shake it out. While some may think this advice is meaningful and carefully sidesteps the difficult conversations of systemic racism that pervades academia, this kind of support is often as damaging as more overt microaggressions. As an Indigenous scholar, when I am told to move on and not care so much about such experiences, it further feels as though this journey is traveled alone in spaces where, university-wide, there may be only four or five other Indigenous faculty spread thinly through dispersant disciplines. In other words, the isolation feels like succumbing to the stereotypes of the lone Indian warrior or the Indian princess on the pedestal, or accepting the narratives and whitewashed histories of assimilation of the Cherokee through their educational institutions.

My story is certainly not unique and could easily be just a small excerpt from a larger series on academic microaggressions. Even as a blip in the series, the story still holds power. In "Narratives from the Margins: Centering Women of Color in Technical Communication," the authors begin by asking their readers to "listen and learn from the narratives" they all share about their experiences of facing Eurocentrism in academic settings in hopes of moving others "toward a more accountable praxis of allyship" (Gonzales et al. 2021, 18). They caution readers that it's often easy to quickly listen to stories and immediately put on the academic lens of analysis, asking why such things occur or who or what caused that specific situation rather than acknowledging micro- and macroaggressions as deeply embedded structures of racism faced on a daily basis by women of color working in academic spaces. Even more, they call for engagement with stories on a deeper level, moving beyond a claimed allyship to an actively engaged accompliceship. They define an accomplice as white "people who *consistently* leverage their privileges to stand up for, support, and amplify marginalized communities without guaranteed recognition" (Gonzales et al. 2021, 16). While they offer robust strategies for practicing accompliceships in technical communication, their call for accomplices had me return back to the archives of the Cherokee National Seminaries. Who were the white accomplices during the nineteenth century that supported the Cherokee, without expecting recognition and instead offering reciprocity and responsibility.

As an accomplice to Indigenous ancestors in the archives, listening to stories is only the first step. To follow in ceremony as an accomplice, I encourage those who seek to be accomplices to recognize the importance of ceremony by developing Indigenous critical practices in your own research. First, by acknowledging the colonial settlerism deeply embedded in archival research, researchers can then begin on the path of ceremonial research and reconciliation (Wilson and Hughes 2019). Like the Cherokee medicine wheel, this path is circular, beginning by making relations and continually maintaining those relations through the stories and wisdoms of the ancestors. Being a circular path resists the Eurocentric focus of linear research methods and engages in a critical and reflective praxis that is continually acted upon, within, and throughout research (Sullivan and Porter 1997). By continually being in ceremony with research, researchers in the archives will strive for *duyuk'ta*, always working toward balance. To start that path, the following are the steps I encourage all to take as they approach archival research as an accomplice.

Focus on Making Relations through Critical Practices

As you enter research from the east, the first step should be to acknowledge ways to make meaning outside of Eurocentric positionings. You can do this by listening to cultural elders and ancestors through stories. During this process, it's important to remember to be accountable to local knowledges and communities by listening with respect, even if that means they may not be willing to share with you at that time. By doing so, you can act responsibly through reciprocity, not only to the humans in the communities by also to the more-than-human relations. All of those relations, once recognized, serve as elders and teachers in stories and in critical practice.

Seek Knowledge through Stories

As you form and maintain relationships through respect and reciprocity, open yourself up to resist embedded Eurocentric systems by listening to the cultural stories and practicing material teachings of the community your work is situated in. By doing so, you may situate your learning in embodied rhetorical and methodological practices of all our relations. This is one of the key steps in grounding your research and writing in the livingness of stories. By seeking knowledge through these pathways, your research and writing is grounded in the response-ability of stories that works with the community to sustain that community. Much of this is begun even before you step into the archives, so that you are attuned and reflect with those cultural stories and practices as you encounter the more-than-human participants of the archives.

Work on Keeping the Wisdom of Ancestors through Loyalty and Continued Reflection

As you begin your archival research, open your learning pathways to the wisdom of the ancestors you encounter through the material objects you analyze. This may mean resituating your own learning as the ancestors pass wisdom on through those materials. By doing so, you are acknowledging the present-ability of ancestors through living and cyclical teachings and stories. Each material artifact (re)acquaints you with the past and the present in ways that inform your knowledge-making. By existing in constant cultural reflection, you respect and remain loyal to ancestors and continue their stories in the present.

Continually Work to Maintain All Our Relations

Since ceremonial research pathways are not linear checklists, you prepare to continually make relations by maintaining those relations in cultural reflective and critical practices. By doing this, engage in making knowledge with all our relations (never just about them), past and present, human and other-than-human. Continue to support these knowledge-making pathways by sharing the knowledge you have gained in ethical ways by honoring those who came before you and those who come after. Most importantly, use that knowledge responsibly to sustain the communities that gifted you that knowledge (even if that community is a community of ancestors, present in the past). Finally, honor the balance you have sought to maintain in your archival research by practicing your knowledge-making in a way that continues around the path of the medicine wheel.

One of the alluring aspects of archival work is that we can often feel like both the puzzlemaker and the completionist as we sift through boxes of letters, artifacts, and other ephemera. Our sense of primary researcher can cloud our abilities to listen and learn, and this identity as researcher is further complicated by the cultural gatekeeping practices of archival assessment and organization still being informed by the Enlightenment's need to separate embodied culture (the body) from the clinical and rational descriptions of artifacts (the mind). In other words, a researcher in the archives is not the first settler to step in; the researcher is already occupying a place that has been colonized and follows a long tradition of Eurocentric settlerism in the archives. Our first steps as researchers are to acknowledge the colonial settlerism in the archives, question the impulses of Manifest Destiny that frame researchers as explorers, and most importantly, understand that you are not alone in the archives. You are entering an already rich and complex cultural place, where the stories and cultural embodiments of the artifacts are not always immediately available to you (and may never be) without some sort of cultural teachings from those within the cultural community.

What I would like to stress at this juncture is that each research path and each archive will enter you into new and varied cultural contexts. Because of this, the role of the accomplice in the archive is never quite set in stone, with an easy-to-follow way marked before them. Because stories are living pathways of knowledge-making, each time you encounter the story, you will learn what you need to learn in that moment. Each time, that knowledge may (and will) change because of the relations you have made with human and other-than-human participants. Respect BIPOC's needs to survive and resist in the academy by working within their community and coalitions. Understand that, as an accomplice, you can provide support for these coalitions and community-building without having to involve yourself directly, even if that means completely stepping away so that these communities can work to sustain themselves without white gatekeeping (Gonzales et al. 2021, 30). Gatekeeping is part of the larger systemic colonial settlerism that is present in all aspects of research, and this one relation will always be present in the systemic Eurocentrism placed deeply in academic structures. Colonial settlers will ignore this relation, because that Eurocentrism maintains the veil that obfuscates and forgives the colonialism that is constantly reinscribed. However, by making relations with colonial settlerism, researchers are aware of the need to resist the hold that Eurocentrism has on archival research.

In the academic spaces that still uphold the systems of Eurocentricity, I turn to my grandmothers for strength and for their stories, and as Lee Maracle calls these moments, my dream space. Her words offer us a much-needed reflection in times like these: "With conditions as they are, it is a luxury for me to wander into my dream space and conceive of post-colonialism. A multitude of faces, all white and too numerous to name, gather around the edges of my dream space. If I enter despite them, their words ignite and nearly melt away the thin line of silver housing my ability to dream. Images of screaming squaws, dirty Indians and weeping women write along the rivers of tears we have shed over these images that continue to meet page, print and reader. And still I imagine new words to deal with old dilemmas that still stand on the way to freedom" (Maracle 2015, 109). The work of listening to grandmothers, to keep alive tradition as the Cherokee seminary students dedicated their learning to, is hard. It's a constant existence of mixed-blooded identity, of having to cross between the dream space and the white space of existences. The Cherokee students who were conceived to be a part of the assimilation machine of federal policy used that space to reimagine and reignite their dream spaces for the nineteenth century. Still, what I find troubling is the notion that nineteenth-century Cherokee could not have access to educational institutions as survival if we frame those institutions as assimilationists, because for them, these systems they adapted and wove together with their own stories and practices became their lived mixed-blood dream space that does not need to exist in the binaries of Eurocentric reasoning and caught between the spaces of traditionalists and assimilationists that we still see repeatedly. Joshua Nelson explains it this way: "Similar reasons could account for the traditional/assimilated binary's staying power among inveterate anti-Indian opposition arguments, but in pro-Indian circles, it may pay off in certain less obvious ways, too (if I can indulge in a little psychosocial speculation). In continuing to blame assimilationist Indians for their complicity in exploitation, for their failure to represent the wishes of the conservative majority of their people, for their alienation by virtue of their wealth and education, could progressive academics today be revealing as much about contemporary anxieties as about scores of tribal histories across hundreds of years?" (Nelson 2014, 28). So, how do we reframe this as occupying a middle space that isn't bound by binaries but lived as a balanced material space of all our relations? We turn to our culture keepers—stories. Our responsibilities to ourselves, our spaces, and our ancestors is to keep recentering on stories and practices as culture keepers. Just like my grandmothers and all of the Cherokee seminary alumni, we know what it means to be both the insider and the outsider (Smith 2012). Those who occupy a middle way, of mixed blood, are teachers who have traveled back and forth, often flying from one identity to another, that can ultimately teach us what it means to live in both identities and to share that knowledge through writing in balance. It's time to listen to the Indians in the archives and do so on their terms.

REFERENCES

Absolon, Kathy. 2020. "Indigenous Wholistic Theory: A Knowledge Set for Practice." *First Peoples Child and Family Review* 5 (2): 74–87. https://doi.org/10.7202/1068933ar.

Agnew, Brad. n.d. "Cherokee Male and Female Seminaries." *The Encyclopedia of Oklahoma History and Culture.* Accessed January 28, 2021. https://www.okhistory.org/publications/enc/entry.php?entry=CH018.

Agnew, Lois, Laurie Gries, Zosha Stuckey, Vicki Tolar Burton, Jay Dolmage, Jessica Enoch, Ronald L. Jackson, et al. 2011. "Octalog III: The Politics of Historiography in 2010." *Rhetoric Review* 30 (2): 109–34. https://doi.org/10.1080/07350198.2011.551497.

Alves, Jaime Osterman. 2009. *Fictions of Female Education in the Nineteenth Century.* New York: Routledge.

Archer, Ada. 1884. "Advocate Correspondence." *Cherokee Advocate,* July 25, 1884.

Archibald, Jo-ann. 2008. *Indigenous Storywork: Educating the Heart, Mind, Body, and Spirit.* Vancouver: UBC Press.

Archibald, Jo-ann, Jenny Lee-Morgan, and Jason De Santolo. 2019. *Decolonizing Research: Indigenous Storywork as Methodology.* London: Zed Books, Ltd.

Armor, Annie Williams. 2013. "Annie Williams Armor Interview." In *Voices of Cherokee Women,* edited by Carolyn Johnston. Real Voices, Real History. Winston-Salem, NC: Blair.

Arola, Kristin L. 2018. "Composing as Culturing: An American Indian Approach to Digital Ethics." In *Handbook of Writing, Literacies, and Education in Digital Cultures,* edited by Kathy Mills, 275–84. New York: Routledge.

Awiakta, Marilou. 1994. *Selu: Seeking the Corn-Mother's Wisdom.* Golden, CO: Fulcrum Pub.

Barad, Karen Michelle. 2007. *Meeting the Universe Halfway: Quantum Physics and the Entanglement of Matter and Meaning.* Durham, NC: Duke University Press.

Barthes, Roland. 1987. "The Death of the Author." In *Image, Music, Text.* Translated by Stephen Heath, 142–48. London: Fontana Press.

Bass, Althea. 1937. *A Cherokee Daughter of Mount Holyoke.* Muscatine, IA: The Prairie Press.

Bennett, Jane. 2010. *Vibrant Matter: A Political Ecology of Things.* Durham, NC: Duke University Press.

Berlin, James A. 1984. *Writing Instruction in Nineteenth-Century American Colleges.* Studies in Writing and Rhetoric. Carbondale: Southern Illinois University Press.

Bieseker, Barbara. 2006. "Of Historicity, Rhetoric: The Archive As Scene of Invention." *Rhetoric and Public Affairs* 9 (1): 124–31.

Brereton, John C., ed. 1995. *The Origins of Composition Studies in the American College, 1875–1925: A Documentary History.* Pittsburgh Series in Composition, Literacy, and Culture. Pittsburgh, PA: University of Pittsburgh Press.

Brooks, Lisa Tanya. 2008. *The Common Pot: The Recovery of Native Space in the Northeast.* Indigenous Americas Series. Minneapolis: University of Minnesota Press.

Brown, Kirby. 2018. *Stoking the Fire: Nationhood in Cherokee Writing, 1907–1970.* Norman: University of Oklahoma Press.

Brown, Kirby. 2019. "OsiyoTV and the Production of Cherokee Nationhood in the Twenty-First Century." Presented at the Native American and Indigenous Studies Association Conference, Hamilton, NZ, June 2019.

Carr, Jean Ferguson, Stephen L. Carr, and Lucille M. Schultz. 2005. *Archives of Instruction: Nineteenth-Century Rhetorics, Readers, and Composition Books in the United States.* Studies in Writing and Rhetoric. Carbondale: Southern Illinois University Press.

Casey, Edward S. 2009. *Getting Back into Place: Toward a Renewed Understanding of the Place-World.* 2nd ed. Studies in Continental Thought. Bloomington: Indiana University Press.

"Catalogue of Cherokee National Male Seminary 1886–87." 1887. Levison & Blythe Stationary. Northeastern State University Archives.

Césaire, Aimé, and Robin D. G. Kelley. 2000. *Discourse on Colonialism.* New York: Monthly Review Press.

Cherokee Advocate. 1847. "Laws of the Cherokee Nation Passed at the Annual Session of the National Council, 1846."

Cherokee Advocate. 1885. "Teachers Institute." June 26, 1885.

Cherokee National Female Seminary. 1906. *An Illustrated Souvenir Catalog of the Cherokee National Female Seminary, Tahlequah, Indian Territory, 1850–1906.* Chiloco, OK: Indian Print Shop.

Cherokee Rose Buds. 1854. "A Dialogue Between Susan and Ellen," August 2, 1854.

Chilisa, Bagele. 2012. *Indigenous Research Methodologies.* Thousand Oaks, CA: SAGE Publications.

Connors, Robert J. 2016. "Dreams and Play: Historical Method and Methodology." In *Landmark Essays on Archival Research*, edited by Lynée Lewis Gaillet, Diana Eidson, and Don Gammill, 50–62. Landmark Essays Series. New York: Routledge/Taylor & Francis Group.

Corrine. 1854. "Rose Buds." *Cherokee Rose Buds*, August 2, 1854.

Cruikshank, Julie. 2005. *Do Glaciers Listen? Local Knowledge, Colonial Encounters, and Social Imagination.* 1st ed. Seattle: University of Washington Press.

Cushman, E. 2010. "The Cherokee Syllabary from Script to Print." *Ethnohistory* 57 (4): 625–49. https://doi.org/10.1215/00141801-2010-039.

Cushman, Ellen. 2011. *The Cherokee Syllabary: Writing the People's Perseverance.* American Indian Literature and Critical Studies Series, v. 56. Norman: University of Oklahoma Press.

Daily American. 1885. "Monteagle: A Summer Home and Health Resort for Christian People," July 12, 1885.

de Certeau, Michel. 2013. *The Practice of Everyday Life.* Berkeley: University of California Press.

Deleuze, Gilles, and Félix Guattari. 1987. *A Thousand Plateaus: Capitalism and Schizophrenia.* Minneapolis: University of Minnesota Press.

Deloria, Vine. 1988. *Custer Died for Your Sins: An Indian Manifesto.* Norman: University of Oklahoma Press.

Deloria, Vine. 1997. *Red Earth, White Lies: Native Americans and the Myth of Scientific Fact.* Golden, CO: Fulcrum Publishing.

Deloria, Vine. 2001. "American Indian Metaphysics." In *Power and Place: Indian Education in America*, 1–6. Golden, CO: Fulcrum Publishing.

Deloria, Vine. 2003. *God Is Red: A Native View of Religion.* 3rd ed. Golden, CO: Fulcrum Publishing.

Deloria, Vine. 2007. *We Talk, You Listen: New Tribes, New Turf.* Bison Books ed. Lincoln: University of Nebraska Press.

Deloria, Vine, Barbara Deloria, Kristen Foehner, and Samuel Scinta. 1999. *Spirit and Reason: The Vine Deloria, Jr., Reader.* Golden, CO: Fulcrum Publishing.

Derrida, Jacques, and Eric Prenowitz. 1995. "Archive Fever: A Freudian Impression." *Diacritics* 25 (2): 9. https://doi.org/10.2307/465144.

Driskill, Qwo-Li. 2010. "Doubleweaving Two-Spirit Critiques: Building Alliances between Native and Queer Studies." *GLQ: A Journal of Lesbian and Gay Studies* 16 (1–2): 69–92. https://doi.org/10.1215/10642684-2009-013.

Driskill, Qwo-Li. 2015. "Decolonial Skillshares: Indigenous Rhetorics as Radical Practice." In *Survivance, Sovereignty, and Story: Teaching American Indian Rhetorics*, edited by Lisa King, Rose Gubele, and Joyce Rain Anderson, 57–78. Logan: Utah State University Press.

Driskill, Qwo-Li. 2016. *Asegi Stories: Cherokee Queer and Two-Spirit Memory*. Tucson: The University of Arizona Press.

Duchein, Michel. 1992. "The History of European Archives and the Development of the Archival Profession in Europe." *American Archivist* 55: 14–24.

Duncan, Barbara R., and Davey Arch, eds. 1998. *Living Stories of the Cherokee*. Chapel Hill: University of North Carolina Press.

Duncan, Elizabeth, and Lucinda M. Ross. 1855. "Exchanges." *Wreath of the Cherokee Rose Buds*, August 1, 1855.

Enoch, Jessica. 2008. *Refiguring Rhetorical Education: Women Teaching African American, Native American, and Chicano/a Students, 1865–1911*. Carbondale: Southern Illinois University Press.

Fierreia-Buckley, Linda. 1999. "Rescuing the Archives from Foucault." *College English* 61 (5): 577–83.

Freshwater, Helen. 2003. "The Allure of the Archive." *Poetics Today* 24 (4): 729–58.

Fry, Maggie Culver, ed. 1988. *Cherokee Female Seminary Years: A Cherokee National Anthology*. 1st ed. Claremore, OK: Rogers State College Press.

Glenn, Cheryl, and Jessica Enoch. 2010. "Invigorating Historiographic Practices in Rhetoric and Composition Studies." In *Working in the Archives: Practical Research Methods for Rhetoric and Composition*, edited by Alexis E. Ramsey, 11–27. Carbondale: Southern Illinois University Press.

Gold, David. 2008. *Rhetoric at the Margins: Revising the History of Writing Instruction in American Colleges, 1873–1947*. Carbondale: Southern Illinois University Press.

Gold, David. 2012. "Remapping Revisionist Historiography." *College Composition and Communication* 64 (1): 15–34.

Gonzales, Laura, Josephine Walwema, Natasha N. Jones, Han Yu, and Miriam F. Williams. 2021. "Narratives from the Margins: Centering Women of Color in Technical Communication." In *Equipping Technical Communicators for Social Justice Work: Theories, Methodologies, and Pedagogies*, edited by Rebecca W. Walton and Godwin Agboka, 1st ed., 15–32. Logan: Utah State University Press.

Gubele, Rose. 2012. "Utalotsa Woni—'Talking Leaves': A Re-Examination of the Cherokee Syllabary and Sequoyah." *Studies in American Indian Literatures* 24 (4): 47–76. https://doi.org/10.5250/studamerindilite.24.4.0047.

Gubele, Rose. 2015. "Unlearning the Pictures in Our Heads: Teaching the Cherokee Phoenix, Boudinot, and Cherokee History." In *Survivance, Sovereignty, and Story: Teaching American Indian Rhetorics*, edited by Lisa King, Rose Gubele, and Joyce Rain Anderson, 96–115. Logan: Utah State University Press.

Haas, Angela. 2007. "Wampum as Hypertext: An American Indian Intellectual Tradition of Multimedia Theory and Practice." *Studies in American Indian Literatures* 19 (4): 77–110.

Haas, Angela. 2012. "Race, Rhetoric, and Technology." *Journal of Business and Technical Communication* 26 (3): 277–310.

Henry, Gordon D., Jr., Nieves Pascual Soler, and Silvia Martínez-Falquina, eds. 2012. *Stories through Theories, Theories through Stories: North American Indian Writing, Storytelling, and Critique*. East Lansing: Michigan State University Press.

Holmes, Ruth Bradley, and Betty Smith Sharp. 1989. *Beginning Cherokee*. 2nd ed. Norman: University of Oklahoma Press.

Huckaby, Anna. n.d. "The Cherokee Rosebuds." Cherokee Nation. Accessed March 1, 2019. www.cherokee.org/About-The-Nation/History/Facts/The-Cherokee-Rosebuds.

Icy. 1855. "The Two Companions." *Wreath of the Cherokee Rose Buds*, February 14, 1855.

Ingold, Tim. 2008. "When ANT Meets SPIDER: Social Theory for Arthropods." In *Material Agency*, edited by Carl Knappett and Lambros Malafouris, 209–15. Boston, MA: Springer US. https://doi.org/10.1007/978-0-387-74711-8_11.

Ingold, Tim. 2011. *The Perception of the Environment: Essays on Livelihood, Dwelling and Skill*. London: Routledge, Taylor & Francis Group.

Jaimes*Guerrero, M. A. 2003. " 'Patriarchal Colonialism' and Indigenism: Implications for Native Feminist Spirituality and Native Womanism." *Hypatia* 18 (2): 58–69.

Johnson, Gene. 2021. "Tribes Sue to Stop Relocation of Rare Documents." *Indian Country Today*, January 4, 2021. https://indiancountrytoday.com/news/tribes-sue-to-stop-relocation-of-rare-documents-3wsWTPgofka-vOAV1Uoj2g?fbclid=wAR1b_85aTI2diFaM_LGsjAiE2dwBdNUovRnTTcx3REKnGMnW8llhmoUuweQ.

Johnston, Carolyn. 2003. *Cherokee Women in Crisis: Trail of Tears, Civil War, and Allotment, 1838–1907*. Contemporary American Indian Studies. Tuscaloosa: University of Alabama Press.

Justice, Daniel Heath. 2006. *Our Fire Survives the Storm: A Cherokee Literary History*. Indigenous Americas. Minneapolis: University of Minnesota Press.

Justice, Daniel Heath. 2018. *Why Indigenous Literatures Matter*. Indigenous Studies Series. Waterloo, Ontario, Canada: Wilfrid Laurier University Press.

Kilpatrick, Jack F., and Anna G. Kilpatrick. 1965a. *The Shadow of Sequoyah: Social Documents of the Cherokee, 1862–1964*. 1st ed. Norman: University of Oklahoma Press.

Kilpatrick, Jack F., and Anna G. Kilpatrick. 1965b. *Walk in Your Soul: Love Incantations of the Oklahoma Cherokees*. Dallas, TX: Southern Methodist University Press.

Kimmerer, Robin Wall. 2013. *Braiding Sweetgrass: Indigenous Wisdom, Scientific Knowledge and the Teachings of Plants*. 1st ed. Minneapolis, MN: Milkweed Editions.

King, Lisa. 2017. *Legible Sovereignties: Rhetoric, Representations, and Native American Museums*. Corvallis: Oregon State University Press.

King, Lisa, Rose Gubele, and Joyce Rain Anderson, eds. 2015. *Survivance, Sovereignty, and Story: Teaching American Indian Rhetorics*. Logan: Utah State University Press.

King, Thomas. 2005. *The Truth about Stories: A Native Narrative*. Indigenous Americas. Minneapolis: University of Minnesota Press.

Kirsch, Gesa. 2008. "Being on Location: Serendipity, Place, and Archival Research." In *Beyond the Archives: Research as a Lived Process*, edited by Gesa Kirsch and Liz Rohan, 20–27. Carbondale: Southern Illinois University Press.

Kitzhaber, Albert R. 1990. *Rhetoric in American Colleges, 1850–1900*. 1st ed. SMU Studies in Composition and Rhetoric. Dallas, TX: Southern Methodist University Press.

Klotz, Sarah. 2021. *Writing Their Bodies: Restoring Rhetorical Relations at the Carlisle Indian School*. Logan: Utah State University Press.

LaDuke, Winona. 2015. *All Our Relations: Native Struggles for Land and Life*. Chicago, IL: Haymarket Books.

Larsen, Soren C., Jay T. Johnson, and Daniel R. Wildcat. 2017. *Being Together in Place: Indigenous Coexistence in a More than Human World*. Minneapolis: University of Minnesota Press.

Latour, Bruno. 2007. *Reassembling the Social: An Introduction to Actor-Network-Theory*. Clarendon Lectures in Management Studies. Oxford: Oxford University Press.

Lee, Kimberli. 2015. "Heartspeak from the Spirit." In *Survivance, Sovereignty, and Story: Teaching American Indian Rhetorics*, edited by Lisa King, Rose Gubele, and Joyce Rain Anderson, 116–37. Logan: Utah State University Press.

Lee, Robert, and Ahtone, Tristan. 2020. "Land-Grab Universities." *High Country News*, March 30, 2020. https://www.hcn.org/issues/52.4/indigenous-affairs-education-land-grab-universities.

Legg, Emily. 2014. "Daughters of the Seminaries: Re-Landscaping History through the Composition Courses at the Cherokee Female Seminary." *College Composition and Communication* 66 (1): 67–90.

Leila. 1855. "Critics and Criticism." *Cherokee Rose Buds*, February 14, 1855.
Locke-Stow, Sarah D. 1887. *History of Mount Holyoke Seminary, South Hadley, Mass., during Its First Half Century, 1837–1887*. Springfield: Springfield Printing Co.
Lyons, Scott Richard. 2000. "Rhetorical Sovereignty: What Do American Indians Want from Writing?" *College Composition and Communication* 51 (3): 447. https://doi.org/10.2307/358744.
Lyons, Scott Richard. 2010. *X-Marks: Native Signatures of Assent*. Indigenous Americas. Minneapolis: University of Minnesota Press.
Lyotard, Jean-François. 1984. *The Postmodern Condition: A Report on Knowledge*. Theory and History of Literature. Vol. 10. Minneapolis: University of Minnesota Press.
Mallon, Florencia E. 2012. "Introduction: Decolonizing Knowledge, Language, and Narrative." In *Decolonizing Native Histories: Collaboration, Knowledge, and Language in the Americas*, edited by Florencia E. Mallon, 1–19. Narrating Native Histories. Durham, NC: Duke University Press.
Mankiller, Wilma, and Michael Wallis. 1993. *Mankiller: A Chief and Her People*. 1st ed. New York: St. Martin's Press.
Maracle, Lee. 2015. *Memory Serves: Oratories*. Writer as Critic 13. Edmonton, AB: NeWest Press.
Mastrangelo, Lisa. 1999. "Learning from the Past: Rhetoric, Composition, and Debate at Mount Holyoke College." *Rhetoric Review* 18 (1): 46–65.
Mastrangelo, Lisa. 2012. *Writing a Progressive Past: Women Teaching and Writing in the Progressive Era*. Anderson, SC: Parlor Press.
McGowan, Kay Givens. 2006. "Weeping for the Lost Matriarchy." In *Daughters of Mother Earth: The Wisdom of Native American Women*, edited by Barbara Alice Mann, 53–68. Native America. Westport, CT: Praeger.
Mignolo, Walter. 2011. *The Darker Side of Western Modernity: Global Futures, Decolonial Options*. Latin America Otherwise: Languages, Empires, Nations. Durham, NC: Duke University Press.
Mihesuah, Devon A. 1998. *Cultivating the Rosebuds: The Education of Women at the Cherokee Female Seminary, 1851–1909*. Urbana: University of Illinois Press.
Mihesuah, Devon A. 2006. " 'Indigenizing the Academy': Keynote Talk at the Sixth Annual American Indian Studies Consortium Conference, Arizona State University, February 10–11, 2005." *Wicazo Sa Review* 21 (1): 127–38.
Moon, Gretchen Flesher. 2007. "Locating Composition History." In *Local Histories: Reading the Archives of Composition*, edited by Patricia Donahue and Gretchen Flesher Moon, 1–13. Pittsburgh Series in Composition, Literacy, and Culture. Pittsburgh, PA: Pittsburgh Press.
Mooney, James. 1982. *Myths of the Cherokee and Sacred Formulas of the Cherokees*. Nashville, TN: Charles Elder.
Moulder, Amanda. 2011. "Literacy Learning among Early Nineteenth Century Cherokee Women." *College Composition and Communication* 63 (1): 75–97.
Mount Holyoke Seminary. 1867. *Thirtieth Annual Catalogue of the Mount Holyoke Female Seminary in South Hadley, Mass, 1866–67*. Northampton: Bridgman & Childs, Publishers.
Na-Li. 1854. "An Address to the Females of the Cherokee Nation." *Cherokee Rose Buds*, August 2, 1854.
Na-Li, and Fanny. 1855. "Two Scenes on Cherokee Land." *Wreath of the Cherokee Rose Buds*, February 14, 1855, sec. 1–2.
Nelson, Joshua B. 2014. *Progressive Traditions: Identity in Cherokee Literature and Culture*. American Indian Literature and Critical Studies Series. Vol. 61. Norman: University of Oklahoma Press.
O'Neal, Jennifer R. 2015. " 'The Right to Know': Decolonizing Native American Archives." *Journal of Western Archives* 6 (1). https://digitalcommons.usu.edu/westernarchives/vol6/iss1/2/.

Ong, Walter J. 2009. *Orality and Literacy: The Technologizing of the Word*. Reprinted. New Accents. London: Routledge.

OsiyoTV. 2020. "Knowledge Is Meant to Be Shared: Cherokee National Treasure Noel Grayson." https://www.youtube.com/watch?v=ACEmMhBZQjo.

Parins, James W. 2013. *Literacy and Intellectual Life in the Cherokee Nation, 1820–1906*. American Indian Literature and Critical Studies Series. Norman: University of Oklahoma Press.

Parker, Richard Green. 1875. *Aids to English Composition Prepared for Students of All Grades*. 20th ed. New York: Harper Brothers.

Parker, William Riley. 1967. "Where Do English Departments Come From?" *College English* 28 (5): 339–51.

Perdue, Theda. 1999. *Cherokee Women: Gender and Culture Change, 1700–1835*. Lincoln: University of Nebraska Press.

Powell, Malea. 1999. "Blood and Scholarship: One Mixed-Blood's Story." In *Race, Rhetoric, and Composition*, edited by Keith Gilyard, 1–16. CrossCurrents. Portsmouth, NH: Boynton/Cook.

Powell, Malea. 2002. "Rhetorics of Survivance: How American Indians Use Writing." *College Composition and Communication* 53 (3): 396. https://doi.org/10.2307/1512132.

Powell, Malea. 2008. "Dreaming Charles Eastman: Cultural Memory, Autobiography, and Geography in Indigenous Rhetorical Histories." In *Beyond the Archives: Research as a Lived Process*, edited by Gesa Kirsch and Liz Rohan, 115–27. Carbondale: Southern Illinois University Press.

Powell, Malea. 2014. "A Basket Is a Basket Because . . . : Telling a Native Rhetorics Story." In *The Oxford Handbook of Indigenous American Literature*, edited by James H. Cox and Daniel Heath Justice, 471–88. Oxford: Oxford University Press. https://doi.org/10.1093/oxfordhb/9780199914036.013.037.

Powell, Malea, Daisy Levy, Andrea Riley-Mukavetz, Marilee Brooks-Gillies, Maria Novotny, and Jennifer Fische-Ferguson. 2014. "Our Story Begins Here: Constellating Cultural Rhetorics." *Enculturation: A Journal of Rhetoric and Culture* 18 (October). http://enculturation.net/our-story-begins-here.

Qua-Tsy. 1855. "Female Influence." *Cherokee Rose Buds*, February 14, 1855.

Reed, Julie L. 2016. *Serving the Nation: Cherokee Sovereignty and Social Welfare, 1800–1907*. New Directions in Native American Studies. Vol. 14. Norman: University of Oklahoma Press.

Rifkin, Mark. 2017. *Beyond Settler Time: Temporal Sovereignty and Indigenous Self-Determination*. Durham, NC: Duke University Press.

Riley Mukavetz, Andrea. 2014. "Towards a Cultural Rhetorics Methodology: Making Research Matter with Multi-Generational Women from the Little Traverse Bay Band." *Rhetoric, Professional Communication, and Globalization* 5 (1): 108–25.

Ritter, Kelly. 2016. "Archival Research in Composition Studies: Re-Imagining the Historian's Role." In *Landmark Essays on Archival Research*, edited by Lynée Lewis Gaillet, Diana Eidson, and Don Gammill, 280–94. Landmark Essays Series. New York: Routledge/Taylor & Francis Group.

Round, Phillip H. 2010. *Removable Type: Histories of the Book in Indian Country, 1663–1880*. Chapel Hill: University of North Carolina Press.

Royster, Jacqueline Jones. 1996. "When the First Voice You Hear Is Not Your Own." *College Composition and Communication* 47 (1): 29–40.

Royster, Jacqueline Jones. 2000. *Traces of a Stream: Literacy and Social Change among African American Women*. Pittsburgh Series in Composition, Literacy, and Culture. Pittsburgh, PA: University of Pittsburgh Press.

Royster, Jacqueline Jones, and Gesa Kirsch. 2012. *Feminist Rhetorical Practices: New Horizons for Rhetoric, Composition, and Literacy Studies*. Carbondale: Southern Illinois University Press.

Schultz, Lucille M. 1999. *The Young Composers: Composition's Beginnings in Nineteenth-Century Schools.* Studies in Writing and Rhetoric. Carbondale: Southern Illinois University Press.
Sequoyah Memorial. 1855. [Editorial remarks], August 2, 1855.
Sequoyah Memorial. 1857a. "Newspapers," July 31, 1857. Beinecke Rare Book and Manuscript Library, Yale University.
Sequoyah Memorial. 1857b. "The American Indian," July 31, 1857.
Sharer, Wendy B. 2008. "Traces of the Familiar: Family Archives as Primary Source Material." In *Beyond the Archives: Research as a Lived Process,* edited by Gesa Kirsch and Liz Rohan, 47–55. Carbondale: Southern Illinois University Press.
Silko, Leslie Marmon. 2012. *Storyteller.* New York: Penguin Books.
Smith, Linda Tuhiwai. 2012. *Decolonizing Methodologies: Research and Indigenous Peoples.* 2nd ed. London: Zed Books.
Starr, Emmet. 1921. *History of the Cherokee Indians and Their Legends and Folk Lore.* Oklahoma City: Warden Company.
Steedman, Carolyn. 2002. *Dust: The Archive and Cultural History.* Encounters. New Brunswick, NJ: Rutgers University Press.
Strantz, Adam. 2015. "Wayfinding in Global Contexts—Mapping Localized Research Practices with Mobile Devices." *Computers and Composition* 38 (December): 164–76. https://doi.org/10.1016/j.compcom.2015.09.008.
Stromberg, Ernest. 2006. "Rhetoric and American Indians: An Introduction." In *American Indian Rhetorics of Survivance: Word Medicine, Word Magic,* edited by Ernest Stromberg, 1–14. Pittsburgh Series in Composition, Literacy, and Culture. Pittsburgh, PA: University of Pittsburgh Press.
Sullivan, Patricia, and James E. Porter. 1997. *Opening Spaces: Writing Technologies and Critical Research Practices.* New Directions in Computers and Composition Studies. Greenwich, CT: Ablex Publishing Corporation.
TBW. 1855. "The Seminaries." *Sequoyah Memorial,* August 2, 1855.
"'Teacher's Institute of the Cherokee Nation: July 5, 1882' Meeting Notes." 1882. Northeastern State University Archives.
Teuton, Christopher B. 2008. "Theorizing American Indian Literature: Applying Oral Concepts to Written Traditions." In *Reasoning Together: The Native Critics Collective,* edited by Janice Acoose, Craig S. Womack, Daniel Heath Justice, and Christopher B. Teuton, 193–215. Norman: University of Oklahoma Press.
Teuton, Christopher B. 2010. *Deep Waters: The Textual Continuum in American Indian Literature.* Lincoln: University of Nebraska Press.
Teuton, Christopher B. 2012. *Cherokee Stories of the Turtle Island Liars' Club: Dakasi Elohi Anigagoga Junilawisdii (Turtle, Earth, the Liars, Meeting Place).* Chapel Hill: University of North Carolina Press.
"Tom Belt: Cherokee Language Teacher." 2011. Western Carolina University Mountain Heritage Center. Accessed May 25, 2023. https://southernappalachiandigitalcollections.org/object/11676.
Toulmin, Stephen. 1992. *Cosmopolis: The Hidden Agenda of Modernity.* University of Chicago Press ed. Chicago: University of Chicago Press.
Trafzer, Clifford E., ed. 1993. *Earth Song, Sky Spirit: Short Stories of the Contemporary Native American Experience.* 1st ed. New York: Anchor Books.
Villanueva, Victor. 2008. "Colonial Memory, Colonial Research: A Preamble to a Case Study." In *Beyond the Archives: Research as a Lived Process,* edited by Gesa Kirsch and Liz Rohan, 83–92. Carbondale: Southern Illinois University Press.
Vizenor, Gerald Robert, ed. 1993. *Narrative Chance: Postmodern Discourse on Native American Indian Literatures.* American Indian Literature and Critical Studies Series 8. Norman: Univ. of Oklahoma Press.
Vizenor, Gerald Robert. 2003. *Wordarrows: Native States of Literary Sovereignty.* Lincoln: University of Nebraska Press.

W. 1856. "A Glance at the Past and Present Condition of the Cherokees." *Sequoyah Memorial,* July 31, 1856.
Walters, Karina L., Selina A. Mohammed, Teresa Evans-Campbell, Ramona E. Beltrán, David H. Chae, and Bonnie Duran. 2011. "Bodies Don't Just Tell Stories, They Tell Histories: Embodiment of Historical Trauma among American Indians and Alaska Natives." *Du Bois Review: Social Science Research on Race* 8 (1): 179–89. https://doi.org/10.1017/S1742058X1100018X.
Wam-Da. 1855. "Literary Societies." *Sequoyah Memorial,* July 31, 1855.
Weaver, Jace. 1997. *That the People Might Live: Native American Literatures and Native American Community.* New York: Oxford University Press.
White, Hayden. 1984. "The Question of Narrative in Contemporary Historical Theory." *History and Theory* 23 (1): 1. https://doi.org/10.2307/2504969.
Whitmore, Ellen. 1953. *The Journal of Ellen Whitmore.* Edited by Lola Garrett Bowers and Kathleen Garrett. Tahlequah, OK: Northeastern State College.
Wieser, Kimberly G. 2017. *Back to the Blanket: Recovered Rhetorics and Literacies in American Indian Studies.* American Indian Literature and Critical Studies Series. Vol. 70. Norman: University of Oklahoma Press.
Wildcat, Daniel R. 2001a. "Indigenizing Education: Playing to Our Strengths." In *Power and Place: Indian Education in America,* 7–19. Golden, CO: Fulcrum Publishing.
Wildcat, Daniel R. 2001b. "The Schizophrenic Nature of Western Metaphysics." In *Power and Place: Indian Education in America,* 47–55. Golden, CO: Fulcrum Publishing.
Wilson, Shawn. 2008. *Research Is Ceremony: Indigenous Research Methods.* Halifax, Nova Scotia: Fernwood Publishing.
Wilson, Shawn, and Margaret Hughes. 2019. "Why Research Is Reconciliation." In *Research and Reconciliation: Unsettling Ways of Knowing through Indigenous Relationships,* edited by Shawn Wilson, Andrea V Breen, and Lindsay DuPré, 5–19. Toronto: Canadian Scholars.
Womack, Craig S. 2008. "Theorizing American Indian Experience." In *Reasoning Together: The Native Critics Collective,* edited by Janice Acoose, Craig S. Womack, Daniel Heath Justice, and Christopher B. Teuton, 353–410. Norman: University of Oklahoma Press.
Wreath of the Cherokee Rose Buds. 1855. [Editorial remarks]. August 1, 1855.
Wreath of the Cherokee Rose Buds. 1857. "A Week at the Female Seminary," February 11, 1857.

INDEX

Page numbers followed by *f* indicate a figure; page numbers followed by *n* indicate an endnote.

academia, 47, 196, 224*n1*, 237
accompliceship, 237–38
accountability, 16, 51, 52, 230, 238
acculturation, 187, 193, 211
actor-network theory (ANT), 19; Grandmother Water Spider/SPIDER and, 92–95
Adam and Eve, 111
Adams Corner, 144
"Address to the Families of the Cherokee Nation, An" (Na-Li), 203
"Address to the Whites, An" (Boudinot), 210
agents, 116; human/nonhuman, 88, 93, 95, 97, 128, 129; material/nonmaterial, 129
Aids to English Composition (Parker), 188–89
Alaska Natives, 225
"American Indian, The," 212–13
American Journal of Education, 155*n7*
ancestors, 9, 21, 134, 230–31, 238; Euroamerican, 56; knowledge-making and, 16, 19; places/spaces and, 75; present-ability of, 239; sharing knowledge with, 226–29; social distancing and, 225; walking with, 223
Anderson, Joyce Rain, 112
Ani-kutani, 22, 169–71, 175, 176, 184, 216
Anishinabe, 233
anotlvsv dunadadudalv, 18, 27
ANT. *See* actor-network theory
Apaches, 76
Archer, Ada, 157–58
Archibald Q'um Q'um Xiiem, Jo-ann, 56, 124
archival locations, 67–71
archival research, 8, 10, 19, 22, 38, 39, 46, 53, 64, 66, 72, 73, 88, 109, 110, 114, 238, 240; cautionary tale of, 29–32; constellating practices in, 83; cultural context and, 86; foundations of, 61; Indigenous approach to, 20; using, 55
archives, 17, 70–71, 83, 100, 114, 116, 177, 217, 240; appealing to, 73; Cherokee context of, 138; classificatory system for, 18; cultural places of, 73; listening to, 186–93; materiality of, 72; more-than-human participants of, 239; Native Americans in, 61–64; (re)membering in, 75–77; rhetorical beings of, 71–77; as storytellers, 114
Archives de France, 66
Archives of Instruction: Nineteenth Century Rhetorics, Readers, and Composition Books in the United States (Carr, Carr, and Schultz), 45
arkhe, 18
Armor, Cynthia "Annie" (Williams), 30, 76, 76*f*, 77
Armstrong, Jeanne, 89
Arola, Kristin, 83–84
artifacts, 63, 114, 117, 179; archival, 64, 73, 89; culling, 71; institutional, 20; living, 75; materiality of, 110; responsibility to, 89
Aspasia, 206
assimilation, 18, 19, 23, 30, 38, 67, 82, 135, 138, 140, 154, 155, 167, 173, 186, 198, 205, 207, 211; academic, 232; civilization and, 210; cultural, 58; erasure and, 43, 49, 123, 134, 183, 194; Eurocentric models of, 21; evidence of, 22; performance of, 212; pressures of, 188; resisting, 217–18; stories of, 136, 143; tradition and, 165; uncomfortable coding of, 133; white-presenting, 14
authority, 18, 69, 73, 108, 111, 112, 125, 182, 224; air of, 124; sharing, 106; slippage in, 126
Awiakta, Marilou, 90, 96, 106, 113, 167

Bacon, Kevin, 30
balance, 101, 107, 157, 176, 182, 198; founding in, 136–43; gender, 144, 187
Banks, Paden, 164
Barnard, Henry, 155*n7*
baskets, 98–101; double-walled, 101, 233*f*. *See also* weaving

Bass, Althea, 150
Basso, Keith, 76, 127*n*2
Battle of Tippecanoe, 68
Bay, Jenny, 12
Bear, stories about, 8
Beaver, 61, 62, 63
Belt, Tom, 61, 119, 120, 122, 228; Kituwah and, 229
Belt That Would Not Burn, 100
Benjamin, aura and, 72, 178
Bergmann, Linda, 72
Berlin, James, 44, 51, 69, 187
bias, 20, 64, 66, 67
Big Daddy, 45
binaries, 133, 143, 165; oral-literate, 37, 124; oral-written, 181
BIPOC (Black, Indigenous, people of color), 36, 51, 240
Bird Clan, 141
Bishop, Allie Beth (Williams), 76*f*
Blackmon, Samantha, 12
Blair, 186
blood quantum, 165*n10*, 195
Boudinot, Elias, 153, 183, 208, 209, 210
Bowers, Lola Garrett, 146
Brahmins, 33, 169
Braiding Sweetgrass: Indigenous Wisdom, Scientific Knowledge, and the Teaching of Plants (Kimmerer), 13
Brereton, John C., 44, 45–46, 51, 69, 187
Brockett, Linus Pierpont, 155*n*7
Brooks, Lisa, 98, 99, 127*n*2
Brown, Kirby, 39, 227, 228
Bureau of Indian Affairs, 178
Burton, LaVar, 125

Campbell, C. H., 186, 201
Carlisle Indian Industrial School, 43, 50, 194
Carr, Jean Ferguson, 188–89
Carr, Stephen L., 188–89
Casey, Edward, 73
ceremonies, 230; Cherokee, 15, 17–25, 104, 227
Césaire, Aimé, 37–38
Chapin, Mary, 147
Cherokee Advocate, 137, 156, 157, 184, 200, 228
Cherokee Constitution (1839), 40
Cherokee Council House, 61
Cherokee Female Seminary, 7, 23, 29, 32, 48–49, 52, 59, 60, 76, 139*f*, 140, 144, 145, 147, 157, 159, 163, 189, 201, 205, 217, 230, 234; attending, 77; colonization/assimilation/gender and, 19; control of, 42–43; course offerings at, 187; fire at, 5, 6, 42; history of, 65; publications by, 197; rebuilding, 6; storytelling and, 16; teaching at, 185, 194
Cherokee Heritage Center, 144, 145*f*, 195
Cherokee Heritage Museum, 217*n*4
Cherokee Language Council, 203
Cherokee Language Program (Western Carolina University), 61
Cherokee Male Seminary, 6, 7, 201, 234; course offerings at, 187, 188; photo of, 138; publications by, 197; teaching at, 194
Cherokee medicine wheel, 16, 33, 83, 104, 238, 239; map of, 15*f*; pathways of, 101–2; as research methodology, 15
Cherokee Nation, 6, 22, 31, 32, 40, 43, 60, 61, 65, 77, 133, 137, 142, 147, 152, 154, 156, 164, 166, 175, 183, 184, 193, 194, 197, 198, 199; assimilation and, 136; brain drain from, 153; citizenship in, 165*n10*; Civil War and, 42, 42*n*4; community gatherings in, 151*n*3; dark ages for, 185; education on, 143–44, 146, 149, 155, 157–58, 159, 167; enrollment in, 11; language/writing and, 173; learning in, 179; Mount Holyoke and, 149, 187; nationhood and, 41; people/citizens of, 228; Pocahontas Club and, 151*n*2; political aims of, 208; political history of, 57; sovereignty of, 172; welfare of, 151
Cherokee Nation Constitution, approval of, 49
Cherokee Nation Heritage Center, 30, 32
Cherokee Nation v. Georgia, 40, 172, 213
Cherokee National Seminaries, 9, 14, 15, 17, 18, 32, 38, 57, 73, 77, 83, 84, 107, 109, 117, 140, 177, 194, 196, 224, 226, 233, 238; archives of, 7, 60, 61, 129, 225; attending, 163–64; collections at, 67; histories of, 7, 16, 21, 56, 58, 166; language and, 181; origin story of, 39, 40–44; research on, 133–34, 150; rhetorical curriculum of, 51; students from, 161*f*; teaching at, 25; timeline of, 41*f*
Cherokee Origin of Stories, 38
Cherokee Orphan Asylum, 153, 154*n*5
Cherokee Phoenix, 183, 184, 197, 203, 208, 227–28
Cherokee Rose Buds, 166, 189, 200, 201, 214, 217, 218, 219; civilization and, 209; copy of, 201*f*; history of, 197–98; ideals in, 207; true womanhood and, 205–7; writing in, 202–5, 207–8
Cherokee society, 137, 145, 212, 216; changes for, 134; decline of, 185; structure of balance and, 140

Cherokee Stories of the Turtle Island Liars' Club (Teuton), 118
Cherokee Trading Post, 236
Cherokee women: divorce and, 141; education and, 144, 146, 147, 148, 156, 159, 206–7; gender expectations for, 205, 206; leadership/equality and, 141, 143; marriage and, 141–42; role of, 206, 215; spiritual/physical strength of, 162; survivance of, 143–53; writing of, 23, 202–5
Cherokee-ness, 149, 167, 177, 178
Chickamauga Wars, 172, 211
Chickasaws, 40, 175$n1$, 209
Chief Wahoo, 236
Chilisa, Bagele, 54
Chiloco Indian Agricultural School, 194
Choctaws, 40, 54, 152, 209, 175$n1$
Civil Rights Act, 185
Civil War, 5, 42, 42$n4$, 186
civilization, 113, 123, 169, 208; assimilation and, 210; nature and, 215; term, 209
civilized society, 175, 186, 209
clan system, 16, 141, 142, 216
classification, 18, 66, 113, 137
Cleopatra, 206
Clingman's Dome, 228
Collins, Mae, 151
colonial structures, 20, 24, 85, 109
colonialism, 30, 56, 57, 60, 66, 82, 123, 218; Indigenous people and, 74; stories of, 129; trauma of, 74
colonization, 37, 49, 57, 67, 73, 75, 108, 140, 143, 154, 155, 163, 178, 180, 208, 210; resisting, 122; thingification and, 38
Common Pot, The (Brooks), 127$n2$
communication, 113, 114, 147, 181; ecologies of, 177; impulse of, 182; method of, 176; technical, 238
community, 74, 88, 146, 160, 164, 185, 223; building, 85, 240; consciousness of, 177; networked, 110; searching for, 90–91; sustaining, 126, 228
composition, 35, 53, 60, 69, 187, 193; Cherokee-centric, 177; classes, 188; current-traditionalist, 186; evidence of, 189; Harvard method of, 51; history of, 36, 46, 55, 56; instruction in, 186, 194; methods of, 190; origins of, 22; public, 183–86; relandscaping, 22; studies, 70, 155; teaching, 188; work of, 69
Connors, Robert J., 64, 65, 70, 71
constellating, 20, 23, 38, 39, 82, 83, 101, 102, 103, 198, 223; importance of, 217–18
Cooper, Marilyn, 90
Cooweescoowee District, 31
Corn Hunter, 119

Corn Mother, 23, 168, 207
Corrine, 190; poem by, 189, 189$n4$
councils of animals, stories of, 27
Creator, 34, 46, 84, 101
Creeks, 40, 152, 175$n1$, 209
critical practices, 177, 238, 239
Crowley, 51, 187
cult of true womanhood. *See* true womanhood
cultural networks, 39, 83
cultural practices, 36, 97, 108, 126, 153; Cherokee, 101, 125, 135, 142, 232
Cultural Rhetorics Theory Lab, 39, 82
culture, 7, 12, 14, 21, 38, 39, 43, 50, 53, 60, 64, 87, 101, 104, 107, 108, 118, 120, 121, 133–37, 142, 143, 145, 150, 151, 152, 153, 164, 165, 166, 167; children's, 8; Christian, 204; Eurocentric, 207; Indigenous, 25, 36, 88, 92, 99, 111, 112, 149, 199; keepers/life-givers of, 134, 163; metaphorical, 23; oral-based, 36, 37, 176, 178; physical, 160; preserving, 174, 197, 198; responsibility to, 89; ritualistic, 163; society and, 98; traditional, 216; written, 176
Culver, Maggie Waters, 160, 161, 162
current-traditionalism, 44–49, 51, 186, 187, 192
curriculum, 148, 150, 151, 155$n6$, 156; changes, 47; language/writing, 152$n4$
Curtis, Edward, 236
Curtis Act (1889), 42
Cushman, Ellen, 22, 173, 178, 180

Daily American, The, 157
Davis, Diane, 90
Dawes Act, 30, 185
Dawes Commission, 43, 165
Dawes Rolls, 11, 30, 165, 165$n10$
De Santolo, Jason, 56
de Stael, Madame, 206
decolonization, 20, 53, 54, 66–67, 71, 82, 231, 232, 234
Deleuze, Gilles, 91, 93
Deloria, Vine, Jr., 54, 86, 91, 97, 99, 113, 129, 134; on American society, 90; ecological thinking and, 114; ecology of participation and, 116; on Indigenous worldview, 127
Delphine (de Stael), 206
Derrida, Jacques, 18
"Dialogue Between Susan and Ellen, A" (*Cherokee Rose Buds*), 166
Digital Archives of Literacy Narratives (DAHL), 70$n3$
digitization, 66, 155, 217, 235, 236

Diligwa, 144
Discourse on Colonialism (Césaire), 37
Disney, Pocahontas and, 212
documentation, 70, 70n3, 72; curriculum-based, 68
Driskill, Qwo-Li, 39, 100, 101, 103, 226, 232; *duyuk'ta* and, 140; on weaving, 102
Duchein, Michel, 66
Duncan, Elizabeth, 200
duyuk'ta, 8, 9, 14, 21, 25, 97, 98, 100, 106, 107, 116, 127, 138, 144, 162, 182, 223, 226, 227, 230; construction of, 136; cultural practices of, 163; focus on, 17; maintaining, 125; ontological foundation of, 101; pedagogies of, 168; practicing, 109, 140, 219; restoring, 158; strive for, 238

Easter Sunday, 142, 164; fire on, 5, 6
Eastern Band of Cherokee Indians (EBCI), 49n5, 61, 101, 166n11, 228
Eastern Shawnee, 56
Eastman, Charles, 74, 75
Easy Exercises in Composition (Frost), 190
EBCI. *See* Eastern Band of Cherokee Indians
Echota, 101
ecology, 87, 91, 93, 95, 96, 106, 115; balancing, 97; biological, 94; closed-loop, 86; cultural, 19, 25, 193–94; Eurocentric, 92; Indigenous, 55, 97, 107, 114, 177; ontological, 86
education, 7, 9, 21, 32, 41, 42, 43, 58, 157–58, 159, 163, 164, 165, 167, 174, 186, 190, 200, 203, 208, 210, 218, 219, 241; approaches to, 57; Cherokee women and, 144, 146, 147, 148, 156, 159, 206–7; as civilized, 216; Eurocentric models of, 21, 58, 144, 149, 153; formal, 230; German model of, 48; higher, 42, 43, 44; importance of, 166, 171, 202, 215; Indigenous, 16, 22, 51; models of, 50, 146, 193; nineteenth-century, 48; promotion of, 40, 146; public, 143–53, 154; reform, 46; socially conscious, 148; sovereignty and, 136, 146; system, 209, 217; teacher, 157
Einstein, Albert, 97
Eliot, Charles, 47
Elizabeth, Queen, 151n2
Enlightenment, 24, 36, 52, 53, 56, 82, 91, 226, 240
Enoch, Jessica, 35, 49, 50, 51, 187
environment, 93, 97, 100, 110, 127
epistemologies, 35, 55, 98, 108, 110, 114, 121, 234; Cherokee, 16, 103; collapsing, 107; Eurocentric, 7, 86; Indigenous, 19, 86, 103, 236

erasure, 7, 23, 55, 74, 135, 143, 144, 149, 197, 198, 199, 208; assimilation and, 43, 49, 123, 134, 183, 194; cultural, 57; forced, 18, 122; policies of, 22, 141, 164; resisting, 207; story of, 142–43
Eurocentrism, 9, 16, 17, 35, 57, 74, 90, 92, 111, 113, 123, 140, 144, 149, 204, 226, 227; resisting, 143; writing/literacy and, 124, 126
Evans, J. B., 169
experiences, 23, 94, 104, 117, 166, 167; cultural, 233; epistemological, 97; Eurocentric model of, 96; Indigenous, 16, 24, 98, 176; ontological, 97

Family Educational Rights and Privacy Act (FERPA) (1974), 52, 53, 59, 59n1
Family History Center, 11
"Female Influence" (*Cherokee Rose Buds*), 205
FERPA. *See* Family Educational Rights and Privacy Act
First Nations, 103
Fite, Mrs. R. L., 230
Five Civilized Tribes, 133, 175n2, 209
Five Civilized Tribes Museum, 30, 175n1
Foreman, Grant, 76
Foucault, Michel, 54
Frederick, Jack, 179
Freshwater, 69
Frost, John, 190, 191
Fry, Maggie Culver, 153, 161, 163, 203n2
Frye, Professor, 157

gadugi, 227, 229
gagoga, 125, 127, 167
Garfield, James, 194
Garrett, Kathleen, 146
Geertz, Clifford, 87
gender, 19, 22, 82, 125, 156, 157, 162, 192, 193; balance, 144, 187; Cherokee understanding of, 136–37, 182, 207; harmony of, 140; social organization and, 137; society and, 140
gender roles, 187, 205, 206; balancing, 136–43
genealogy, 11, 30, 134, 195, 197
genocide, 36, 134, 225
Genung, John Franklin, 186
George, King, 172
gha, 179, 180, 181, 182
"Glance at the Past and Present Condition of the Cherokees, A" (W.), 213
Glenn, Cheryl, 35
Gold, David, 49, 50, 51, 56, 187

"Good, the Beautiful, and the True, The" (*Cherokee Rose Buds*), 205
Goodale, Ida Collins, 5
Graban, 51
grammar, 156, 187, 188, 192
Grandmother Water Spider, 19, 102, 135, 232; ANT and, 92–95; baskets and, 98–101, 107; relations and, 95–98; SPIDER and, 92–95; story of, 96, 99; weaving and, 97–98
Grayson, Noel, 226–27, 228
Great Smoky Mountains National Park, 228
Green Corn Ceremony, 23, 216
Green Corn Dance, 215
Gries, Laurie, 90
Guattari, Félix, 91, 93
Gubele, Rose, 112, 149, 203, 208
Guess, Sequoyah, 63*n*2, 83, 123

Haas, Angela, 103, 234
harmony, 158–59, 162, 167; balance and, 90, 96, 100, 204; collective, 128; philosophy of, 140
Harvard, 46, 49, 50, 51, 56, 69, 146; current-traditionalism and, 48; English program at, 47; model, 188, 189, 193
Harvard Plan, 47, 186, 188
Harvard Reports, 186, 187
Haskell Environmental Research Studies Center, 94
Haskell Indian Nations University, 194
Hawk, Byron, 90
Helen of Troy, 206
Henry, Gordon, Jr., 233
heritage, Cherokee, 7, 11, 30, 31, 64, 65, 144
Hill, Adams Sherman, 186
historiography, 19, 35, 36, 109, 179, 234; Indigenous dimensions of, 54
history, 31, 65, 71, 109, 118, 143, 151, 175, 176, 177, 193, 205, 208; disciplinary, 47, 55, 168; educational, 9, 232; Eurocentric, 23, 151*n*2; family, 11; Indigenous, 18, 19, 21, 35, 36, 38, 51, 223; oral, 70*n*3, 74; pedagogical, 9, 44, 68; publication, 197; revisionist, 51, 168; undocumented, 70; writing, 37
History and Progress of Education, from the Earliest Times to the Present: Intended as a Manual for Teachers and Students (Philobiblius), 155
Hobbs, 51
how, building, 127–29
Huckaby, Anna, 203
Hughes, Margaret, 51, 52

i:gawe:sdi, 181, 182
Icy, 203*n*2, 204
identity, 7, 21, 23, 58, 59, 163, 172, 184, 197, 202, 217, 240, 242; correct, 214; cultural, 173, 208; developing, 203, 208; group, 225; keepers/life-givers of, 134; legitimizing, 212; national, 39, 213; Native, 210, 218; performance of, 208
igatihaigvnedi dunadadudalv, 23, 221, 223
Iiv:n(e)dhi, 181, 182
Indian Allotment Act, 185
Indian Print Shop, 194
Indian Removal Act (1830), 40
Indian Removal strategy, 30–31
Indian Territory, 31, 40, 43, 58, 77, 142, 144, 145, 184, 184*n*3
Indiana Miami, 56
Indigenous Research Methodologies (Chilisa), 54
Indigenous scholars, 7, 24, 56*n*6, 112, 234, 236, 237
industriousness, 15, 16, 131
Ingold, Tim, 92, 96, 97; environmental meshworks and, 19; social theory of, 93; SPIDER and, 93, 94
intelligence, 15, 16, 40, 146
intercultural praxis, 102, 107, 129
isolation, 83, 84, 90, 102, 237

Jackson, Andrew, 22, 41, 49, 173, 210; Cherokees and, 40; defiance of, 217; removal policies of, 178
Jaimes*Guerrero, M.A.: racism/sexism and, 163
John the Baptist, 27
Johnston, Carolyn, 141
Justice, Daniel Heath, 39, 60

kalvgv, 17, 27, 33, 57, 58, 85
Kananeski Ama'i'yehi, 95. *See also* Ulisi Ama Kanonesgi
Kana'ti, 6, 23, 119, 137, 139, 140, 143, 145, 163, 215, 216; Selu and, 162; stories of, 22; teachings of, 155
kanuchi, 214–15*n*3
Keetowah Society, 42*n*4
Keetowahs, 61, 166, 166*n*1
Kilpatrick, Anna Gritts, 177, 179, 181, 182
Kilpatrick, John, 177, 181; on i:gawe:sdi, 182
Kimmerer, Robin Wall, 13, 14, 17, 88–89, 97–98
King, Lisa, 36*n*2, 112
King, Thomas, 34, 89–90, 110, 111, 128, 230; on time/place, 119
kinship, 86, 88, 100, 118, 124, 142, 227, 228; clan, 12, 162; communal, 166;

matrilineal, 141, 163; survivance of, 143–53
Kituwah, 61, 63, 119, 122, 228, 229
Kitzhaber, Albert, 44, 48, 51, 69
Klotz, Sarah, 50, 51
knowledge, 14, 60, 84, 94, 104, 123, 126, 128, 135, 173, 232; access to, 171; binary, 133; captured, 171; colonial, 117; cultural, 15, 176; disseminating, 112, 116, 170, 234; engaging with, 51; Eurocentric, 53, 63; imposing, 105; Indigenous, 54, 58, 100, 115, 138, 176, 184, 224; local, 117–18; relationships and, 100, 115; sharing, 33, 184, 226–29; stories and, 118, 238–39; unreliable, 178
knowledge-making, 13, 17, 19, 24, 38, 53, 79, 82, 95, 103, 108, 110, 112, 113, 116, 118, 125, 126, 135, 167; as active force, 88; ancestors and, 16, 19; balance with, 107; Cherokee, 7–9, 16, 89, 103, 136, 174; coloniality of, 66–67; community of, 223; ecological model of, 90; growth/adaptation and, 93; Indigenous, 12, 51, 60, 104, 124; networked, 96; non-Western, 67; participatory, 9, 20, 21; praxis, 20, 21, 102, 105*f*, 109, 114, 115, 117, 119, 128, 194, 226; responsibility to, 89; storytelling and, 104–5, 127, 128; sustaining, 225; work of, 7

LaDuke, Winona, 85, 88
landscapes, 35, 81, 193; cultural, 43, 72; disciplinary, 49–51; Indigenous, 22; red bricked, 44–49
Lane, Rosa Gazelle, 153
language, 34, 50, 156; body, 33; Cherokee, 21, 22, 23, 25, 120–21, 124, 134, 137, 152, 153, 173, 174, 179, 181, 184, 185, 192, 196, 197, 198, 202–3, 205, 219, 225, 228; cultural practices of, 218; English, 147, 188, 192, 197, 202–3, 205; importance of, 123, 171; meaning-making of, 188; natural habitat of, 176; perseverance through, 216; revitalization of, 121; storytelling praxis and, 120–26; written, 173, 178
Latour, Bruno, 19, 92, 93, 96
learning: brave/mighty warrior and, 198–200; experiential, 191
Lee, Kimberli, 234
Lee-Morgan, Jenny Bol Jun, 56
Legg, Eldon, 30
Legg, Mary Leota (Holmes), 11, 12
Lerner, Neal, 72
Lessons on Common Things (Schultz), 190
listeners, 9, 110; storytellers and, 116, 124, 128

listening, 51–56, 111, 115; telling and, 128
literacy, 22, 148, 171, 172, 174, 176, 183, 184, 186, 198, 200, 218; English-language, 144; Eurocentrism and, 124, 126; orality and, 124; practices, 59; spread of, 173
Little People, 120, 120*n1*
loyalty, 15, 16, 172, 239–42
Lucille (great-grandmother), death of, 31–32
Lyon, Mary, 148, 189
Lyons, Scott, 208, 210, 211, 212; on sovereignty, 149, 180
Lyotard, Jean-François, 91

McGee, Nannie Waters, 165
McGowan, Kay Givens, 141
Manifest Destiny, 72, 199
Maracle, Lee, 103, 115, 240–41
marginalization, 8, 140
Mastrangelo, Lisa, 51, 148, 192–93
materiality, 55, 70*n3*, 71, 76, 110, 118, 177–82, 235
Mayes, Joel B., 201
Mayo, Elizabeth, 190, 191
medicine, Cherokee, 14, 170, 182
memories, 112, 114; ownership of, 72
mental health issues, 225
metaphysics, 94, 100; Indigenous, 57, 86, 94
methodologies, 37, 56, 70, 99, 102, 116, 128, 219, 233, 239; archival, 64, 106, 107, 109; decolonial, 53, 129; Enlightenment-reformed, 226; Indigenous, 8, 16, 20, 21, 25, 52, 53, 85, 103, 109; knowledge-making, 112; research, 38, 88, 109, 110, 193; rhetorical, 82, 96; storytelling, 16, 20, 103, 104, 110, 114, 115, 126, 128, 129, 193, 194
Mignolo, Walter, 66–67
Mihesuah, Devon, 53–54
mission schools, 146, 152
Mole, 8
Momaday, N. Scott, 199
Monteagle Teacher's Resort, 157
Moon, Mary Lee (Haury), 10, 11–12
Moon People, 120*n1*
Mooney, James, 121–22, 177
morality, 40, 159, 206
Morrill Act, 48
Mother Earth, 100–101, 140
Moulder, M. Amada, 143, 144
Mound Builders, 169, 170
Mount Holyoke College, 59, 145, 146, 147, 191, 192, 193; Cherokee Nation and, 149, 187; curriculum at, 148, 189

Mukavetz, Andrea Riley, 38, 230, 234
Muscogees, 30, 77, 94, 175*n1*
Myths of the Cherokee and Sacred Formulas of the Cherokees (Ross and Evans), 169
Myths of the Cherokees (Mooney), 121–22

Na-Li, 203, 203*n2*, 204, 214, 215
Napoleon, 206
narratives, 48, 135, 161, 204, 210, 237; colonized, 51; composition, 56; discursive, 37; historical, 67, 70; multifaceted, 49; oral, 37, 76; recovery of, 193; removal, 106; white, 23, 216
"Narratives from the Margins: Centering Women of Color in Technical Communication," 237
National Council, 41
National Geographic, 236
National Museum of the American Indian, 218
nationalism: Cherokee, 198, 200–202, 217*n4*, 227; Christian, 204; developing, 183–86
nationhood, Cherokee, 43, 108, 183, 227
Native Americans, 35, 40*n3*, 54, 96, 100, 180, 225; Anglo-Saxonization of, 134–35; colonization of, 57
"Native Narrative" (King), 111
Native Womanism, 163
Nelson, Joshua B., 23, 39, 124, 133, 143, 162, 173, 186, 205, 209, 210, 211, 217, 241; Ani-kutani and, 170; on education, 152–53, 215
New Kituwah Academy, 228
Newberry Library, 75
newspapers, 22, 23, 44, 59, 117, 137, 152, 157, 166, 173, 183, 184, 189, 196, 198, 205, 207, 211, 214, 216, 217, 219, 227, 228; Cherokee, 200–202; dual-language, 184; student, 197, 203, 203*n2*, 208, 212, 229
Newton Theological Seminary, 147
Nicotani, 169
Nix, Lucille Irene, 30, 76
noble savage, 23, 212, 216
Northeastern State University, 19, 42, 52, 58, 59, 63, 137, 156, 185; archives at, 189; research at, 82–83

objectification, 56, 84, 91, 113
objectivity, 35, 36, 55, 103
Okanagan people, 89
Ong, Walter J., 37, 176
ontologies, 16, 18, 57, 58, 98, 103, 108, 114, 121; collapsing, 107; Eurocentric, 86; Indigenous, 20, 55, 82, 85, 90, 95, 235, 236; object-oriented, 235

orality, 121, 125–26, 176; Cherokee, 124, 174, 177–82, 185, 186; Eurocentric, 123; language and, 178; literacy and, 124; material, 22, 192; rhetorical sovereignty and, 181; storytelling, 114
Origins of Compassion Studies in the American Colleges, 1875–1925, The (Brereton), 44
Osiyo TV, 228
Oswego Normal School, 190, 191
"Our Wreath of Rose Buds" (Corrine), 189
Overhill Cherokees, 31, 173

Parins, James, 152, 153
Park Hill, 5, 30, 144–45, 147, 167, 195, 196, 217*n4*; printing press for, 152
Park Hill Press, 152
Parker, Richard Green, 47, 188, 189, 190
participation, 99, 110, 127; ecology of, 116; telling/listening as, 115
pedagogy, 44, 51, 55, 68, 108, 187, 191, 194; active, 148; analyzing, 69; composition, 45; current-traditionalist, 186; *duyuk'ta*, 153–68; Eurocentric, 149; forgetfulness of, 45; Pestalozzian, 190, 192; process-driven, 83; reshaping, 50; rhetorical, 22; socially driven, 193; writing, 230–42
Perdue, Theda, 136, 139, 142, 207
Pericles, 206
Pestalozzi, Johann Heinrich, 190
Philobiblius, 155, 155*n7*
philosophy, 86, 176; educational, 57; Enlightenment, 91; Eurocentric, 90, 91, 96; Indigenous, 19
physical education, women and, 160
Pilgrims, 134
Pocahontas, 150–51*n2*, 212
Pocahontas Club, 150, 150–51*n2*, 151
politics, 19, 23, 162, 197, 211; Cherokee, 165, 169; Eurocentric, 16
Porter, James E., 109, 110
Possum, stories about, 8
Powell, Malea, 36, 45, 56, 73, 74, 106, 226, 231, 234; Eastman and, 75; on multiple subjects/discourses, 82–83; on places/spaces, 75
power: civil, 172; domestic, 141; economic, 141; Eurocentric, 18; political, 141
power structures, 53, 122, 129, 143
Powhatan, 150*n2*
prejudices, 64, 65, 163, 211
priesthood, 169–71
print: storytelling praxis and, 120–26; supremacy of, 178
process, 68; praxis and, 127–29
Progressive Traditions: Identity in Cherokee Literature and Culture (Nelson), 39

Qua-Tsy, 203*n2*, 205, 206, 207

Rabbit, 6, 8, 9, 61, 62, 63
race, 22, 50, 236, 237
racism, 163, 237
Raven, 84, 95
reality, 37, 117, 126, 193
reciprocity, 9–14, 17, 238
recovery work, 44, 68, 109, 186–93, 234
"Red Men" societies, 150*n2*
red-brick explosion, 44–49
Reed, Julie, 39
Refiguring Rhetorical Education (Gold and Enoch), 50
relationship-building, 19, 22, 38, 52, 53, 82, 90, 100, 101, 112, 148
relationships, 18, 83, 85, 89, 100, 104, 105, 115, 118, 119, 158, 159; balanced, 176; critical practices and, 238; cultural, 97; ecology and, 97; Eurocentric, 91, 109, 113, 182; faculty-student, 193; familial, 142; Indigenous, 20, 106, 129; maintaining, 221, 221*f*, 238, 239–42; making, 27*f*; material, 73, 90, 193; metonymic, 87; more-than-human, 100; ontological, 95, 96; other-than-human, 123; part-to-whole, 87, 97; power, 182; storytelling, 88, 107, 116; synecdochic, 87, 88, 89; understanding of, 127, 129
Removable Type: Histories of the Book in Indian Country, 1663–1880 (Round), 183
removal, 73, 123, 178, 207; Indigenous, 18; policies, 40
research, 37, 58, 60, 65, 66, 71, 72, 127, 224, 225, 239; ceremony, 230; colonial, 18, 61, 108; community-based, 234; as critical praxis, 110; decolonial, 56, 110; Eurocentric, 7, 18, 19, 54, 55, 57, 83, 198, 226, 227, 238; genealogy, 134, 197; historical, 45, 71; Indigenous, 52, 54–55, 56, 99, 106, 109, 110, 171, 226; intercultural, 235; methodologies and, 38, 88, 109, 110, 193; retooling methods of, 21; stagnation in, 12; stories about, 10; storytelling, 9. *See also* archival research
Research Is Ceremony (Wilson), 54
resistance, 122, 143; methods of, 136; survival and, 24
Revolutionary War, 173
rhetoric, 21, 35, 53, 55, 60, 68, 70, 75, 108, 114–20, 155, 190, 202, 239; Cherokee, 118–19, 124, 167, 198, 214; civilized, 209; colonial, 234; cultural, 103, 232, 234; current-traditionalist, 186; history of, 36, 46, 55; Indigenous, 38, 56, 112, 177, 234, 235; material stories and, 110–14; oral, 124; practical, 84; relandscaping, 22; teaching, 188; trickster, 209–16
Rhetoric in American Colleges, 1850–1900 (Kitzhaber), 44
Rhetoric at the Margins (Gold), 49
rhizomes, 88–92, 94
Rice, Jeff, 90
Rickert, Thomas, 12, 90
Rifkin, Mark, 118, 213–214
Ritter, Kelly, 51, 70, 72
rituals, 180, 181, 182; student, 161–62
Rogers, Will, 30, 151, 174
Roosevelt, Theodore, 184*n3*
Ross, Betsy, 151*n2*
Ross, Chief, 169
Ross, John, 65, 142, 147, 208, 209; plan by, 153–54
Ross, Lucinda M., 200
Ross, William Potter, 147
Round, Phillip, 183
Royster, Jacqueline Jones, 46, 48

Said, 54, 123
Sanders, Charlotte Mayes, 163, 164
savage, civilized and, 207
scholarship, 51, 102, 135, 224
Schultz, Lucille M., 188–89, 190, 191
self-determination, 174, 182, 205, 207, 218
Selu, 6, 23, 119, 137, 139, 140, 141, 142, 143, 145, 163, 167, 168, 215, 216; Eve and, 207; Kana'ti and, 162; stories of, 22; teachings of, 155
Seminary Hall, 43
Seminoles, 40, 175*n1*, 209
Sequoyah, 6, 171, 178, 180, 184–85*n3*, 197, 219; story of, 58, 174, 175; syllabary of, 6, 22, 124, 170, 172–73, 179, 180, 181, 194
Sequoyah, Lloyd, 101
Sequoyah Memorial, 150, 200, 201, 202, 211, 214, 217, 218, 219; civilization and, 209; history of, 197–98; writing in, 207–8
settler colonialism, 60, 108, 214
settlerism, colonial, 70, 238, 240
sgadug, 21, 86, 103, 104
Shade, Hastings, 128, 170, 175, 185
Shadow of Sequoyah, The (Kilpatrick and Kilpatrick), 178, 179
Shakespeare, William, 167
Sharer, Wendy, 69
Shorey, Elizabeth Bessey, 142
Shorey, William, Jr., 141, 142
Shorey, William, Sr., 141
Sky Woman, 33, 98
Sky World, 98
smallpox, impact of, 172

Smith, Linda Tuhiwai, 8, 53, 54
Smith College, 146
Smithsonian National Museum of the American Indian, 39*n3*
social organization, 137, 169
social structures, 138, 169, 173
Socrates, 206
sovereignty, 143, 149, 172, 210, 211, 216, 227; education/writing and, 136, 146; Indigenous, 24, 36*n2*; maintaining, 122; orality and, 181; rhetorical, 124, 181, 182, 232; temporal, 118; tribal, 36, 185
spaces: archival, 74; creation of, 200; democratic, 148; Indigenous, 234; male-dominated, 168
Spearfinger, 218
SPIDER: Ant and, 92–95; Grandmother Water Spider and, 92–95
spirituality, 15, 16, 29, 174
Squirrel, 61
Starr, Doctor Orange, 153
Starr, Emmett, 30, 158, 160
Steedman, Carolyn, 71
stereotypes, 163, 212, 237
Stop Dance, 153
stories, 8, 19, 20, 25, 27, 38, 53, 64–67, 123, 134, 168, 177, 192, 225; as accomplices in archives, 232–42; assimilation, 136; colonization of, 178; communal, 226; creation, 88, 111; cultural, 218, 238, 239; ecology of, 117; Eurocentric, 9, 112, 113, 127; hearing, 33–34; importance of, 89; Indigenous, 61, 90, 96, 112, 116, 129, 178, 234; institutional, 59; knowledge and, 79, 79*f*, 221, 238–49; knowledge-makers and, 128; listening to, 29–32; maintaining, 230–42; material, 92–95, 110–14; oral, 23, 37, 124, 178, 216; origins and (dis)locations of, 32–39; (re)searching for, 74–77; telling, 10, 34–35, 101–7, 109, 111, 122–23; as theory, 92, 234; time/place and, 119; traditional, 7, 106; weaving, 234
storytellers, 8, 9, 106, 110, 115, 119, 120, 178; archives as, 114; changes from, 124–25; Cherokee, 7–8, 119, 121, 122, 125; contemporary, 88; explanations from, 125; knowledge-making by, 127; knowledge transfer by, 125; listeners and, 116, 124, 128; orality of, 178; traditions of, 123
storytelling, 10, 57, 74, 88, 99, 102–3, 106, 110, 123, 126, 170, 229; act of, 87, 112, 113; agential realism of, 117; continuum, 115; Eurocentric, 111; hows of, 109; Indigenous, 16, 20, 21, 24, 25, 38, 51–56, 103, 108, 111, 112, 125, 127–29; kairotic moment of, 102, 104; knowledge-making and, 104–5, 109; as living/reflective, 124; lying and, 125; methodologies of, 16, 20, 103, 104, 110, 114, 115, 126, 128, 129, 193, 194; oral, 111, 114, 121, 124, 128; origins of, 35; participation in, 90, 114–15; praxis, 104, 120–26, 127–29; process and, 127–29; relations and, 88, 107, 116; (re)positionings of, 114–20; rhetoric of, 108, 118, 119, 124, 125, 127, 229; shifts in, 33, 124–25; understanding, 113, 125; weaving and, 106–7
Strantz, Adam, 12
Strum, Circe, 134
students, 14, 23, 158, 159, 160, 162, 211, 216, 217, 231, 231*f*, 232, 241; photo of, 161; teachers and, 189
Suli, 84
Sullivan, Pat, 12, 109, 110
survivance, 59, 75, 122, 124, 198, 199, 226; cultural, 123, 208; material mode of, 174; perseverance through, 216; resistance and, 24; strategy of, 234
syllabary, 170–75, 179, 180, 181, 194, 197, 218, 229, 240; development of, 59

Tahlequah, 6, 29, 31, 42, 43, 58, 67, 144, 231
teachers, 110, 152, 155, 158, 189
Teacher's Institute, 156, 187
Teacher's Institute of the Cherokee Nation, 156
teaching, 157, 193; Pestalozzian, 192
technology, 10, 87, 106, 110, 118, 123, 125, 173, 182, 234; adapting, 149, 227
Tennessee River Valley, 31
Tennessee Valley Authority, 101
Teuton, Christopher, 9, 118, 123, 125, 128, 167, 169–70, 182, 184, 226; balance and, 176; community/we-ness and, 177; *sgadug* and, 86
theory, 55, 103, 109; cultural, 104; Indigenous, 19, 54, 127; literary, 112, 113; materialist-driven, 91; philosophical ends of, 90; rhetorical, 176; stories-as-, 92
Toulmin, Stephen, 91
tradition, 135, 174, 195, 198, 213, 218, 219, 241; assimilation and, 165; Native, 88, 123, 199; revitalization, 123
Trail of Tears, 24, 29, 41, 65, 77, 144, 159, 210
tribal councils, 137–38
tribal government, 137, 146, 152, 173, 183, 195, 211; Cherokee, 40, 145; decentralized, 172; education and, 153

trickster figure, 208
true womanhood, 140, 143; rhetorics of, 205–7
Truth about Stories: A Native Narrative, The (King), 89
Tse:gh(i)sini, 180
Turtle Island, 83, 84
Turtle Island Liars' Club, 9, 125, 128, 226
"Two Should Walk Together," 204

uganawu, 23, 221, 223
ugohvi vgatahvi, 21, 79
Ulisi Ama Kanonesgi, 94, 96. See also Kananeski Ama'i'yehi
Unanti, 169, 170, 175
United Keetoowah Band, 49n5
US Supreme Court, 40
usquanigodv agadohvsdi, 21, 131
uyvtlv, 19, 79, 81, 84, 85, 86

Van Horn, Thomas, 147
Vann, David L., 147, 201
Vassar College, 146
Villanueva, Victor, 74
Vinita, 31, 77
"Visit to the Fortune Teller, A," 189
Vizenor, Gerald, 121, 125–26, 198, 199
Voices of Cherokee Women (Johnson), 76

W. (student), 211, 212, 213
Walk in Your Soul (Kilpatrick and Kilpatrick), 179
Wam-Da, 150
wampum, 100, 234
"Wampum as Hypertext" (Haas), 234
Washington, George, 206
Washington, Martha, 151n2
Water Spider, 95, 96
"We Are Still Here," 218–19
Weaver, Jace, 86, 87; on colonialism/Native traditions, 123; colonization and, 178; *communitism* and, 88; on reality, 126
weaving, 16, 20, 97–98, 101–7, 135, 140, 234; double-, 101, 102; practice-as-theory of, 135; storytelling and, 106–7
weddings, 119, 184n3, 217
"Week at the Female Seminary, A" (Corrine), 190
Wellesley College, 146
Welter, Barbara, 205
Wendell, Barrett, 186
Western Carolina University, 61, 228
Western Histories Collection, 77
Whately, 186

"When ANT meets SPIDER" (Latour), 92
White, Hayden, 37
Whitmore, Ellen, 147, 148
Wieser, Kimberly, 100
Wild Boy, 139
Wildcat, Daniel, 86, 94–95
Williams, Cynthia Anne, 142
Williams, Jenny (Cowart), 76*f*
Williams, Mat, 77
Wilson, Ann Florence, 43, 52, 63, 145, 146, 161, 191; Cherokee Female Seminary and, 5; female seminary and, 190; remembering, 159–60
Wilson, Shawn, 51, 103, 171, 226; Eurocentric research and, 55; on Indigenous ways of knowing, 54–55
Winged One, 169, 175
winiduyuk'ta, 14–17
wisdom, 224; keeping, 131, 131*f*; loyalty/reflection and, 239; passing, 239
Wisdom Sits in Places (Basso), 76
Wolf, 6, 9, 56, 70, 71; shoes of, 61–64
"Wolf Wears Shoes," 20, 61, 64
Womack, Craig, 37
Woodford, Oswald, 147
Woolaroc Wildlife Preserve, 29–30
Worcester, Sarah, 147
Worcester v. Georgia, 40
Works Progress Administration, 76
worldviews, 92, 128, 192, 193; American Indian and Alaska Native (AIAN), 225; Eurocentric, 19, 87, 91, 117, 144, 175, 177; Indigenous, 19, 55, 87, 89, 90, 91, 94, 95, 97, 99, 116, 124, 126, 127, 129; metonymic, 96–97; polycentric, 126; synecdochic, 87, 88, 99
Wreath of Cherokee Rose Buds, A, 200
writing, 12, 58, 134, 174, 178, 179, 182, 190, 192, 200–205, 217, 218–19, 224, 225, 239; brave/mighty warrior and, 198–200; decolonizing, 177; Eurocentrism and, 124, 126; historical/cultural location of, 51; importance of, 171, 173, 183; materiality of, 15, 37, 180, 186; oral, 181; positioning of, 176; as reciprocity, 13; as restorative, 14; sovereignty and, 136, 146; teaching, 22
Writing Instruction in Nineteenth Century American Colleges (Berlin), 44
Writing Their Bodies: Restoring Rhetorical Relations at the Carlisle Indian School (Klotz), 50
wudeligv, 21, 131, 135, 171

Young Astronauts Club, 81

www.ingramcontent.com/pod-product-compliance
Lightning Source LLC
Chambersburg PA
CBHW020521080526
44583CB00013B/690